Routledge Perspectives on Development Series

An Introduction to Sustainable Development

Third edition

Jennifer A. Elliott

 Routledge
Taylor & Francis Group

LONDON AND NEW YORK

First published 2006
by Routledge
2 Park Square, Milton Park, Abingdon, Oxon OX14 4RN

Simultaneously published in the USA and Canada
by Routledge
270 Madison Ave, New York, NY 10016

Routledge is an imprint of the Taylor & Francis Group

Typeset in Times and Franklin Gothic by
RefineCatch Ltd, Bungay, Suffolk
Printed and bound in Great Britain by
TJ International Ltd, Padstow, Cornwall

British Library Cataloguing in Publication Data
A catalogue record for this book is available from the British Library

Library of Congress Cataloging in Publication Data
Elliott, Jennifer A., 1962–
    An introduction to sustainable development / Jennifer A. Elliott.–
    3rd ed.
        p. cm. -- (Routledge perspectives on development)
    Includes bibliographical references and index.
    ISBN 0–415–33558–2 (hardcover : alk. paper) –
        ISBN 0–415–33559–0 (papercover : alk. paper) 1. Sustainable
        development – Developing countries. 2. Environmental policy –
        Developing countries. I Title. II Series.
    HC59.72.E5E43 2005
    338.9′27′091724–dc22
                                                            2005004404

ISBN10: 0–415–33558–2 (hbk)
ISBN10: 0–415–33559–0 (pbk)

ISBN13: 9–78–0–415–33558–4 (hbk)
ISBN13: 9–78–0–415–33559–1 (pbk)

In memory of my Dad

Contents

Plates

Figures

Tables

Boxes

Acknowledgements

I was pleased to be asked to write this third edition of this text. Most importantly, I am pleased that it is proving to be a useful introduction for students and others interested in this challenge of sustainable development in the developing world. I wrote the first edition whilst employed as a Lecturer in Geography at the University of Zimbabwe in Harare; the bulk of it completed whilst the university was closed by the government as students engaged in demonstrations over resources for their study. The materials on which I drew to compile that original edition (and indeed those of the students with whom I was working in the early 1990s) were very limited; sustainable development was a relatively new idea for everyone and the impact of two successive years of drought were bigger concerns amongst my colleagues and for the people of Zimbabwe than the recently negotiated 'Economic and Structural Adjustment Programme'. There was certainly no electronic access to academic journals nor online materials emanating from major institutions like the World Bank.

Writing this third edition from Brighton in 2004, I think regularly on whether the aspirations of those students of geography in Zimbabwe whom I came to know are being realised now; whether the proliferation of writings and experiences on sustainable development, the structural reforms that their country has gone through, and the advances in information technology that I have access to, have made a positive difference in their lives. I am sure that many people could answer in the negative (without even reading this book). However, that is another book.

I hope that this edition will continue to provide a useful introduction to some of the principal ideas, debates, changes seen, lessons being learnt and future challenges and opportunities underpinning the notion and practice of sustainable development as understood in relation to developing countries. With each edition the task of writing has become harder as the literature has expanded and fundamentally as the geographies of those components are revealed.

In writing this third edition, I continue to be thankful for the supportive environment in which I work at the University of Brighton and particularly the friendship of my colleagues. My biggest thanks are to my family who will be those most pleased that this edition has been completed.

The author and publisher would like to thank the following for granting permission to reproduce material in this work: David Simonds for Figure 3.2; Earthscan Publications Ltd for Figure 5.6; the *Guardian* newspaper for Table 3.4.

Introduction

This book is concerned with the continued challenges and opportunities of finding sustainable patterns and processes of development within the international community for the future. Since the publication of the first edition of this text in 1994, it is evident that much has been learnt in terms of the principles behind and the characteristics of policies, programmes and projects that appear to be more sustainable than previous such interventions, and certainly in terms of how such trends can be monitored and evaluated. However, whilst the idea of sustainable development may be widely recognised by the public, academics and practitioners in many disciplines and fields, both in the developing and more industrialised countries, there continue to be many patterns of human welfare and the status of environmental resources worldwide that suggest that further scrutiny and efforts are required. Too often, development processes are characterised by the loss or degradation of primary environmental resources. In many countries, 'development reversals' are being seen, with rising proportions of people below basic poverty lines and falling life expectancies, for example. The concern continues to be that many of the patterns and processes of development will not be able to supply the needs of the world's population into the future and cannot deliver the higher standards of living to the rising numbers of people essential to the conservation of the environment.

The pursuit of sustainable development is now stated as a principal policy goal of many of the major institutions of the world including the United Nations, the World Bank and the World Trade

Organisation. This is confirmation of how understanding of the global challenge of sustainable development has moved on to encompass the complex interdependencies of environmental, social and economic development. In addition, the context in which sustainable development is being sought in the twenty-first century is quite different from that of the 1990s. In particular, an increasingly globalised world has brought new challenges as well as opportunities for the environment and for development. New actors (such as transnational corporations and civil society organisations) and new technologies (particularly in communications), for example, now shape outcomes in resource development and management to a much greater extent than previously. Ensuring that processes of globalisation operate to reach the needs of the poor rather than to marginalise particular groups and places further, is central to the challenge of sustainable development currently.

The primary focus of the book is the challenges and opportunities for sustainability in the less economically developed regions of the world. Fundamentally, this is because it is here that the majority of the world's poor reside. This is not to suggest that sustainability is mostly a problem for the poor. Indeed, most pollution, for example, is a result of affluence, not poverty. Furthermore, the prospects of sustainable development in any one location are in part shaped by forces and decision-making which are often situated at great distances away such that it is impossible to consider the developing world in isolation from the wider global community. However, there are also particular and distinct issues of sustainability in the developing world that will be seen to lie in factors of both the natural and the human environment. For example, many countries of what can be termed the developing world are in the tropics where the boundary conditions on development, particularly in agriculture, are often quite different from those of temperate regions. These regions also encompass many of the world's 'fragile lands', such as the major arid and semi-arid zones and forest ecosystems, where bio-physical factors in combination with social characteristics may make them particularly susceptible to degradation and make recovery from disturbance difficult. Large sections of the populations of these countries live in environments in which securing basic needs is extremely problematic and which may even be detrimental to human health. Not only do rising numbers of people in the developing world suffer the multiple deprivations associated with poverty, but they also live in countries that are becoming economically poorer and more indebted, for example. These factors of the human environment further combine to create particular challenges and opportunities for sustainable development.

In order to understand the characteristics of resource use or human conditions in the developing world and to allow more sustainable patterns to be supported, it is essential to identify the underlying processes of change. Some of these processes may operate solely at a local level, whilst others may impact across many places and constitute global forces of change. All to some degree, and in combination, shape the interactions between people and the environment (wherever they live) and the relationships between people in different places. It is for these reasons that sustainable development is a common challenge for the global community as a whole. In the course of this book, it will be seen that sustainable development in the future requires actions for change at all levels, addressing both the human and physical environments, through interventions in physical, political-economic and social processes.

One of the primary aims of the book is to highlight the progress that has been made towards establishing new patterns and processes of development which are more sustainable in terms of the demands they make on the physical, ecological and cultural resources of the globe, and the characteristics of technology, societal organisation and economic production which underpin them. Understanding the characteristics of successful sustainable development projects will be essential for meeting the worldwide ongoing and evolving challenges of balancing present needs against those of the future. Since the publication of the first edition of this book, a lot has been learnt from 'practice on the ground' concerning the principles for actions that are more sustainable and the nature of the continued challenges.

As the term 'sustainable development' reaches further into popular consciences worldwide and more institutions are stating sustainability as a major policy goal, there is a need to reflect critically on what is trying to be achieved and the inherently political nature of interventions in resource management towards these ends. The meaning and origins of the notion of sustainable development is traced in Chapter 1 within an analysis of thinking and practice in development theory and in environmentalism. Whilst the interdependence of future environment and development ends is recognised in both literatures, it is seen that substantial debate and contestation characterise both the theory and practice of sustainable development. The historical overview presented also confirms that the context within which environment and development are being pursued is changing rapidly, requiring continuous re-evaluation of

1 What is sustainable development?

Summary

- There are many different definitions of sustainable development coming from various disciplines and with different assumptions about the basic relationship between society and nature.
- Ideas of sustainable development have a long history in the literatures of both development and environmentalism.
- There have been a number of important international conferences within which actions towards sustainable development have been debated (and contested) at the highest levels of government.
- Sustainable development is widely accepted as a desirable policy objective amongst many institutions concerned with the future development of the resources of the globe.
- Ideas concerning the best way of achieving development have changed over time, but are rarely replaced entirely. Mainstream environmentalism encapsulates the dominant ideas surrounding society–environment relationships, but are not subscribed to by all interests, equally.
- Sustainable development is currently being pursued in the context of an increasingly globalised world, but one which is also characterised by poverty. The global challenge of sustainable development lies in complex interdependencies of environment, social and economic development.

Introduction

In 1984, the United Nations established an independent group of 22 people drawn from member states of both the developing and developed worlds, and charged them with identifying the long-term environmental strategies for the international community. In 1987, the World Conference on Environment and Development published their report entitled, 'Our Common Future' (WCED, 1987), often known as the 'Brundtland Report', after its chair, the then Prime Minister of Norway, Gro Harlem Brundtland. The report used the term 'sustainable development' widely and defined it as 'Development that meets the needs of the present without compromising the ability of future generations to meet their own needs' (p. 43). The report is said to have put sustainable development firmly into the political arena of international development thinking. Certainly, it has been translated into more than 24 languages (Finger, 1994) and its definition of the term continues to be that which is most widely used.

In 1992, the United Nations Conference on Environment and Development, the 'Earth Summit', took place in Rio de Janeiro, Brazil. At the time, it was the largest ever international conference held, with over 170 governments represented (Adams, 2001) and a further 2,500 NGOs and 8,000 accredited journalists attending (O'Riordan, 2000). The central aim was to identify the principles of an agenda for action towards sustainable development in the future. The challenge was seen to require consensus at the highest level, so that, for the first time, heads of state gathered to consider the environment. By this time, the term 'sustainable development' had also 'gained a currency well beyond the confines of global environmental organisations' (Adams, 1990: 2). Certainly in the developed world, the substantial media attention given to the serious environmental disturbances surrounding forest fires in Indonesia, flooding in the Americas, China and Bangladesh, and typhoons in South-East Asia, for example, brought questions of conservation and ideas of sustainability into the public vocabulary. In the fields of development and the environment, an evident consensus was emerging that sustainable development was an important rallying point for research and action and a desirable policy objective which should be striven for.

However, it was evident through the decade of the 1990s, that there was substantial debate and contestation concerning the meaning and practice of sustainable development. For example, whilst the primary output of the Rio Conference, the huge 'Agenda 21' document, carried much political authority and moral force (Mather and Chapman, 1995) important tensions were evident through the proceedings at Rio such as between the environmental concerns of rich and poor countries, between those who wished to exploit resources and those who wished to conserve them, and between the development needs of current generations and those of the future. For some, the term 'sustainable development' has subsequently been redefined so many times and used to cover so many aspects of society–environment relationships that there are now 'doubts on whether anything good can ever be agreed' (Mawhinney, 2001: 1). For others, sustainable development is an idea that 'makes a difference' precisely because it is contested, requires debate and compromise and because it challenges both researchers and policy-makers (McNeill, 2000).

In 2002, 104 heads of state once again met in Johannesburg, South Africa, for the World Summit on Sustainable Development (WSSD). The global challenge of sustainability is now understood to lie in the complex interdependencies of environmental, social and economic development (Potter *et al.*, 2004). New understanding has emerged of the linkages between environmental resources and conflict and the threats to environment of globalisation (as well as opportunities) as discussed in more detail here and in Chapter 2. In addition, a much more diverse range of interest groups was engaged in activities at Johannesburg than at Rio. In particular, there were many more non-governmental organisations (NGOs) from the developing world representing issues of human rights, social justice and business accountability, for example. These activities suggested new ways of addressing sustainable development at a global level and a 'more decentralized understanding of where change comes from' (Bigg, 2004: 5).

This chapter identifies in some detail the origins of the concept of sustainable development and its current 'meaning' in terms of finding alternative patterns of progress to meet the needs of the global community. Through an analysis of the key debates in the previously separate literatures of development thinking and environmentalism, it is possible to understand the sources of continued conflict regarding sustainable development in theory and practice and the broad political economic context in which sustainable development is being sought into the twenty-first century.

The concept of sustainable development

Literally, sustainable development refers to maintaining development over time. By the early 1990s, it was suggested that there were more than 70 definitions of sustainable development in circulation (Holmberg and Sandbrook, 1992). Figure 1.1 lists just a small number of such definitions and the varied interpretations of the concept which have flowed from these different ideas. Definitions are important, as they are the basis on which the means for achieving sustainable development in the future are built.

Evidently, different disciplines have influenced and contributed to the sustainability debate, 'each making different assumptions about the relation between environment and the human subject' (Lee *et al.*, 2000: 9). Differences are even more important when thinking about policy development: how the human and environmental 'condition' is

Figure 1.1 *Defining and interpreting the contested concept of sustainable development*

....

Definitions of sustainable development

'In principle, such an optimal (sustainable growth) policy would seek to maintain an "acceptable" rate of growth in per-capita real incomes without depleting the national capital asset stock or the natural environmental asset stock.'

(Turner, 1988: 12)

'The net productivity of biomass (positive mass balance per unit area per unit time) maintained over decades to centuries.'

(Conway, 1987: 96)

'Development that meets the needs of the present without compromising the ability of future generations to meet their own needs.'

(World Commission on Environment and Development, 1987: 43)

Interpretations of sustainable development

'A creatively ambiguous phrase . . . an intuitively attractive but slippery concept.'

(Mitchell, 1997: 28)

'Like motherhood, and God, it is difficult not to approve of it. At the same time, the idea of sustainable development is fraught with contradictions.'

(Redclift, 1997: 438)

'It is indistinguishable from the total development of society.'

(Barbier, 1987: 103)

'Its very ambiguity enables it to transcend the tensions inherent in its meaning.'

(O'Riordan, 1995: 21)

'Sustainable development appears to be an over-used, misunderstood phrase.'

(Mawhinney, 2001: 5)

....

thought about, viewed or understood underpins subsequent planning and interventions in the form of development and conservation projects, yet different disciplines and philosophies may assign quite divergent 'orders of priority' to these policies and programmes. During the course of this text, it will be apparent that, although there are many signs of progress, there is also much debate and uncertainty as to the most appropriate strategies to foster sustainable change. Indeed, as suggested in the quotations in Figure 1.1, the attractiveness (and the 'dangers') of the concept of sustainable development may lie precisely in the varied ways in which it can be interpreted and used to support a whole range of interests or causes.

The challenges of understanding what this idea of sustainable development may mean, and how people can work towards it, are evident in a brief analysis of the definition of sustainable development provided by the WCED. Their apparently simple definition of sustainable development is immediately seen to contain a distinction and a potential conflict between the interests of the present and those of future generations. Further, very challenging notions can be identified such as those of needs and limits. Questions emerge such as: what is it that one generation is passing to another? Is it solely natural capital or does it include assets associated with human ingenuity, language or other aspects of culture? What and how are the limits set – by technology, society or ecology, for example? What of the fact that, currently, needs in one place or amongst particular groups are often fulfilled at the expense of others? Fundamentally, 'needs' mean different things to different people and are linked to our ability to satisfy them, i.e. are closely aligned to 'development' itself. So, society is able to define and create new 'needs' within certain groups (that could be interpreted as 'wants'), without satisfying even the basic needs of others. These questions highlight the many sources of conflict in the debates over the meaning of sustainable development: conflict between the interests of present generations and those of the future; between human well-being and the protection of nature; between poor and rich; and between local and global.

Furthermore, the substantial challenges of operationalising the concept of sustainable development were clear in the report of the WCED, back in 1987. Figure 1.2 displays the critical objectives identified by the Commission and the necessary conditions for sustainable development in the future, evidently encompassing a huge breadth and scale of activity. A more prosperous, more just and more secure global future was seen to depend on new norms of behaviour at all levels and in the interests of all. The conditions for such a future encompass all areas of human activity, in production, trade, technology and politics, for example, and encompass cooperative and mutually supportive actions on behalf of individuals and nations at all levels of economic development.

Most definitions of sustainable development encompass the idea that there are three interdependent pillars of sustainable development: environmental, economic and social. In 1987 Barbier presented these as three interlocking circles as seen in Figure 1.3. The objective of sustainable development is to maximise the goals across all three systems and is illustrated by the intersection of these circles. Critically, the model encompasses the understanding that each of the system goals (examples of which are identified in the figure) is socially

Plate 1.1 *Promoting the messages of sustainable development*

a. Sign on entry to Kang, Botswana

Source: David Nash, University of Brighton.

b. VOYCE (Views of Young Concerned Environmentalists) Four Seasons Mural, Brighton, England

Source: Kim Jackson, Brighton and Hove City Council.

Figure 1.2 *Critical objectives and necessary conditions for sustainable development as identified by the World Commission on Environment and Development (WCED)*

....

Critical objectives

● Reviving growth
● Changing the quality of growth
● Meeting essential needs for jobs, food, energy, water and sanitation
● Ensuring a sustainable level of population
● Conserving and enhancing the resource base
● Reorientating technology and managing risk
● Merging environment and economics in decision-making

Pursuit of sustainable development requires:

● A political system that secures effective citizen participation in decision-making
● An economic system that provides for solutions for the tensions arising from disharmonious development
● A production system that respects the obligation to preserve the ecological base for development
● A technological system that fosters sustainable patterns of trade and finance
● An international system that fosters sustainable patterns of trade and finance
● An administrative system that is flexible and has the capacity for self-correction

....

Source: WCED (1987).

Figure 1.3 *The objectives of sustainable development*

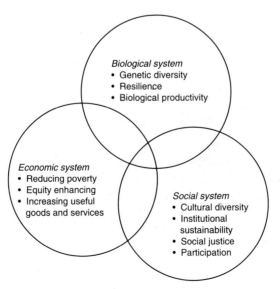

Biological system
• Genetic diversity
• Resilience
• Biological productivity

Economic system
• Reducing poverty
• Equity enhancing
• Increasing useful goods and services

Social system
• Cultural diversity
• Institutional sustainability
• Social justice
• Participation

Source: compiled from Barbier (1987).

constructed and that achieving sustainable development requires trade-offs; choices have to be made at particular points in time and at particular scales as to what is being pursued and how, and sustainable development requires recognition of the costs involved for particular interests and for groups of people. ✳

Whilst many of the early contributions to defining sustainable development came from the disciplines of economics and ecology, it is the third sphere that has accommodated much recent work. For Starkey and Walford (2001), for example, sustainable development is a moral concept that seeks to define a 'fair and just' development. They suggest that since the environment is the basis of all economic activity, and of life itself, 'it is surely only right that the quality and integrity of the environment be maintained for future generations' (p. xix). Notions of 'environmental justice' are now a prominent part of contemporary discussions of the meaning and practice of sustainable development and take the moral concerns further: in addition to environmental protection, the concern is for how environmental bads (such as pollution) and goods (such as access to green space) are distributed across society. Environmental justice also encompasses a concern for the equity of environmental management interventions and the nature of public involvement in decision-making. Understanding is mounting of the political nature of sustainable development in practice; how the solutions proposed (and the choices and trade-offs made) can carry different costs for different groups of people.

Clearly, whilst common sense would seem to tell us that our development should not be at the expense of that of future generations, the challenges in practice are substantial. In order to identify the challenges of implementing sustainable development actions and to realise the opportunities for sustainable development, it is necessary to understand the changes in thinking and practice from which the concept has developed. As Adams (2001) suggests, sustainable development cannot be understood in 'an historical vacuum' (p. 22). Of particular importance are the changes in thinking about what constitutes 'development' and how best to achieve it, and changing ideas about the 'environment'. Indeed, the current conflicts surrounding sustainable development today could be considered a legacy of the substantially separate nature of these two debates in the past (Lee *et al.*, 2000). Furthermore, it is considered that the debates on sustainable development have been important in reshaping understanding in both these arenas (McNeill, 2000).

Changing perceptions of development

> Poverty, hunger, disease and debt have been familiar words within the lexicon of development ever since formal development planning began, following the Second World War. In the past decade they have been joined by another, sustainability.
>
> (Adams, 2001: 1)

Development is often discussed in relation to 'developing countries', but is a concept which relates to all parts of the world at every level, from the individual to global transformations (Potter *et al.*, 2004). Development is something to which we all aspire and, certainly in the more developed world, 'self-development' has become something that is actively encouraged and an endeavour on which large amounts of money are spent, for example. Ideas about the best means by which to achieve our aspirations and needs are potentially as old as human civilisation. The study of development, however, has a relatively short history, really dating back only as far as the 1950s. Since then, the interdisciplinary field of development studies has seen many changes in thinking regarding the meaning and purpose of development (ideologies) and in development practice in the field (strategies of development). Although these shifts are considered chronologically here, in reality existing theories are rarely totally replaced; rather, new ones find relative favour and contestation over the prescriptions for development flowing from them continue.

Optimistic early decades

During the 1960s, development thinking (encompassing these aspects of ideology and strategy) prioritised economic growth and the application of modern scientific and technical knowledge as the route to prosperity in the underdeveloped world at that time. In short, the 'global development problem' was conceived as one in which less developed nations needed to 'catch up' with the West and enter the modern age of capitalism and liberal democracy. Underdevelopment was seen as an initial stage through which western nations had progressed and the gaps in development that existed could be gradually overcome through an 'imitative process' (Hettne, 2002: 7), significantly, through a sharing of the experience of West in terms of capital and know-how. In short, development was seen in terms of modernisation and, in turn, modernisation was equated with westernisation (and an associated faith in the rationality of science and technology) during this period. This 'modernisation thesis' dominated mainstream theories of economic development from the late 1950s through to the early 1970s. It was an optimistic time: it was thought that underdevelopment could be overcome through the spatial diffusion of modernity from the West to less developed countries and from urban centres to rural areas, for example. It was assumed that many development problems of the underdeveloped world would be solved quickly through the transfer of finance, technology and experience from the developed countries.

Insights from neo-classical economics as modelled by authors such as Rostow (1960) were very influential in development thinking at this time. Rostow's model of the linear stages of economic development is shown in Figure 1.4. On the basis largely of the experience and history of the more developed societies (i.e. a Eurocentric stance), it was suggested that, through assistance in reaching a critical 'take-off' stage in levels of savings and investment, the benefits of development and characteristics of 'modernisation' (including of society, politics and culture) would inevitably and spontaneously flow from the core to less-developed regions. Industrialisation through capitalist growth was seen as the central requirement in order for development to take place and through this strengthening of the material base of society, all countries had an equal chance to develop. Whilst there were differences in emphasis regarding the nature of the strategies to deliver industrial growth, there was an absolute faith within development thinking at this time that there was a linear, unconstrained path to economic development and an 'unswerving faith in the efficacy of urban-based industrial growth' (Potter *et al.*, 2004: 94). There was an active role envisaged for the state in creating the conditions needed to achieve 'take-off' (such as setting policy to stimulate local demand and savings) and in setting appropriate rates of taxes. Aspects of these ideas, such as the importance of the free market and the priority given to the European experience, found renewed emphasis in the 1990s within structural adjustment programmes as detailed below.

The optimism of the theorists of the 1960s, however, was generally not borne out by experience of development on the ground in that decade. By the 1970s, inequality between and within countries had in fact worsened. The empirical evidence concerning economic growth as measured by gross national product (GNP) suggested that, whilst change had been achieved, this 'development' was not shared equally amongst the populations of these nations. For example, in Brazil in 1970, the poorest 40 per cent of the population received only 6.5 per cent of the total national income, in contrast to the 66.7 per cent of

Figure 1.4 *The stages of economic development as modelled by Rostow*

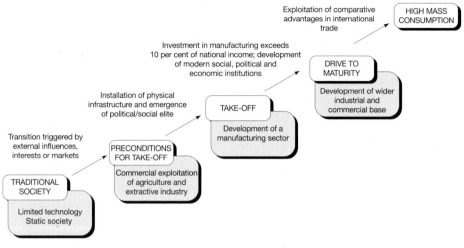

Source: Rostow (1960).

the total national income received by the richest 20 per cent of the population (Todaro, 1997). Into the 1980s, rising levels of debt, the oil crisis and the problems for oil-importing countries led to growing dissatisfaction with ideas of modernisation as development. The optimism of a speedy end to underdevelopment faded on the basis of such emerging 'real-world observations' (Potter *et al.*, 2004: 97).

During the 1970s, development thinking was influenced strongly by the writings of scholars within the developing world itself, particularly from Latin American and the Caribbean (notably those regions most strongly linked to the United States). They considered the socioeconomic structures and economic conditions of their countries in terms of the exploitative/dependent relations with other parts of the world, particularly through colonialism in the past and with the capitalist economy generally. The politics of development came to the fore within such writings. In Europe too at this time, there was a reinvigorated interest in the work of Marx and an emerging 'New Left' movement that linked with the struggles of the Third World anti-colonial movements (Potter *et al.*, 2004). Through the 1970s, what became known as the radical or 'dependency' school of thought became dominant in development. This school is perhaps most closely associated with the work of Andre Gunder Frank (1967), a European economist trained in America, but who carried out much research in Central and Latin America.

Fundamentally, the assertion in dependency theory was that underdevelopment was not the result of any inadequacies in economic, social or environmental conditions within those countries themselves, but the direct outcome of development elsewhere and the manner in which those countries were incorporated into the operations of the international capitalist system, i.e. the structural disadvantages of these countries and regions. Rather than seeing the US and Europe as the source of a cure for the ills of the developing world, dependency theorists saw the role of these regions as the source of those ills, i.e. in actively creating the problems of underdevelopment. To use Frank's terminology, development and underdevelopment were two sides of the same coin. As illustrated in Figure 1.5, peripheral or satellite regions and countries are integrated into the world system through processes of unequal exchange and dependent relations with the metropolitan core. In consequence, the further entrenched they become in such processes, the more they are held back in development, rather than enabled to progress. This 'development of underdevelopment' was modelled as applying to processes of unequal exchange operating both internationally and internally within countries, and was used to explain patterns of regional and national underdevelopment in countries like Brazil.

The barriers to development as modelled by dependency theorists, therefore, lay in the international division of labour and the terms of trade, rather than a lack of capital or entrepreneurial skills, as within modernisation thinking. One of the principal policy responses to flow from the dependency ideas was import substitution industrialisation (ISI). ISI is a strategy to enable peripheral countries to industrialise through looking inward (setting up domestic industry and supplying markets previously served by imports). It depends on a strong role for the state in protecting new industries via import tariffs and quotas and controlled access to foreign exchange. Many Latin American countries such as Brazil and Argentina had established substantial industrial bases by the 1960s using this strategy towards providing consumer goods such as clothing, cars, food and drinks to sizeable home markets. However, ISI has proven less successful in relation to the production of intermediate and capital goods which are more capital than labour intensive (Hewitt, 2000) and where problems of the lack of domestic capital to invest in such production and a lack of purchasing power on behalf of local, relatively poor, citizens have emerged. Other means towards 'withdrawal' from the international capitalist economy such as through the formation of regional trading areas (as a means for expanding domestic markets) have generally not

Figure 1.5 *The Frank model of underdevelopment*

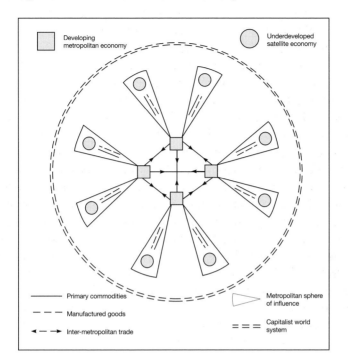

Source: Corbridge (1987).

been sustained over time. In short, dependency theory did much to expose the structural disadvantages of peripheral countries in relation to the capitalist core, and therefore how unlikely it was that they would follow the stages of economic growth mapped out on the basis of early experiences in Europe and North America (as modelled by modernisation theorists). However, the internal problems of local economies were generally underestimated within dependency theory.

The lost decade of the 1980s?

By the 1980s, dependency theory had to a large extent moved out of fashion within development thinking, criticised in particular for its rather deterministic emphasis on the role of external economic structures in shaping society and development. Many commentators by this time were starting to consider the basic development conditions and needs of people within countries of the developing world, to focus on issues of self-reliance in development and on the internal forces of change. The expression, 'another development' is

Plate 1.2 *The inevitable consequences of development? Industrial air pollution*

Source: Gordon Walker, Lancaster University.

often used as an umbrella term to include a broad sweep of changes in thinking regarding development and how best to achieve it from the late 1970s. As a whole, proponents of 'another' or 'alternative' development make less recourse to theorising social change and are more concerned with *how* development should occur (Thomas, 2000). Phrases such as 'growth with equity' or 'redistribution with growth' emerged in the 1970s and encapsulated the recognition that economic growth remains a fundamental ingredient within development thinking and action, but that it was critical to ensure that the benefits do not fall solely to a minority of the population. Similarly, the International Labor Organisation World Employment Conference in 1976 is considered to have been particularly important in raising issues of employment generation and a redistribution of wealth over and above economic growth. By the 1980s, 'development' was seen as a multidimensional concept encapsulating widespread improvements in the social as well as the material well-being of all in society.

In addition, it was recognised that there was no single model for achieving development; certainly it required investment in all sectors, including agriculture as well as industry. Rural-based strategies of development were particularly important amongst those promoting 'development from below' such as Stohr and Taylor (1981). Rather than a single, 'top-down' (and linear) model, it was asserted that development needs to be closely related to the specific local, historical,

Plate 1.3 *The pollution of poverty*

a. Hazardous housing on a Calcutta roadside
Source: author.

b. Washing in the Jakarta floods
Source: author.

sociocultural and institutional conditions, focused on mobilising internal natural and human resources, appropriate technologies and give priority to basic needs. In stark contrast to the theories of development up to that time, development was to be more inclusive, with individual and cooperative actions and enterprises becoming the central means for (or 'agents' of) development. Strong and enduring notions (as will be seen through subsequent chapters) of 'participatory development' emerged at this time in recognition of the shortcomings of top-down, externally imposed and expert-oriented research and development practice (Cooke and Kothari, 2001). Above all through the 1980s, it started to be understood that development needed to be sustainable; it must encompass not only economic and social activities, but also those related to population, the use of natural resources and the resulting impacts on the environment.

Table 1.1 *Income ratios between rich and poor nations*

Year	Income of richest 20% divided by income of poorest 20%
1960	20:1
1980	46:1
1989	60:1
1999	74:1

Sources: Schurmann (2002); UNDP (1999).

The 1980s, however, have been referred to as the 'lost decade' in development. The suggestion is that, with the exception of the 'Asian Tigers', the widespread experience in the developing world was of 'development reversals', i.e. previous gains were lost and in many cases went into reverse. 'Per capita national incomes in Latin America and Africa, for example, declined, investment declined (resulting in the deterioration of infrastructure and transport, communications, education and health care) and unemployment and underemployment grew' (Hewitt, 2000: 301). Furthermore, global inequality increased in the 1980s: the income ratio of rich to poor nations worsened in this decade and continues to do so as seen in Table 1.1.

For many developing countries through the 1980s, development had to be pursued in the context of global economic recession and a mounting 'debt crisis'. Starting in Latin America, with Brazil and Mexico announcing that they could no longer service their official debts, concern spread through the commercial banks and northern governments (that had previously lent huge monies in a context of low interest rates and global expansion) about widespread defaulting and the possible collapse of the international monetary system. Figure 1.6 illustrates the persistent and generally mounting challenge throughout the 1980s and into the 1990s of servicing debt in relation to export performance of regions of the developing world. Economic recession impacted on developing countries through a combination of declining international demand, increasing protectionism in the industrialised countries, deteriorating terms of trade, negative capital flows, continuing high interest rates, and unfavourable lending conditions. These factors had serious implications for the environment, as considered in Chapter 3, and were primary aspects of

Figure 1.6 *Debt service as a percentage of exports of goods and services by world region*

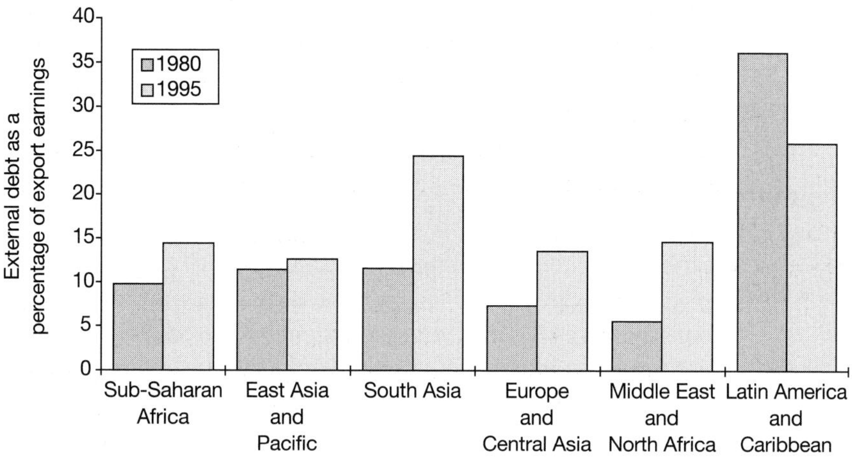

Source: World Bank (1997).

the context in which sustainable development was pursued in the 1980s (and remain so). Not only did huge interest repayments mean money going out without any direct impacts on productive development internally, but savings had to be made, typically in the finance for environment departments and through cuts in social services.

The growing inequality globally and the increasingly diverse experiences of development and underdevelopment in the South through the 1980s were important factors in shaping what has been termed the 'impasse in development studies' (Schurmann, 2002) that was also considered to have characterised this period. The suggestion was that 'old certainties' concerning understanding development were 'fading away' and that existing theories 'could ever less adequately explain experiences of development and underdevelopment' (p. 12): i.e. there was a concern about how development was being theorised as well as the concerns over the development impacts on the ground. A number of factors continued to underpin such concerns through the 1990s. For example, the end of the Cold War and the collapse of communism undermined the strength of Marxist analyses (that had underpinned dependency theories, for example). A 'post-modern' critique within the social sciences generally at this time was also fundamentally about moving away from an era dominated by notions of modernisation and modernity. Both these factors had profound implications for development theory and practice. Furthermore, the rise of globalisation (as considered below and in Chapter 2) was changing the position of the nation state and national governments across economic, social and political spheres. Yet the nation state was central within existing theories of development as seen above. Evidently, all these factors raised many questions for those involved in both development thinking and practice through the 1990s.

The neo-liberal 1990s

In the North, disillusionment with the record of state involvement in the economy (and social life more broadly) also mounted from the late 1980s. This was illustrated in the ascendancy of conservative governments and the politics of Reagan and Thatcher in the US and UK, for example. A belief in what Simon (2002: 87) terms the 'magic of the market' developed and neo-liberal ideas of development took hold. Neo-liberalism is essentially an approach to development that considers the free market to be the best way to initiate and sustain economic development. Typical policy implications of such an approach therefore centre on removing the influence of the state in markets; in removing tariffs on imports and subsidies on exports, for example, and denationalising public industries and service provision. The roots of neo-liberalism are in the neo-classical economics of Adam Smith and 'this ideology rapidly became the economic orthodoxy in the North and was exported to the global South via aid policies and the measures formulated to address the debt crisis' (Simon, 2002: 87).

For many nations in the developing world, their entry into the world economy through the 1990s was increasingly defined by the neo-liberal policies of the World Bank (WB) and the International Monetary Fund (IMF). As already suggested, many developing countries began to experience severe balance of payments difficulties in the 1980s that were considered to threaten the international financial system as a whole. Debt became the concern of the two 'mainstays of the global economic order', the WB and the IMF. The assessment in the early 1980s was that the economic crisis in developing countries was more than a temporary liquidity issue (as it had been conceived in the 1970s). Rather, comprehensive, longer-term solutions were required, based on packages of broad policy reforms in indebted nations. The term structural adjustment programme (SAP) is used to refer to the generic activities of the IMF and WB in this arena. The central objective of SAPs as defined by the World Bank was to 'modify the structure of an economy so that it can maintain both its growth rate and the viability of its balance of payments in the medium term' (Reed, 1996: 41), i.e. to address issues of debt.

The first SAP was implemented in Turkey in 1980 and by the end of the decade 187 SAPs had been negotiated for 64 developing countries (Dickenson *et al.*, 1996: 265). Most countries today have some kind of SAP since they are the basis for receipt of WB lending that now reaches most countries of the world as shown in Figure 1.7. Although each package of policy reform is tailored for the particular country, SAPs generally have included many or all of the elements listed in Figure 1.8. It has been argued that the impacts of SAPs quickly went far beyond the original national contexts for which they were designed, to become an instrument for global economic restructuring (Reed, 1996) and through the conditions attached, they enabled the IMF and WB to 'virtually control the economies' of many developing nations (Hildyard, 1994: 26). Certainly, these international institutions currently influence development policy and planning in the developing world to an unprecedented extent and are important actors in determining the prospects for sustainable development in the future, as seen in Chapter 3.

Through the 1990s, recognition also grew of the unprecedented changes of a global character occurring in all arenas of economic, social, political (and environmental) activity. The term 'globalisation' became:

> widely used to explain the causes and effects of most aspects of life at the turn of the century ... While open to different interpretations, globalisation captures a description of the widening and deepening of economic, political, social and cultural interdependence and interconnectedness.
>
> (Willett, 2001: 1)

In short, globalisation encompasses the various processes of change through which interactions between different regions are increasing and the world becomes ever more global in character. Whilst global links and interconnections between places and peoples around the world have existed previously (through colonial ties, for example), the nature, extent and depth of contemporary processes of globalisation are relatively new. As Allen and Hamnett (1995) suggest, it is not the global scope of movements of people or resources currently, but the immediacy and intensity with which we can now experience other parts of the globe, which is unprecedented and is part of what distinguishes globalisation from earlier periods of 'internationalism'. Furthermore, processes of global integration now extend to much

Figure 1.7 *The global reach of the World Bank*

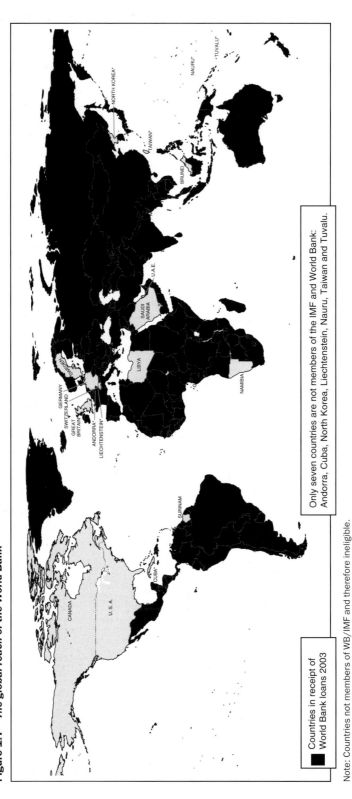

Countries in receipt of
World Bank loans 2003

Only seven countries are not members of the IMF and World Bank:
Andorra, Cuba, North Korea, Liechtenstein, Nauru, Taiwan and Tuvalu.

Note: Countries not members of WB/IMF and therefore ineligible.
Source: *New Internationalist*, no. 365, March 2004.

Figure 1.8 *The principal instruments of*
structural adjustment
....

Cuts in:
● government expenditure
● public sector employment
● real wages

Pricing policies designed to:
● eliminate food subsidies
● raise agricultural prices
● cost recovery in public services

Trade liberalisation involving:
● currency devaluation
● credit reform
● privatisation of state-owned institutions
● higher interest rates
....

more than the flow of goods and services, for example, as illustrated further in Chapters 2 and 3. However, whilst the world is becoming more global, it does not necessarily mean it is becoming more uniform, as discussed in Box A.

Into the twenty-first century, one of the most radical reactions within development thinking to the dilemmas of development on the ground and to the limitations of both conventional and alternative schools of thought came from what's known as the 'post-development' school (most closely associated with Escobar, 1995). Within this thinking, the concept of development as a desirable process itself is contested for the ways in which it 'involves a dependent and subordinate process, creates and widens spatial inequalities, harms local cultures and values, perpetuates poverty and poor working and living conditions, produces unsustainable environments, and infringes human rights and democracy' (Hodder, 2000: 17). Not only is development considered to have failed, but the development project itself is condemned for creating and producing the opposite of what it promised (Corbridge, 1999). In short, a post-development era depends on breaking the 'holds of westernisation' be it as organised by the aid industry or activities of western private capital. 'Defending the local' (such as through ecological, women's and people's organisations) and resisting the forces of globalisation are core prescriptions for change. Post-developmentalists emphasise grassroots participation and the capacities of organisations at the local level as agents of change (the suggestion being that the state has failed for the way that it has facilitated the westernisation of the development project). Whilst the post-development school can be criticised for focusing on the 'worst' experiences of the last decades (Rigg, 1997) and for ignoring the improvements shown in longer-term data sets, post-development thinking has helped reaffirm the importance of the local in development processes (Potter *et al.*, 2004), which will be seen to be a feature of more sustainable development processes in later chapters.

Box A

The unevenness of globalisation

Despite the global character of many major processes of economic, political, environmental and social change in the world currently, it should not be taken that globalisation affects all people or all areas of the globe equally. It is evident that some parts of the world are 'left out' in the sense that they are not part of a network of communications or do not receive multi-national investment, for example. A simple illustration is that half of the world's population has never made a telephone call.

(Potter *et al.*, 2004)

Figure 1.9 highlights the geographical differences in the use of the Internet. Over half of the population of the United States is now online, whereas in countries like Thailand, only a minority of the urban population is able to access this network. Approximately 70 per cent of all traffic on the Internet originates from or is addressed to North America (Knox and Marston, 2004). Furthermore, 80 per cent of all global websites are in English, yet only 10 per cent of the world's population speaks English (UNDP, 2001).

Figure 1.9 *Internet users per 1,000 population, 2001*

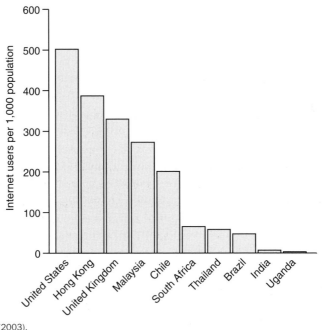

Source: UNDP (2003).

The uneven reach of globalisation is also illustrated in terms of foreign direct investment – investment made by private companies that is a major driving force of economic globalisation. The developed world accounts for two-thirds of the world's FDI stock (UNCTAD, 2003). In particular, it is firms from the EU, the US and Japan which are the major owners and sources of outward FDI. In large measure, these major investors overseas are also investing in each other. Table 1.2 confirms that the great proportion of inward FDI flows are to the high-income countries of the world. In contrast, the African continent, for example, could be suggested to be only loosely connected to this globalising economy.

Table 1.2 *Inward foreign direct investment, by major world region, 2000*

	Total flows, millions of dollars	% of world total
World	1,167,337	
Low income countries	6,812	0.6
Middle income countries	150,572	12.9
High income countries	1,009,929	86.5
East Asia and Pacific	42,847	4
Europe and Central Asia	28,495	2.4
Latin America and Caribbean	75,088	6.4
Middle East and North Africa	1,209	0.1
South Asia	3,093	0.3
Sub-Saharan Africa	6,676	0.6

Source: Compiled from World Bank (2003a).

Changing perceptions of the environment

The history of environmental concern is quite similar to that of development studies: although people have held and articulated varying attitudes towards nature stretching back many years, it is only since the 1960s that a coherent philosophy and language surrounding the environment ('environmentalism' as defined by Pepper in 1984) can be identified. In continuity with 'development thinking', it is possible to identify significant differences and changes over time concerning ideas about the environment; regarding society's relationship with nature and in terms of the prescribed conservation requirements within modern environmentalism. Although the focus here is largely on 'mainstream' environmentalism, i.e. the broad consensus that can be identified as forwarded for example within successive conferences and publications of international institutions, the continued diversity within modern environmentalism should not be denied or underestimated. For example, there is a persistent and fundamental divergence between 'reformist/technocentric' and 'radical/ecocentric' environmentalism which is the source of much contemporary debate within sustainable development. Box B

Box B

Modes of thought concerning humanity and nature

It is argued that society's desire to manipulate nature, concomitant with an acceptance that the Earth nurtures our own existence, is inherent in the human condition. 'Technocentric' and 'ecocentric' refer to the two extreme positions. In reality, the distinction between these different perspectives is often blurred. As O'Riordan (1981) suggests, rarely is the world so neatly divided into two camps; rather we all tend to favour certain elements of both modes, depending on such factors as our changing economic status and the institutional setting or issue at hand. The categories should not, therefore, be thought of as rigidly fixed or mutually exclusive.

	Technocentric	Ecocentric
Environmental philosophies:		
	Human-centred: humanity has a desire to manipulate nature and make the world a more certain place in which to live.	Earth-centred: the Earth nurtures humanity's existence and should be treated with respect and humility.
Green labels:	'Dry Green'	'Deep Green'
	Reformist in that the present economic system is accepted, but considered to require some gradual revision.	Radical in that quite rapid and fundamental changes in economy and society are desired.
	Belief in political status quo, but more responsible and accountable institutions. Self-regulation through 'enlightened conscience'.	Supports devolved, political structures with emphasis on self-reliant communities and pursuit of justice and redistribution across generations.
Environmental management strategies:	Reliance on scientific credibility, modelling and prediction.	Management strategies geared to retaining global stability based on ecological principles of diversity and homeostasis.
	Promotes the appropriate manipulation of markets to create cost-effective solutions to environmental improvements.	New and fundamentally different conservation solutions required which are flexible and adaptable.
	Sustainable development through rational use of resources, better planning and clean technologies, for example.	Alternative and appropriate technologies.

Sources: compiled from Pepper (1996), O'Riordan (1981) and O'Riordan (1995).

highlights the principal differences between these two philosophical standpoints on nature and society and the varied implications of each for conservation action.

Development as environmentally destructive

In the 1960s, environmentalism was largely a movement reflecting European and American white, middle-class concerns. The undesirable effects of industrial and economic development were beginning to be seen via a number of 'conspicuous pollution incidents' (Bartelmus, 1994: 5) and people were worried about the effects on their own lifestyles and health: 'after two centuries of industrialism and urbanisation, people now began to rediscover the idea that they were part of nature' (McCormick, 1995: 56). Environmentalists campaigned on issues such as air pollution and whaling and often received substantial support from the media. In contrast to earlier nature protection or conservation movements within these regions, environmentalism was overtly activist and political. The combination of actual changes in the environment and people's perceptions generally at this time brought widespread public support for the environmental movement, particularly amongst the younger groups. As Biswas and Biswas (1985) suggest, 'the environment and Vietnam became two of the major issues over which youth rebelled against the establishment' (p. 25).

For the new environmentalists, it was not solely their local outdoor environments which were perceived to be under threat, but human survival itself. A number of very influential 'global future studies' were published in the early 1970s which served to reinforce and spread the fears and influence of western environmentalists. For example, texts such as *The Population Bomb* (Ehrlich, 1968), *Blueprint for Survival* (Goldsmith *et al.*, 1972) and *The Limits to Growth* (Meadows *et al.*, 1972) modelled an ever-expanding population and mounting demands of society on a fundamentally finite resource base. In order to 'avoid the disastrous consequences of transgressing the physical limits of the Earth's resources' (Bartelmus, 1994: 5), urgent conservation actions (particularly population control in the developing world) and 'zero-growth' in the world economy were required.

Not surprisingly, this environmental movement found little support in the developing nations. Many developing nations (outside Latin America) had only just gained independence and were sceptical regarding the motives behind proposals which seemed to limit their development objectives and remove sovereign control over resources. These underdeveloped nations saw their development problems as being linked to too little industry rather than too much and contrasted this with the position of the developed countries which used the bulk of resources and contributed most to the resulting industrial pollution. Similarly, it was hard for representatives of the developing world to consider how their relatively impoverished citizens could compete with affluent consumers of the West in terms of responsibility for the depletion of resources.

Development and conservation at this time were portrayed as incompatible: resources were thought to be finite, and pollution and environmental deterioration were considered the inevitable consequences of industrial development. In conceiving the 'environment' as the stocks of substances found in nature, by definition these resources were ultimately considered to be limited in quantity. In turn, therefore, the global future predictions gave little attention to the social, technological or institutional factors which affect the relationship between people and resources (Biswas and Biswas, 1985). Further to such environmental determinism, these reports were ahistorical in the sense that they gave no attention to how or why the world is divided into rich and poor, for example. They were also apolitical in considering the future of the Earth (rather than people) as the overriding and paramount concern, with no consideration of how the solutions advocated would favour some nations or groups over others.

By the time of the UN Conference on the Human Environment in 1972, the environmental movement had 'come of age' and environmental issues were clearly on the international political agenda, as evidenced by the participation in Stockholm of 113 countries. However, as Adams (2001) suggests, whilst the Stockholm meeting is often identified as the key event in the emergence of sustainable development, 'it was only partly, and belatedly, concerned with the environmental and developmental problems of the emerging Third World' (p. 54). The primary impetus for the conference had been the developed world's concerns about the effects of industrialisation (Sweden, for example, being particularly concerned about acid rain). In the event, the dialogue between government representatives, and within parallel meetings of non-governmental organisations (NGOs) at the conference, soon moved to wider issues including the relationship between environment and development issues. The term 'pollution of poverty' was used for the first time at

Stockholm to refer to the environmental concerns of the poor, such as lack of clean water or sanitation, which threatened life itself for many in the developing world. It also encompassed the emerging recognition that a lack of development could also cause environmental degradation, a notion which is now shaping much thinking and action towards sustainability, as detailed in subsequent chapters. However, discussions of the links between poverty and environmental degradation were limited at Stockholm (Adams, 2001), as were the causes of poverty (Middleton and O'Keefe, 2003), and whilst it was made clear that environment and development *should* be integrated, it was left unclear as to *how* this should happen.

Following the Stockholm conference, there continued to be mistrust on behalf of the developing nations regarding the extent to which ideas of development and environment were indeed understood as interdependent and truly 'shared' problems of global resource management. Furthermore, environmental concern continues to be very uneven within regions of both developing and developed worlds, as considered in subsequent sections. Perhaps the most significant outcome of the Stockholm conference was the creation of the United Nations Environment Programme (UNEP) in the following year. The intention established at the conference, was that a new intergovernmental body should be established within the UN to focus environmental action and to serve as an 'international environmental watchdog' to be responsible for the monitoring of global environmental change. Although its monitoring role is considered to have been limited (Werksman, 1996), UNEP remains the UN's primary environmental policy co-coordinating body and its role has been strengthened in subsequent international fora. UNEP has also been instrumental in overseeing a rising number of multilateral environmental agreements in the last few decades, as seen in Chapter 3. However, its activities continue to be hampered by problems of international coordination and scarce funding.

Finding policies for action

In summary, by the late 1970s, important changes in thinking regarding both the environment and development were causing the two previously separate issues to be seen as more interconnected concerns and an improved understanding of the interdependence of the developed and developing worlds was also recognised. The challenge for the 1980s was to translate the substantial rhetoric into policies and actions in practice. In 1977, UNEP commissioned the International Union for the Conservation of Nature and Natural Resources (IUCN) to consider and report on the conservation problems of the world and to identify effective solutions to them. Historically, the IUCN had been concerned with wildlife conservation and nature protection. Their report, the World Conservation Strategy (IUCN, 1980), has been referred to as the 'launchpad' for the concept of sustainable development (Mather and Chapman, 1995: 248) and the 'nearest approach yet . . . to a comprehensive action-oriented programme for political change' (Adams, 2001: 65). Within the WCS, for the first time, development was suggested as a major means of achieving conservation rather than as an obstruction to it: 'human benefits would follow from appropriate forms of environmental management' (Mather and Chapman, 1995: 247). The WCS identified three objectives for conservation, as shown in Figure 1.10. It is evident in the figure that conservation itself was defined as being more than nature preservation through the ways in which human survival, future needs in science, medicine and industry are linked to ecological processes and genetic diversity, for example.

Figure 1.10   *The World Conservation Strategy objectives of conservation*

1 **The maintenance of essential ecological processes and life-support systems** such as soil, forests, agricultural systems, and coastal and freshwater systems. This meant managing cropland, protecting watersheds and coastal fisheries, and controlling the discharge of pollutants.

2 **The preservation of genetic diversity** for breeding projects in agriculture, forestry and fisheries. This meant preventing the extinction of species, preserving as many varieties as possible of crop and forage plants, timber trees, animals for aqua-culture, microbes and other domesticated organisms and their wild relatives, protecting the wild relatives of economically valuable and other useful species and their habitats, fitting the needs of ecosystems to the size, distribution and management of protected areas, and co-coordinating national and international protected area programmes.

3 **Ensuring the sustainable use of species and ecosystems.** This meant ensuring use did not exceed the productive capacity of exploited species, reducing excessive yields to sustainable levels, reducing incidental take, maintaining the habitats of exploited species, carefully allocating timber concessions and limiting firewood consumption, and regulating the stocking of grazing lands.

Source: McCormick (1995).

However, the WCS has been criticised for continuing to portray a very neo-malthusian future in which escalating numbers of people are identified as the source of short-sighted approaches to natural resources management and the root of degradation. In continuity with earlier publications, there was little attention to the political, social, cultural or economic dimensions of resource use or, indeed, obstacles to development (Reid, 1995). Adams (2001: 60) summarises the WCS as 'a conservation document that addressed the issues and problems raised by economic development, rather than a document about development and environment as such'. Whilst stressing global responsibility and strategy, the failure of a global agenda for environmental action to recognise the political nature of the development process was particularly problematic. As Reid (1995: 43) states,

> To suggest solutions based on such 'self-evident' principles as 'population increase must be halted' and 'carrying capacity must be respected' without considering the political realities affecting the chances of their being implemented is to ignore the rights of local people, neglect the impact of social and economic forces on their access to and use of resources, and deny the reality of the effort needed to surmount the many political difficulties associated with negotiating 'improvements' that have recognisable similarity with 'obvious' global solutions.

Recognising the politics of sustainable development

In 1987, the report of the World Commission on Environment and Development extended the ideas of sustainable development significantly beyond those of the WCS and did much to disseminate the popular and political use of the term as identified at the outset of this chapter. Principally, the WCED started with people (rather than the environment) and gave greater attention to human development concerns and the kinds of environmental policies needed to achieve these: to the challenge of overcoming poverty and meeting basic needs and to integrating the environment into economic decision-making. It recognised that the 'environment' did not exist as a sphere separate from human actions and ambitions and explicitly considered the political and social requirements of sustainable development in practice. It was underpinned by a strong ideology that nature and the Earth could be managed (i.e. there was no spectre of economic disaster as portrayed by the WCS within the WCED report) and for this, reviving economic growth was considered essential. No longer was it a question of whether development was desirable: economic growth was central to the Commission's proposals for environmental protection and 'degraded and deteriorating environments were seen to be inimical to continued development' (Mather and Chapman, 1995: 248). It was also clear that it was futile to continue to tackle environmental problems without considering the broader issues of factors underlying world poverty and international inequality. But new forms of economic growth would be the key to sustainable development; growth must be less energy intensive and more equitably shared, for example.

The mix of 'environment' and development concerns of the WCED are evident in the critical objectives identified in Figure 1.2. Whilst ensuring a sustainable level of population is one of those objectives, the WCED gives a very different message from that of WCS. For example, the WCED recognises the differentiated impact on resources of current international patterns of consumption: 'an additional person in an industrial country consumes far more than an additional person in the Third World. Consumption patterns and processes are as important as numbers of consumers in the conservation of resources' (WCED, 1987: 95). Similarly, in relation to the objective of a changed quality in economic growth in the future, the Commission acknowledged varied responsibilities:

> if industrial development is to be sustainable over the long term, it will have to change radically in terms of the quality of that development, *particularly in industrialised countries* ... industries and industrial operations should be encouraged that are more efficient in terms of resource use, that generate less pollution and waste, that are based on the use of renewable rather than non-renewable resources, and that minimise irreversible adverse impacts on human health and the environment.
>
> (WCED, 1987: 213, emphasis added)

For some commentators, however, the continued prominence given in the Brundtland Report to economic growth has suggested a 'comfortable reformism' in respect of the suggestion that it can be reconciled with environmental conservation without any significant adjustments to the capitalist market system. Although the substantial political and economic changes required in future to achieve sustainable development were identified by the WCED (see Figure 1.2), it has also been suggested that it did not go far enough in terms of identifying the barriers or obstacles to change in these sectors (Starke, 1990).

The WCED was commissioned by the United Nations and reported directly to its General Assembly. In 1989, it was announced that a conference would be held five years hence to report progress on environment and development since the report. This was the 'Earth Summit' held in Rio de Janeiro in 1992. It is important to evaluate the conference as a process rather than a single event (Adams, 2001). In Chapter 3 the specific agreements reached at Rio and the *continued* impacts on the actions of varied institutions of development are discussed. Commentators on the Rio conference have presented strong and often opposing reactions (O'Riordan, 2000). For Middleton and O'Keefe (2003: 7), it put the environment at the 'centre stage of politics' and in placing the concept of sustainable development at the centre of the debate, it prompted new ways of thinking regarding the links between poverty and the environment. For Adams (2001), however, the agenda remains dominated by northern priorities focused on issues of the global commons that are more amenable to political and technical solutions than poverty or global inequality. There was certainly substantial optimism at the conference that new global commitments between North and South could be achieved around the common interests of these regions: the end of the Cold War and of the economic recession of the 1980s, for example. However, many of the problems of environment and development identified at Rio got worse through the 1990s and the finances identified as necessary to implement Agenda 21 (A21) generally did not materialise. It was estimated by the UNCED secretariat that US$600 billion annually was required between 1993 and 2000 (O'Riordan, 2000) to implement A21. But by that end date, official development assistance had in fact fallen to its lowest level ever (Banuri *et al.*, 2002), as discussed in Chapter 3.

The World Summit on Sustainable Development

In 2002, the World Summit on Sustainable Development was held in South Africa. The aim was to reinvigorate at the highest political level, the global commitment to a North–South partnership to achieve sustainable development. It has been referred to as 'by far the most inclusive summit to date' (Seyfang, 2003: 227) for the way in which more stakeholder groups were brought into formal meetings (including a bigger presence for business, for example), but also for the extensive informal participation of many individuals and groups in parallel civil society events. An estimated 40,000 people attended the Civil Society Global People's Forum. However, it has also been suggested that it may be the last of the 'mega-summits' whereby success is measured by the number of participating heads of state and the summit is preceded by years of negotiation to develop a text that reflects a consensus of common purpose for the international community (Bigg, 2004). The suggestion is that the gap between the expectations of these summits and the results produced is now too wide.

The official outcomes of WSSD were the Declaration on Sustainable Development and the Plan of Implementation. It is evidenced in the Declaration reproduced in Figure 1.11 that social and economic development (poverty and inequality, for example) are now firmly within international thinking on the environment: 'the eradication of poverty is now seen as an underlying theme in all work on sustainable development' (Bigg, 2004: 7). Similarly, Seyfang (2003) suggests, one success of the summit was the way in which it facilitated such 'joined-up' thinking on environment and development. It was also the first time that the implications of globalisation (that were not discussed at the Rio Conference) were identified as principal challenges for the future. However, early reflections on the WSSD Plan of Implementation are that it is substantially a recommitment to

Figure 1.11 *The Johannesburg Declaration on Sustainable Development: the challenges we face*

....

- We recognise that poverty eradication, changing consumption and production patterns, and protecting and managing the natural resource base for economic and social development are overarching objectives of, and essential requirements for, sustainable development.
- The deep fault line that divides human society between the rich and the poor and the ever-increasing gap between the developed and developing worlds pose a major threat to global prosperity, security and stability.
- The global environment continues to suffer. Loss of biodiversity continues, fish stocks continue to be depleted, desertification claims more and more fertile land, the adverse effects of climate change are already evident, natural disasters are more frequent and more devastating and developing countries more vulnerable, and air, water and marine pollution continue to rob millions of a decent life.
- Globalisation has added a new dimension to these challenges. The rapid integration of markets, mobility of capital and significant increases in investment flows around the world have opened new challenges and opportunities for the pursuit of sustainable development. But the benefits and costs of globalisation are unevenly distributed, with developing countries facing special difficulties in meeting this challenge.
- We risk the entrenchment of these global disparities and unless we act in a manner that fundamentally changes their lives, the poor of the world may lose confidence in their representatives and the democratic systems to which we remain committed, seeing their representatives as nothing more than sounding brass or tinkling cymbals.

....

the implementation of existing commitments, those of Agenda 21 and of the Millennium Development Goals (MDGs).

The MDGs are listed in Figure 1.12. Their origin is in the Millennium Declaration adopted by the United Nations General Assembly in 2000. In September of that year, 189 member states had met 'at the dawn of a new millennium, to reaffirm our faith in the Organisation and its Charter as indispensable foundations of a more peaceful, prosperous and just world' (UN, 2000: 1.1). A host of commitments were encompassed within the Declaration and a number of specific, monitorable targets for achievement by 2015 were identified that have become known as the MDGs. One of those goals refers specifically to sustainable development and the actions of governments in preparing national strategies. Many others are clearly central to sustainable development in that they demand better outcomes in many areas that affect poorer groups. Although international goals and targets have been set before, the MDGs are considered to be

> unprecedented in the range of goals and targets chosen, in the recogni-
> tion that most are interconnected, and in the public commitment from
> international agencies that they will be judged by whether these goals
> and targets are achieved.
>
> (Satterthwaite, 2003: 8)

A new millennium target, to halve the number of people without access to basic sanitation by 2015, was added at the 2002 World Summit on Sustainable Development. However, many international non-governmental organisations (INGOs) are generally disappointed by the lack of specific monitorable and binding commitments to emerge from the conference. Furthermore, as Middleton and O'Keefe (2003: 30) warn, 'a third of the period in which these goals are to be achieved has elapsed already and . . . so far, there is little sign of change'. However, in addition to the commitment and agreements negotiated by governments in Johannesburg, a new type of partnership was also formalised at the summit, officially termed 'Type II outcomes'. These are alliances comprising interested governments, international organisations, corporations and major groups in society aimed at translating the multinationally agreed outcomes into concrete actions. Hundreds of such partnerships were announced and are suggested as a major innovation of WSSD (Guttman, 2003). There is, however, a concern regarding what impact these regional and sectoral agreements will have on the future of international intergovernmental decision-making (this is considered further in Chapter 3). Governments of southern countries have also expressed concern as to how this kind of development could reduce pressure on

Figure 1.12 *The Millennium Development Goals and Targets*

....

Goal	Target

....

Goal	Target
1 To eradicate extreme poverty and hunger	1 To halve, between 1990 and 2015, the proportion of people whose income is less than US$1 a day 2 To halve, between 1990 and 2015, the proportion of people who suffer from hunger
2 To achieve universal primary education	3 To ensure that, by 2015, children everywhere, boys and girls alike, will be able to complete a full course of primary schooling
3 To promote gender equality and empower women	4 To eliminate gender disparity in primary and secondary education, preferably by 2005 and in all levels of education no later than 2015
4 To reduce child mortality	5 To reduce by two-thirds, between 1990 and 2015, the under-five mortality rate
5 To improve maternal health	6 To reduce by three-quarters, between 1990 and 2015, the maternal mortality ratio
6 To combat HIV/ Aids, malaria and other diseases	7 To have halted by 2015 and begun to reverse the spread of HIV/Aids 8 To have halted by 2015 and begun to reverse the incidence of malaria and other major diseases
7 To ensure environmental sustainability	9 To integrate the principles of sustainable development into country policies and programmes and reverse the loss of environmental resources 10 To halve, by 2015, the proportion of people without sustainable access to safe drinking water and basic sanitation 11 To have achieved, by 2020, a significant improvement in the lives of at least 100 million slum dwellers
8 To develop a global partnership for development	12 Develop further an open, rule-based, predictable, non-discriminatory trading and financial system 13 To address the special needs of the least developed countries 14 To address the special needs of landlocked countries and small island developing states 15 To deal comprehensively with the debt problems of developing countries through national and international measures in order to make debt sustainable in the long run 16 In cooperation with developing countries, to develop and implement strategies for decent and productive work for youth 17 In cooperation with pharmaceutical companies, to provide access to affordable, essential drugs in developing countries 18 In cooperation with the private sector, to make available the benefits of new technologies, especially information and communication

....

Source: *www.developmentgoals.org*

more developed countries to provide additional direct financial support for sustainable development.

Indeed, the optimism that was at Rio concerning the common interests of different parts of the globe does not appear to have been justified across the period between the two conferences. For example, there were significant problems within the PrepComs in arriving at the statements that are intended to provide the framework for subsequent debates at the summit: 'it was astonishing that agreement on either document was possible' (Middleton and O'Keefe, 2003: 23). It has to be acknowledged that the opportunities for constructive dialogue and engagement at the summit were compromised by the fact that it was being held at a time when the US and the UK were engaging in war on Iraq and displaying a 'patent contempt for the UN' (Middleton and O'Keefe, 2003: 24). Many 'gaps' rather than 'commonalities' were also evident within the proceedings of the summit (Bigg, 2004); efforts to establish new targets for proportional increases in renewable energy use were thwarted and for mandatory standards on corporate accountability downgraded. Regularly it was the US who were often 'out of step with developments' (p. 7).

Conclusion

Evidently, the idea of sustainable development is not new but has a substantial history. However, what was new in the 1980s was the way in which the two literatures of development and environmentalism came closer together, recognising the significant and interdependent nature of these goals. Into the 1990s, it has been seen that the concept of sustainable development encapsulated notions of development based in the reality of local environments and the needs of the poorest sectors in society that were far removed from the unilinear, econometric development models of the 1960s. Insight also came through both literatures concerning the multidimensional nature of this challenge through expanded notions of the environment and the functions it plays in human societal development. Critically, sustainable development was recognised as a *global* challenge: ultimately, the achievement of environment and development ends in any single location or for any group of people is connected in some way to what is happening elsewhere, for others. By the end of the 1990s, the widespread suggestion was that the world itself was characterised by unprecedented rates and degrees of economic, political and social change and the understanding of sustainable development currently encompasses the challenges and opportunities presented by a globalising world.

It has been confirmed, through this analysis of mainstream sustainable development, that it remains central to international agendas as encompassed in the outputs of major UN conferences, for example. In subsequent chapters, it will be seen that sustainable development is also being claimed as a major policy goal by other institutions such as the World Bank and even the World Trade Organisation. However, there remains substantial contestation as to how best to secure sustainable development. Once again, such debate is evidently not new, as established through this chapter. Whilst neo-liberal development ideas and faith in market globalisation remain strong, they are not entirely uncontested, as illustrated in the work of the post-development school. Whilst issues of the global environment itself remain at the centre of environmental debates and can be considered a northern agenda focused on intergenerational issues (Adger *et al.*, 2001; Adams, 2001), there are also signs that poverty today in the developing world is moving higher up that agenda. Further details of how these debates (as well as the rapidly changing context for sustainable development) are shaping the challenges of sustainable development and the nature of actions taken by the now varied agencies in development are considered in the following two chapters. The outcomes of these for local experiences in rural and urban areas are the focus of Chapters 4 and 5.

Discussion questions

* Summarise the role of the state as modelled within modernisation theory, dependency approaches and by post-developmentalists.
* Have the principal development and environmental concerns of the developing world been recognised in the outcomes of major international conferences of recent decades?
* Consider how debt may affect the prospects for sustainable development as defined by the WCED.

Further reading

Adams, W.M. (2001) *Green Development*, Routledge, London, second edition.

Allen, T. and Thomas, A. (eds) (2000) *Poverty and Development into the Twenty-first Century*, Oxford University Press, Oxford.

Bigg, T. (ed.) (2004) *Survival for a Small Planet: The Sustainable Development Agenda*, Earthscan/IIED, London.

Lee, K., Holland, A. and McNeill, D. (eds) (2000) *Global Sustainable Development in the Twenty-first Century*, Edinburgh University Press, Edinburgh.

Willis, K. (2005) *Theories of Development*, Routledge, London.

World Commission on Environment and Development (1987) *Our Common Future*, Oxford University Press, Oxford.

The challenges of sustainable development

Summary

- Whilst the challenge of sustainable development is a global one, the unsustainable nature of past patterns and processes of development have had marked geographical patterns.
- Human development (including freedom from conflict) continues to be linked closely to natural resources.
- There are multiple dimensions to 'poverty' and the relationship between poverty and environmental degradation is complex.
- Questions of power and voice are central in understanding the persistence of environmental degradation and the prospects for sustainable development in the future.
- Many processes of globalisation work through existing patterns of environmental difference and can make them worse.

Introduction

Chapter 1 showed that ideas about how best to achieve development and about society's relationship with the environment changed over time, in part as evidence emerged 'on the ground' about the successes and failures therein. The following sections provide greater detail on the limitations of past patterns and processes of development across the globe which have underpinned the call for sustainable development. They also provide a closer examination of aspects of the contemporary context of sustainable development in the twenty-first century such as the nature and impacts of globalisation. In so doing, greater insight into what sustainable development means in practice: for example, the nature and extent of the challenges for action, for whom and where. That is the focus of Chapter 3.

Sustainable development is fundamentally about reconciling development and the environmental resources on which society depends. Economic development processes in the past have been closely associated with rising extraction of the resource stocks of the globe and continue to be so. But the creation of a sustainable society also depends fundamentally on the absence of violent conflict, yet it is now widely recognised that many human rights abuses, humanitarian disasters and civil wars are closely linked to environmental resources. Whilst the linkages between poverty and the environment are complex, the numbers of people in poverty worldwide remains large and it is the poorest groups who suffer the impacts of environmental degradation most extensively and acutely. As seen in the previous chapter, at the turn of the twenty-first century, human well-being, which includes individual civil and political liberties, as well as meeting the physical and material needs of human society, is an accepted concern for development. It is both a goal and a condition for sustained progress.

The patterns of past development are important. Although the challenges for sustainable development can be considered to be those of the global community as a whole, it is evident through the analysis of the integrated economic, social and environmental outcomes of development in the past, that many of the challenges and opportunities for the future are manifested spatially. Fundamentally, people live in places. In understanding that certain groups of people have been historically excluded from accessing the basic opportunities for development and an acceptable quality of life, it is important to know where they live (now and in the future), the barriers they face and the capacities that they bring towards changing these processes of development. But people pursue different activities and practices in different places, for example in rural and urban areas, which generate different environmental and socioeconomic challenges and opportunities. Furthermore, different places are characterised by different resource endowments and by unique ecologies that emerge through adaptation to local conditions and processes of change. Once again, this ensures that the nature of the challenges and opportunities for sustainable development is going to be locally distinct and, indeed, may firstly become evident at this scale.

The centrality of resources in future development worldwide

All forms of economic and social activity make demands on the resource base: as raw materials such as soil and water within agricultural production, as sources of inputs and energy into industrial production or in the construction and maintenance of human settlements and urban lifestyles, for example. Whilst absolute resource scarcities (as predicted in several of the global future scenarios discussed in Chapter 1) have not generally materialised, economic development in the past has been closely correlated with mounting rates of resource extraction. This is seen in the case of global water withdrawals which expanded throughout the twentieth century and at rates in excess of population growth, as shown in Figures 2.1 and 2.2. Water issues may now be at the top of public environmental consciousness, at least in the more developed world (Adeel, 2004). This is due to a number of patterns observed in the 1990s such as record-breaking floods in many parts of the world (including the UK), extreme climate impacts related to El Niño, major hurricanes in the Americas, major droughts in many arid and semi-arid regions of the world and the extensive arsenic poisoning of drinking water in Asia (see Box C). For many countries, worldwide, accessing quality water supplies in the future will depend on the resolution of complex political and institutional challenges associated with harnessing the sources of river and lake systems that extend across more than one national boundary. These challenges may threaten already fragile ties between states, aggravate long-standing international political stand-offs or fuel new ones. Indeed, many similarities were noted in 1992 by Biswas, between what he termed the 'impending water crisis' and the issues surrounding oil in the 1970s and early 1980s, particularly in terms of the implications for political and economic stability in regions such as the Middle East. As Clarke and King (2004: 12) observe, 'in a water-short world, mistrust and insecurity are what mark most relations between countries that share rivers. There are many of them: more than 260 river basins are international and 13 are shared by five or more countries.'

Figure 2.1 *Total global water use, 1940–2000*

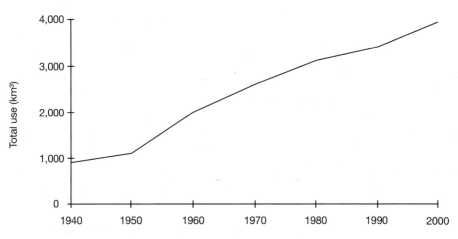

Sources: Mather and Chapman (1995); Clarke and King (2004).

Figure 2.2 *Per capita global water use, 1940–2000*

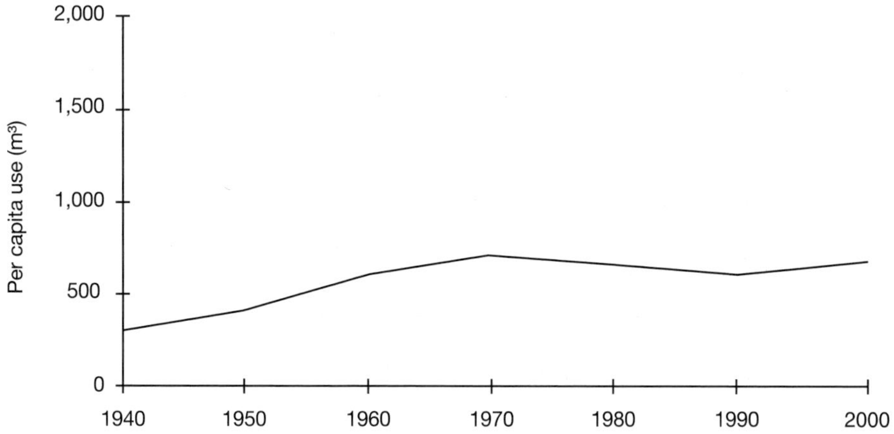

Sources: Mather and Chapman (1995); Clarke and King (2004).

Box C

The unexpected environmental impacts of development

In the early 1970s, multilateral and bilateral donors assisted Bangladesh in sinking thousands of tubewells to provide clean water drawn from the sands and silt of the Ganges floodplain. Currently, the majority of drinking water in Bangladesh is provided through over 11 million tubewells (Zaman, 2001). It was found in the mid-1990s, however, that people using many of these wells are, in fact, being slowly poisoned by naturally occurring arsenic in the alluvial sediments of the delta, which appear to be released by chemical changes prompted by the fluctuations in water levels caused by pumping.

It was estimated by Professor Chakraborti of the University of Calcutta, who first uncovered the problem, that as many as 30 million people in Bangladesh may be drinking contaminated water. A fifth of the nation's drinking water was considered to contain up to one hundred times the maximum level of arsenic recommended by the World Health Organisation (Pearce, 1998). Zaman (2001) suggests that as many as 85 million Bangladeshis may be currently at risk from arsenicosis. However, there is a problem in determining the numbers of people affected in that the early symptoms of increased skin pigmentation take at least ten years to develop. Many of those who develop these skin conditions, however, go on to develop internal cancers. Whilst both the government of Bangladesh and the WHO were informed of the problem in 1993 and the WHO has since revised downwards its assessed 'safe' levels of arsenic in drinking water, the sinking of tubewells has continued in Bangladesh.

There is no effective treatment for arsenic poisoning: poisonous wells need to be identified and alternative sources of water found. Testing is relatively simple, but needs to be done regularly and repeatedly. The task of reaching so many households and communities is considerable, as are the social implications of determining a source as unsafe. There remains much uncertainty in the scientific and development communities as to what the response should be, including the ethics of stopping further tubewells, switching to surface sources (and risking other negative health impacts) and the viability of alternative sources such as rainwater harvesting.

All production and consumption activities also produce wastes in the form of various gases, particulate matter, chemicals and solid matter. Past development processes have depended substantially on the capacity of natural systems to absorb, transport and dissipate such wastes. Where the rate of waste generation exceeds the natural capacity of the atmosphere, oceans, vegetation or soils to absorb these, there are detrimental effects to human health and to the operation of ecological systems. In 1991, the first deaths from air pollution in Britain for more than thirty years occurred in London, where smog levels due to traffic fumes built up over four particularly windless days in December and 160 people died as a result (Bown, 1994). Many more people suffer ill-health and premature death due to air pollution in the developing world currently (McGranahan and Murray, 2003). In recent years, the health effects of particulate and lead levels above World Health Organisation standards in Jakarta, Indonesia, are considered to cost US$2.2 million annually based on the number of deaths, asthma attacks and hospital visits attributed to such pollutants (UNDP, 1998).

There is an ongoing challenge of finding the space to dispose of solid wastes, particularly in the more developed world where rates of production are highest. In England and Wales, commerce and households produce over 100 million tonnes each year, a figure that is growing by around 3 per cent every year (DEFRA, 2004). On average, each person in the UK in 2001 was producing around 590 kg of waste each year. Not only does the UK have higher than average figures for waste production in the European Union, but it also has lower levels of recycling, as shown in Figure 2.3.

New challenges for sustainable development are also emerging as the nature of production and consumption in the contemporary world changes. For example, the electronics industry is now the world's fastest growing manufacturing industry. Such growth, combined with rapid product obsolescence (the average lifespan of a computer in the US is now two years as individuals, businesses and government institutions replace stocks in the light of new technological developments), makes 'e-waste' the fastest growing waste stream in

Figure 2.3 *Municipal waste management in the European Union*

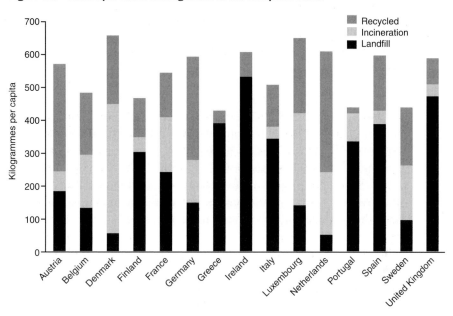

Source: www.defra.gov.uk/environmentalstatistics/waste, accessed 2.4.04.

the industrialised world (Basel Action Network, 2002). The UK alone produces nearly a million tonnes of 'electro-scrap' annually, less than half of which is recycled (Hirsch, 2000). 'E-waste' includes a broad range of electronic devices from household appliances like refrigerators and air conditioning units, to cellular phones, personal stereos and computers. Not only is the volume of waste generated larger than for many other consumer goods, but many of these products contain toxic substances that create serious pollution on disposal. The challenge of finding a means for safe disposal of refrigerators was seen in the UK when European Union rules on the disposal of fridges came into force in 2002. This legislation required the removal of insulating foam prior to scrapping in order to prevent harmful CFC gases being released. Major retailers in the UK cancelled their previous service to customers to remove old appliances on purchase of new and 'fridge mountains' emerged locally as it was found that facilities for dealing with foam linings were so limited. As a result, the government had to provide extra funding to local authorities for storage of fridges, whilst such facilities were developed.

The challenges of sustainable development also include 'cleaning up' the pollution impacts of past development. In the case of many countries of Eastern Europe and the former Soviet Union, it has only been since the collapse of the communist regimes between 1988 and 1991 that previously restricted information has brought to light the substantial pollution legacy of past development. The financial challenge alone is considerable. UNEP recently granted US$30m towards cleaning up pollution in the Russian Arctic where an estimated total of US$40 billion is required to tackle a range of problems associated with decades of industrial and military activity including heavy metal contamination of soils and the dumping of nuclear submarines (Connor, 2003). Twenty years on from the accident at the nuclear reactor in Chernobyl in 1986, work started on a US$750 million project to build a huge structure to enclose the ruins of the reactor so that experts can start to remove 200 tonnes of radioactive material there and make the site safe.

Often pollution impacts do not occur immediately, but may take many years to build up or be recognised. Box C highlights the unexpected problem of arsenic contamination of water caused by development initiatives which had been aimed very directly at improving the health of people in Bangladesh. Providing alternative water supplies to as many as 85 million (Zaman, 2001) Bangladeshis currently at risk from contaminated water is a substantial challenge, not least because of the powerful government and aid interests tied to the continued sinking of tubewells. The political nature and challenge of sustainable development were exemplified in this case when, in 2001, Bangladeshi villagers were given legal aid to sue scientists from the British Geological Survey (a government research agency) for failing to analyse for arsenic when undertaking a survey of drinking water supplies in the early 1990s despite known problems of contamination in neighbouring Indian states (Pearce, 2001).

Whilst past development processes have been closely linked to the rising exploitation of physical resources, there is also evidence of a negative relationship between natural resource endowment and development trajectories. Auty (1993) was one of the first to investigate what he termed this 'resource-curse'. In recent years there has been substantial attention to this relationship between natural resources, economic growth, democracy and civil war and in terms of the contemporary geo-strategic significance of oil to capitalism and to US hegemony in particular (Watts, 2004). In 1995, a study was conducted by Harvard University on the links between natural resources and economic performance encompassing the experience of 97 countries. It identified that over time, the more a country depended on those resources, the lower their economic growth rate (with oil-producing countries amongst the worst performers). A stark illustration of the resource curse thesis is Nigeria, where, despite being the world's seventh largest oil exporter, the proportion of households living on less than a dollar a day increased from 27 per cent in 1980 to 66 per cent in 1996 (Christian Aid, 2004: 8). In 2004, Christian Aid took the analysis further in comparing the economic, poverty and human development statistics over four decades for six oil-producing nations (Angola, Iraq, Kazakstan, Nigeria, Sudan and Venezuela), with six non-oil-producers (Bangladesh, Bolivia, Cambodia, Ethiopia, Peru and Tanzania). The oil economies were found to have achieved slower growth (1.7 per cent per annum on average compared to 4 per cent in non-producing countries). Life expectancy and literacy rates also both improved slightly more in non-oil economies than oil economies. Figure 2.4 summarises the negative relationship between mineral dependence and development indicators based on research by the World Bank and Oxfam.

It is now increasingly recognised that many of the world's persistent and grave conflicts are resource-related and also that they are being fought in areas of great environmental value, particularly in terms of biodiversity (Renner, 2002). Such conflicts sweep away decades of development efforts as well as creating long-term economic, political and environmental impacts (Bannon and Collier, 2003). In countries like the Congo, Sudan, Colombia and Afghanistan, whilst the trigger for civil unrest in a country may not have been the minerals, gems,

Figure 2.4 *Resource dependence and development*

....

- **Conflict**: States dependent on primary resource exports are over 20 times more likely to suffer civil war than non-dependent
- **Human development**: The greater a country's reliance on mineral exports, the lower its Human Development Index ranking, 1991–8
- **Inequality**: The greater a country's reliance on mineral exports, the lower the share of income accruing to the poorest 20 per cent of the population
- **Economic growth**: The greater a country's reliance on mineral exports, the greater the reduction in economic growth

....

Average annual growth, 1990-9 (%)	*Total exports which are minerals (%)*
Between 0 and −1	6–15
−1 to −2	15–50
−2 to −3	>50

....

Sources: adapted from *New Internationalist*, no. 367, 2004.

timber or oil per se, the pillaging of those resources generates the finances that allow conflict to continue and make the conflict harder to resolve. Often, those resources represent one of the few sources of wealth in otherwise very poor societies and conflicts are very much centred on gaining and maintaining control over those lucrative resources. Yet regularly, 'the resources over which so much blood is being shed have consumers in the richest countries as their destinations' (Renner, 2002: 155). In the Democratic Republic of Congo, civil war has killed over 1.7 million people and displaced another 1.8 million (2002). It is estimated that there are over 100,000 foreign troops in the country, from Uganda and Rwanda (in support of rebels trying to overthrow Kabila) and Zimbabwe and Namibia (supporting the government). Evidently, these conflicts occurring within particular countries have both longer-term and wider regional and international implications: 'many of the costs of the war continue to accrue long after the fighting has stopped' (Bannon and Collier, 2003: 1). It is now understood how conflict creates territories outside the control of a recognised government which often become havens for drugs and terrorism and presents concerns for the global community as a whole.

There is also widening concern that resource extraction in many parts of the developing world, whilst not fuelling full-fledged civil war, is having profound consequences. In many instances, the benefits of logging, mining, etc, go to government elites and foreign investors, whereas the burdens are felt by local people (and more insidiously) in terms of loss of land, environmental devastation, social impacts and the abuse of human rights. One of the most widely known examples is in the Niger delta of Nigeria (Adams, 2001; Watts, 2004). Since the early 1970s, oil corporations (most notably, Shell) and the government have received the benefits of oil extraction and the Ogoni people have suffered degradation of the resources on which their livelihoods depend (such as the loss of land, sterilisation of soils and water pollution) and are living in increasingly dangerous and unhealthy environments. Shell was largely able to evade paying compensation to delta communities or abiding by Nigeria's environmental laws (Renner, 2002). Mass protests by the Movement for the Survival of the Ogoni People (MOSOP) in the 1990s were met with violence and a state campaign of encouragement of ethnic violence on behalf of the military dictatorship that was the government at the time (and receiving 80 per cent of its revenues from oil). Over 2,000 Ogoni people were killed, including Ken Saro-Wiwa (the internationally known spokesman for MOSOP) and eight other leaders who were executed by the government itself. Shell has subsequently undertaken a major review of its activities in the delta and Nigeria now has a democratically elected government, although human rights abuses against those who raise grievances in the oil-producing areas continue (Renner, 2002).

Beyond these more obvious, high-profile resource conflicts, many more conflicts occur at local levels centred around access to basic resources for livelihood. Too often development patterns in the past have served to remove, or compromise in some way, the opportunities for some groups of people over others. As Buckles and Rusnak (1999) suggest, 'conflict over natural resources such as land, water and forests is ubiquitous' (p. 2). Indeed, natural resource use, by the very nature of biophysical and ecological processes, connects the actions of one individual or group to another through impacts on erosion, pollution or loss of habitat and thereby contains the potential for conflict. The intensity and level of resource conflict varies hugely, as do the factors underpinning them; indeed, many conflict have multiple causes occurring as resources become more scarce, as new interests enter an area and raise competition over resources or where particular ethnic identities or ways of life that are linked to those resources become threatened (or through any combination of these and other dimensions). In Box N in Chapter 4, conflict between one local community and the state over the use of protected areas is illustrated. The political dimensions of resource use are also confirmed in the current situation in Zimbabwe where historical conflicts (between Africans and European farmers) over land are being used to maintain political alliances (between the black, African peoples). Whether political, class or social and cultural dimensions dominate,

> power differences between groups *(of resource users)* can be enormous and the stakes a matter of survival. The resulting conflicts often lead to chaotic and wasteful deployment of human capacities and the depletion of the very natural resources on which livelihoods, economies, and societies are based. They may also lead to bloodshed . . . As in other fields with political dimensions, those actors with the greatest access to power are also best able to control and influence natural resource decisions in their favour.
>
> (Buckles and Rusnak, 1999: 3)

Inequalities in access to resources

The influence of issues of population in shaping modern environmentalism was seen in Chapter 1. Currently, it is not doubted that in some countries the ability of governments to provide basic needs of shelter, food, water and employment for their populations becomes increasingly difficult with rising numbers. For example, between 1990 and 2001, the population of Kenya increased every year by over 600,000 (an average of 2.5 per cent per year). In contrast, the population of Spain (a country of similar geographic area) grew by only a little over this (702,000) in the total period at an average growth rate of 0.2 per cent per year (World Bank, 2003b). However, it is generally appreciated that inequalities in people's access to resources and the resultant ways in which they use them constitute the greater challenge for sustainable development than issues of population numbers per se (WCED, 1987). As will be seen throughout this text, there is tremendous diversity in people's access to resources of all kinds, from land to investments in health care, for example.

The case of commercial energy sources illustrates how inequalities in access to resources can be considered at a number of levels. Whilst energy can be derived from various sources, a conventional distinction is made between commercial fuels, such as oil, coal, gas and electricity, which have a commercial value and are often traded between countries, and non-commercial fuels, such as wood, charcoal and plant/animal residues, which are less widely bought or sold, certainly within formal markets. Figure 2.5 illustrates how the consumption of commercial energy (oil, natural gas and coal) worldwide is concentrated in the regions of Europe, North and Central America, and Asia. Whilst recent data for sub-Saharan Africa is incomplete, in the mid-1990s, it was estimated that the annual commute by car into New York City alone used more oil than the whole of Africa (excluding South Africa) in one year (Edge and Tovey, 1995: 319). In Africa, traditional biomass fuels often accounted for an average of 35 per cent of total consumption (World Resources Institute, 1996) with levels in the non-oil-producing countries being very high.

Tables 2.1 and 2.2 emphasise further inequalities in access to the basic opportunities for development. In Table 2.1, it is seen that generally the wealthier regions have delivered basic environmental improvements in terms of access to clean water supplies and sanitation for the majority of their populations. Table 2.2 also shows how regional differences within a country can occur such as between

Figure 2.5 *Share of world population and fossil fuel consumption*

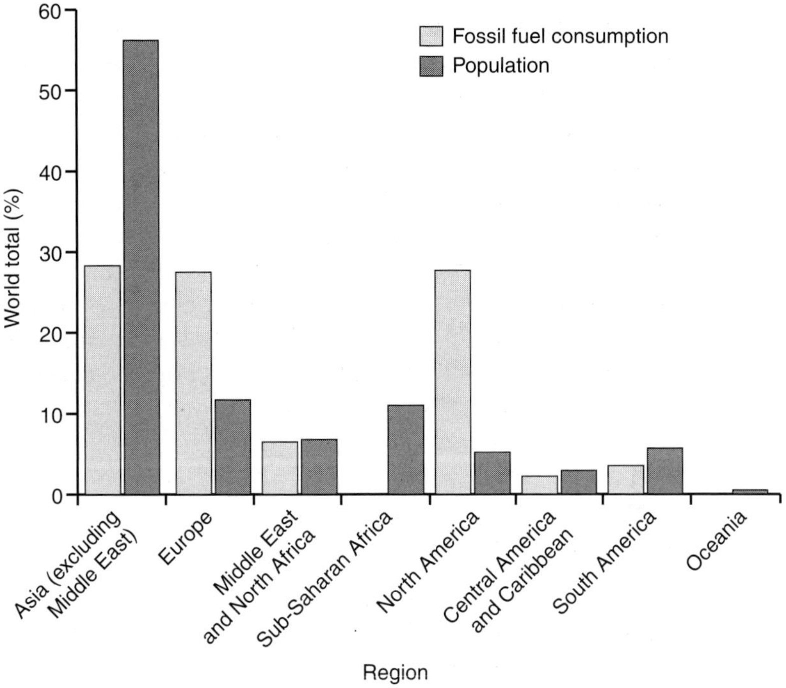

Note: data insufficient in relation to Oceania and sub-Saharan Africa.
Source: compiled from World Resources Institute (2003).

Table 2.1 *International gaps in access to safe water supply and sanitation*

Region	Percentage with access, 1999	
	Water	Sanitation
Africa	62	60
Asia	81	48
Latin America and Caribbean	83	76
Oceania	87	93
Europe	96	92
North America	100	100
Total	82	60

Source: Compiled from DFID (2001).

urban and rural people. In all cases shown (and almost ubiquitously worldwide), urban residents are better served. Inequalities in access can also exist within a community, as seen in Table 2.3, between socioeconomic groups in a city, where wealthier suburbs of Accra fare

Table 2.2 Rural–urban gaps in access to improved drinking water (percentage of population served) 2002

Country	Rural	Urban
Bangladesh	72	82
Brazil	58	96
Ghana	68	93
India	82	96
Kenya	46	89
Peru	66	87
Philippines	77	90
Zambia	36	90

Source: http://unstats.un.org/unsd

better than poorer on a number of environmental dimensions. However, it will also be seen in subsequent sections of this chapter that wealth is not the only factor determining access to resources and opportunities for development. Differences may also exist within the household: women, for example, regularly 'own a very small proportion of the natural resources and often face discrimination, when compared with men, in obtaining land, education, employment and housing' (Satterthwaite *et al.*, 1996: 16).

Inequality in access to resources threatens the prospects for sustainable development in many ways. Such inequalities allow a minority of people globally, within each nation and even at the community level, to use resources in a wasteful manner or in ways which cause environmental damage. Primarily, such patterns of inequality confine large numbers of people to poverty which often leaves them with no choice but to degrade and destroy the resource base on which their future livelihood depends. The call for sustainable development stems from the fact that such inequalities not only are morally wrong but also threaten the environmental basis for livelihoods and development aspirations across the globe.

Table 2.3 Access to basic water services in poor, middle-class and wealthy neighbourhoods of Accra, Ghana, 1991–2 (% of sample households)

	Poor	Middle class	Wealthy
No water at source of residence	55	15	4
Share toilets with more than ten households	60	17	2

Source: World Resources Institute (1996).

The geography of poverty

> An undue emphasis on poverty and poor peasants must recognize that impoverishment is no more a cause of environmental deterioration than its obverse, namely affluence/capital.
>
> (Watts and Peet, 2004: 11)

In 1990, the World Bank (using 1985 data) estimated that almost 30 per cent of the population of the developing world, more than one billion people, lived on less than 'a dollar a day'. At that time, it was predicted that global poverty would decline through the 1990s. In fact, the numbers of people in poverty barely changed, remaining at over one billion at the turn of the twenty-first century. Particular regions also fared very badly through that decade, as seen in Figure 2.6. In Europe and Central Asia the numbers of people in poverty rose rapidly from 1.1 million in 1987 to 4 million in 1998 (World Bank, 2000). The number in sub-Saharan Africa also increased from an already high figure of 217 million to 291 million. Seventy per cent of the world's poor are now resident in South Asia and sub-Saharan Africa combined, as shown in Figure 2.6. High per capita incomes per se, on any scale, do not guarantee the absence of significant numbers of poor, however. For example, an estimated 3.8 million children are currently living in poverty in Great Britain, defined as living in households with incomes below 60 per cent of the median (Flaherty et al., 2004).

'Poverty' is itself a contested term, open to many different definitions and interpretations. Whilst the World Bank's definition as presented above prioritises income or levels of private consumption (and is very widely cited), other institutions and authors incorporate a number of components of 'human development' and deprivation. For example, since 1990, the United Nations Development Programme has developed a 'Human Development Index' encompassing measures of real purchasing power (adjusted income per capita in terms of 'Purchasing Power Parity' dollars), education (adult literacy and combined primary, secondary and tertiary enrolment) and health (life expectancy). In a background study to their World Development Report focusing on poverty in 2000, the World Bank undertook a participatory study of 40,000 poor women and men in 50 countries and itself identified the multi-dimensional nature of well-being, as shown in Figure 2.7. It is evident that factors of security, autonomy and self-esteem as well as income feature in how people themselves define their well-being (and lack of poverty). Similarly, in the UK context reported above, the Child Poverty Action Group found that 'poverty is not only about basic needs and material deprivation but also about engagement and participation in society' (Flaherty et al., 2004: 2).

Concepts of poverty in the developing world now also include environmental dimensions: the command over resources which people have (through their ownership or via membership of particular social

Figure 2.6 *The changing distribution of poverty in the developing world*

Distribution of population living on less than $1 a day

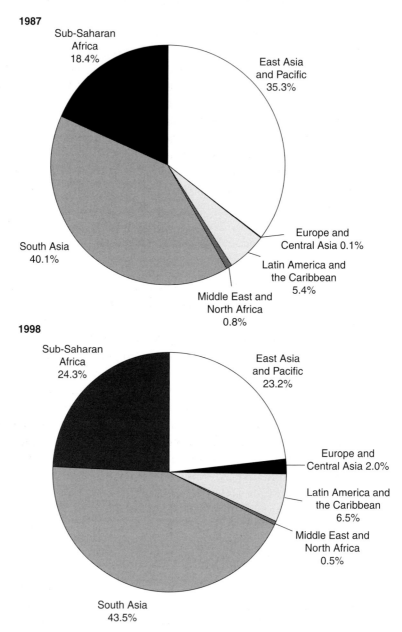

Source: World Bank (2000).

Figure 2.7 *Well-being as revealed through participatory poverty assessments*

....

- **Material well-being**: food, shelter, clothing, housing and certainty of livelihood in terms of possession of assets
- **Physical well-being**: physical health and strength (in recognition of how quickly illness can lead to destitution)
- **Security**: peace of mind and confidence regarding personal and family survival. Includes issues relating to livelihood, but also war, corruption, violence lack of protection from police and access to justice and lawfulness
- **Freedom of choice and action**: power to control one's life, to avoid exploitation, rudeness and humiliation. Ability to acquire education, skills, loans and resources to live in a good place. Having means to help others and fulfil moral obligations
- **Social well-being**: good relations with family and community, being able to care for elderly, raise children, marry. Ability to participate fully in community/society, in gift-exchange, festivities, weddings, etc.

....

Source: Narayan *et al.* (2000).

groups), coupled with their capacity to withstand environmental stresses and shocks, and including the ability people have to make effective and sustainable use of these 'entitlements' (Leach and Mearns, 1991). Poor people are regularly portrayed as both the 'victims and unwilling agents' of environmental degradation in developing regions. It is suggested that 'one of the greatest environmental vulnerabilities that poverty brings is a high dependence on natural resources for subsistence' (WRI, 2002: 16). Living in poverty restricts the options people have for resource management: they may have to cultivate marginal lands, live in unsafe housing or remove remaining woodlands in order to survive in the short term, often with detrimental effects on the resource base and their own longer-term livelihoods (Figure 2.8). Their environmental concerns are those associated with immediate survival needs, such as for fuel, access to clean water and sanitation, or in securing productive lands.

In the mid-1980s, it was suggested that 57 per cent of the rural poor and 76 per cent of the urban poor were resident in areas where ecological destruction and/or severe environmental hazards threatened their well-being. In 2003, the World Bank reported that one-quarter of all people in the developing world, 1.3 billion people in total, survive on fragile lands and this proportion had doubled since the 1950s. Such lands were defined in terms of soil characteristics, aridity and slope constraints (or combinations thereof) and it does not take into account other weather-related factors such as susceptibility

Figure 2.8 *The poverty and environment connection*

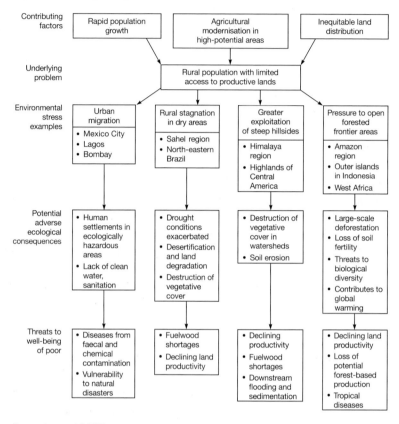

Source: Leonard (1989).

to flooding, storm events or extreme cold, for example. The regional distribution of these people and these lands is shown in Table 2.4. It was found that these areas still 'account for a large share of people in extreme poverty' (World Bank, 2003a: xvi).

Evidently, poverty has also become associated with ecological marginality. Worldwide, across urban and rural areas, the poor are often concentrated in environments that are 'inherently' poor. These include lands where agricultural productivity is limited or subject to large swings as conditions change. These lands require high levels of investment in order to become productive (the resources that the poor don't have), but are also where people's links to land are critical for the sustainability of those communities and for the conservation of the resource base. In urban areas, the concentration of the poor in environments impoverished through their 'acquired' characteristics, such as alongside hazardous installations or railway tracks, often

Table 2.4   *Regional distribution of people living on fragile land*

Region	Population in 2000 (millions)	Population on fragile lands by region	
		Number (millions)	Share of total (%)
Latin America and the Caribbean	515.3	68	13.1
Eastern Europe and Central Asia	474.7	58	12.1
Middle East and North Africa	293.0	110	37.6
Sub-Saharan Africa	658.4	258	39.3
South Asia	1,354.5	330	24.4
East Asia and Pacific	1,856.5	469	25.3
OECD group[a]	850.4	94	11.1
Other	27.3	2	6.9
Total	**6,030.1**	**1,389**	**24.7**
Total less OECD	**5,179.7**	**1,295**	**26.9**

a OECD: Australia, Austria, Belgium, Canada, Denmark, Finland, France, Germany, Greece, Iceland, Ireland, Italy, Japan, Luxembourg, Netherlands, New Zealand, Norway, Portugal, Spain, Sweden, Switzerland, United Kingdom, United States (23 original members).
Source: World Bank (2003a).

reflects the operation of market forces, these environments having low commercial value (i.e. demand from other uses) because they are poor. For low-income groups who are often also politically marginalised, this situation may enable them to afford to live there and be less vulnerable to eviction.

Work in the field of political ecology has done much to explore how and why the poor are so often marginalised ecologically, economically and politically (see for example, Blaikie and Brookfield, 1987; Watts and Peet, 2004). The causes are found to be diverse and specific to particular places and times but emphasise the political structures and relations that influence access and control over resources (rather than poor land practices, culture or population growth as in other explanations of environmental degradation). The exposure of the significance of wider external structures on land management has confirmed the complex, multi-dimensional (and multi-level) challenges of sustainability identified in Chapter 1. It also ensures that there are no simple blueprints for sustainable development, as illustrated in Chapters 4 and 5.

To date, rural poverty has exceeded urban poverty. However, as the world's population becomes more urbanised (as seen in Chapter 5), poverty is also becoming increasingly an urban phenomenon. Cities,

Plate 2.1 *The challenges of aridity to human settlements*

a. Northern Nigeria

Source: Hamish Main, Staffordshire University.

b. Southern Tunisia

Source: author.

for historical reasons, have often been located on prime agricultural land or within valuable ecosystems near rivers, lakes or coasts. Through such pressures of increased population densities, agricultural production often becomes more intense to compensate for losses and/or is pushed into more unsuitable areas, becoming potentially more damaging in turn. Furthermore, urban developments expand onto steep slopes or wetland areas and threaten remaining natural vegetation such as mangrove forests. Whilst the threat of urban poverty to valued ecosystems is clear, it is also evident that the urban poor are regularly the victims of environmental decline. Ten years ago, an estimated 600 million urban residents of developing countries were considered to have their lives threatened every day by the health impacts associated with the inadequate provision of quality water supplies, sanitation and sewage disposal, and the lack of health and emergency services (Hardoy *et al.*, 1992). Furthermore, there are many recent cases of poorer households suffering more losses than wealthier residents when heavy rainfall causes landslides or when earthquakes strike urban environments (Hewitt, 1997). In such circumstances, money tends to afford access to the resources on which safety depends, to the building technologies and the early warning systems, and also to relief services and insurance compensation. The impacts of sudden-onset events like hurricanes can be devastating for poor countries and poor people. When Hurricane Mitch hit Central America in 1998, an estimated 20,000 people were killed and it put the economy of Honduras back twenty years according to their president (International Federation of Red Cross and Red Crescent Societies, 2002). The costs inflicted on individuals in terms of disruption to livelihoods may be almost incalculable as a Mozambiquan woman suggested after the extensive floods in that country in 2000: 'we lost everything we had worked for during our lives. We do not know when and where to start' (2002: 10–11). Clearly, these issues are hugely pertinent as the short- and longer-term impacts of the tsunami of 26 December 2004 are being revealed throughout many countries in South Asia currently.

However, whilst it is readily understood that increased wealth can create many opportunities for more secure livelihoods, recent work in hazards research suggests that many people are being rendered vulnerable to disaster though development: 'disasters are not simply the product of one-off natural phenomena . . . but are equally the result of environmentally unsustainable development projects over time' (Bankoff *et al.*, 2004: 3). The International Federation of Red Cross and Red Crescent Societies has assessed that 56 per cent of recent disasters occurred in countries classified as of 'medium human development' compared to 19 per cent in 'low' and 25 per cent in 'high'. Work within vulnerability analyses is also showing how development processes are aggravating 'everyday risks'. Heijmans (2004), for example, reports work with communities in upland Philippines;

> Nowadays, local people also observe that even normal monsoon rains trigger adverse disastrous events such as landslides and floods, which never occurred before. In their view, the conceptual difference between a typhoon (hazard, extreme event) and monsoon rain (normal climatic condition) has become negligible since effects at the community level have become similar. The increasingly vulnerable condition, in which people live, can now turn not only extreme events, but even normal events, into disaster situations.
>
> (pp. 119–20)

Poorer groups in society also have less power to resist and prevent 'detrimental developments', those that make their environments more impoverished in some way. As identified in Chapter 1, notions of environmental justice developed in the US and European context now include the capacity of low-income groups to influence decision-making regarding management interventions. Research in England and Wales, for example, based on the ranking of areas according to an Index of Multiple Deprivation, found that the most deprived communities were 8 times more likely to live on tidal floodplains; 6 times more likely to live within 1 km of an Integrated Pollution Control Site; and suffered the highest concentrations of five air pollutants (Walker *et al.*, 2004). The lack of voice that poor people often have in environmental decision-making has also been identified in China: for citizens with similar levels of pollution exposure and education, those living in high-income provinces were more than twice as likely to file complaints as those residing in low-income provinces (WRI, 2003). Empowering local voices to enable communities to resist detrimental developments is seen in Chapters 4 and 5 to be a critical feature of more sustainable development processes.

This evidence for the close association between poverty and the environment should not distort an understanding that the linkages are complex and rarely direct in rural or urban settings. Poverty has many dimensions, as seen, and impoverishment is only one factor in influencing behaviour and decision-making regarding environmental resource management. There is a need to search for the deeper underlying causes of poverty and, in turn, local-level environmental decline (as in the work of political ecology). In subsequent chapters, a whole host of factors, including tenure arrangements, capital assets and gender relations, are seen to influence the decisions poor people make and to mediate the relationship between poverty and the environment. Regularly, particular groups (not necessarily the poorest) may be especially vulnerable to environmental and other changes, even in geographical areas beyond those which would be defined as most hazardous in terms of their physical or acquired characteristics.

Plate 2.2 *Delivering basic urban needs*

a. Water in Jakarta, Indonesia
Source: author.

b. Fuel in Kairouan, Tunisia
Source: author.

It is evident, however, that sustainable development in the future will require a commitment to overcoming poverty through a focus on the welfare issues of the poorest sectors of society, particularly in the developing countries. Their environmental concerns and their development needs are certainly often in stark contrast to 'wealthy' or 'northern' priorities, and typically are associated with securing the most basic levels of economic and social well-being. Poverty denies millions of people basic rights in the short term and the potential to achieve development aspirations in the future.

The human cost of contemporary development

The need for sustainable development in the future is also confirmed by the human cost of patterns and processes of development to date. Over 10 million children currently die every year before they reach the age of five. Some 98 per cent of these children are born in the developing world (WHO, 2003). Figure 2.9 presents a stark illustration of how contemporary development is failing the future generation. Whilst average life expectancy at birth has increased globally from 46.5 years in 1950 to 65.2 years in 2002, increasingly the gap in life expectancy is between the very poorest developing countries and the rest of the world (2003). For example, a baby girl born in Japan today can expect to live for about 85 years, whilst a girl born in Sierra Leone has a life expectancy of 36 years. In 14 African countries, current levels of child mortality are higher than they were in the 1990s. Adult health at the turn of the century is also characterised by a slowing of gains previously made and widening health gaps: in parts of sub-Saharan Africa adult mortality rates now exceed those of the 1970s (Bloom *et al.*, 2004).

'Wealth determines health' is a phrase which is often used to explain the spatial pattern of ill health and premature death and to contrast, for example, how a child born in sub-Saharan Africa in 2001 was 25 times more likely to die before the age of five than in OECD countries (the major industrialised countries of Europe and North America). Table 2.5 contrasts under-five mortality rates for particular countries. Whilst patterns may be broadly consistent with the phrase, Table 2.5 shows that good health is not necessarily assured by higher levels of national wealth, as in the case of Brazil, which has a significantly higher GNI than Sri Lanka, but higher under-five mortality. The table also shows the worsening situation over time in countries like Nigeria, despite continued economic expansion. In broad terms, the poorer

Figure 2.9   *Children caught in conflict*

An estimated 300,000 children under 18 are involved in more than 30 armed conflicts around the world as soldiers, porters, messengers and ex-slaves. The number of child refugees increases by 5,000 a day (of 23 million refugees worldwide, over 50% are children). Through the 1990s, over 2 million children have died as result of war, and approximately 5 million have been left disabled. Some 12 million children have been left homeless by armed conflict and over 1 million have been orphaned or separated from their parents by conflict.

Source: compiled from DFID, *Developments Magazine*, no. 12, p. 26, 2000.

Table 2.5   *Child mortality, selected countries*

Country	GNI per capita, 2001 (US$s)*	Under-five mortality (deaths per 1,000 live births)**	
		1990	2001
Niger	170	320	265
Ghana	290	126	100
India	460	123	93
Zimbabwe	480	80	123
Indonesia	680	91	45
Peru	2,000	75	39
Brazil	3,060	60	36
Ecuador	1,240	57	30
Sri Lanka	830	23	19
USA	34,870	11	8
UK	24,230	9	7
Japan	27,430	6	5

Sources: *World Bank, (2003a); **UNDP (2003a).

groups within a country or region also tend to suffer more premature deaths than richer groups. Figure 2.10 shows the differences in infant mortality rates (deaths before age of one year) in England and Wales between classes distinguished on the basis of income. Infant mortality of babies born inside marriage are seen to be twice as high in unskilled manual social classes than in professional.

Children are amongst the poorest groups in all societies. Every year, at least 3 million children under five die of environment-related diseases (WHO, undated); 2 million from diarrhoeal diseases (80–90 per cent of these cases are related to environmental conditions and contaminated water and inadequate sanitation in particular), a

Figure 2.10 *Infant mortality in England and Wales*

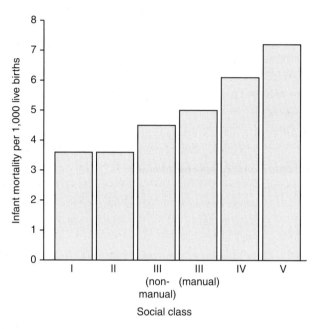

Source: Flaherty *et al.* (2004).

further 2 million children die through acute respiratory infections (60 per cent of these infections worldwide are considered to be related to environmental conditions) and almost 1 million children die of malaria before they are five years old (90 per cent of malaria cases are attributed to environmental factors). Children tend to suffer most from the effects of pollution (Satterthwaite *et al.*, 1996). A resting three-year-old consumes twice as much oxygen and therefore twice the pollution weight for weight as a resting adult. In addition, children's underdeveloped kidneys, livers and enzyme systems are less able to process such pollutants. Children's activities may also place them at particular risk: babies instinctively suck much of what they pick up in their hands and young children play in dangerous places such as streets or waste tips, aggravating the risk of contact with contaminated sources. In short, young children are responsible for very little pollution but are themselves extremely vulnerable to the pollution effects caused by others and, once again, it is impoverished children who are most at risk. However, children should not be considered to be entirely passive victims of degradation, but can also be significant actors in progressing sustainability (Hart, 1997).

Whilst inequalities in wealth may go some way towards explaining spatial patterns of ill health at several levels, other factors are also important. For example, more children die before the age of five in West Africa than in East Africa. This has been linked to the prevalence of malaria in the former for which there is no reliable vaccine (Hill, 1991). In this instance, it is the particular environmental conditions of West Africa, rather than regional differences in wealth, which explain such patterns. Gender is another factor which cuts across inequalities in wealth to influence health. Around the world, there are an estimated 100 million 'missing women', women who would be alive if it were not for practices of infanticide, neglect and sex-selective abortion (UNDP, 2002). In many areas of the developing world, for example, male children are valued more highly than female, leading to a number of practices which may result in premature deaths of girls, as illustrated in Box D. The UNDP now calculates a gender-related development index (GDI) that adjusts the Human Development Index for inequalities in the achievements of men and women. With gender equality in human development, the GDI and the HDI would be the same,

> But for all countries the GDI is lower than the HDI, indicating gender inequality everywhere . . . worse outcomes for women in many aspects of human development result from the fact that their voices have less impact than men's in the decisions that shape their lives.
>
> (UNDP, 2002: 23)

The extent of premature death and ill-health, particularly amongst children, is stark evidence that current development patterns and processes are not meeting the needs of current or future generations. Spatial inequalities in health have been seen to exist at various scales and show strong links with the distribution of wealth internationally between the developed and developing worlds, but also within nations. However, in much of the developing world, with few exceptions, the recent trend has been for declining overall expenditure on health and on education in recent decades. Some of the forces underpinning such patterns will be discussed in detail in Chapter 3. Health has also been seen to be closely tied to the physical environment, particularly in the developing world where poverty is so widespread and entrenched. The challenge of overturning the human cost of unsustainable development patterns is clearly closely related to the elimination of poverty and the provision of basic welfare needs for large numbers of people in the developing world.

Box D

India's missing millions

> India has 40 million fewer women than it would have, if the sexual balance had been left to nature.
>
> (Popham, 1997)

For centuries, various techniques have been used in India to kill baby girls who are considered a financial burden. Although dowries are forbidden under the Anti-Dowry Act, the law is rarely enforced and even in the poorest areas of India, the bride's family is often expected to pay as much as £500 and to provide a lavish wedding feast, which can ruin poorer families or those with several daughters (Lees, 1995). In contrast, sons are considered saviours in that they carry on the family line and are indispensable economically. Although female babies are generally born stronger, statistics from hospitals reveal that girl children get less priority in nutrition and health care, and are breast-fed less than boys. Within a month of birth, the death rate of India's female babies is much higher than that of its males (Chissick, 1990). Girls are an estimated four times more likely to suffer from acute malnutrition in India and boys forty times more likely to be taken to hospital (Todaro, 1997: 158).

Although female infanticide has been banned in India for more than a century, the advent of the amniocentesis test has enabled the practice of selective abortion of female foetuses. Clinics in major cities advertise pre-natal sex-determination tests and, in 1988, a sample survey carried out in Bombay (now known as Mumbai) revealed that, of 8,000 abortions carried out, 7,999 were female foetuses. This prompted an Act in Maharashtra state to regulate the use of pre-natal sex determination (the only state in India to do so), but many clinics continue to use the technique for other than the purpose of identifying genetic defects for which it was designed (Chissick, 1990).

In rural areas, women's status is particularly poor and female deaths are higher. In 1985, UNICEF funded a survey of midwives working in rural areas and found that female infanticide was extremely common:

> Dukni, 60, is a *dai*, a traditional midwife from Bihar, Northeast India. Every month, on average, she delivers six babies and kills three of them because they are girls and the families do not want them. She prefers the quickest, cleanest methods. Usually she strangles the baby with a length of rope, poisons her with fertiliser or puts a lump of black salt in her throat. Sometimes she snaps her spine by bending it backwards or suffocates her by stuffing her into a large clay pot and closing the lid. The baby is usually dead within two hours. Dukni then wraps the body in an old cloth and carries it away under her sari. She either throws it into a river, buries it or leaves it in undergrowth knowing it will quickly be found by wild animals.
>
> (Lees, 1995)

UNICEF also estimated that a further 5,000 women every year were burnt to death by their in-laws in retribution for their families' failure to provide sufficient dowry (Popham, 1997).

In 1997, the Indian government launched a £12.4 million scheme to reward couples for having daughters. Families who earn less than £190 per year who produce a daughter will be rewarded with a payment of £9 and also receive financial incentives to encourage them to send their daughters to school. They also announced a ban on tests to determine whether an expectant mother is carrying a boy or a girl child. The scheme has been given a cautious welcome by those who work with girls and women in poor communities in India; it is the first time the authorities have pledged money, but much more is needed in terms of ensuring a proper educational infrastructure in the rural areas for example, and further incentives to advance the position of women in Hindu society.

The environment cannot cope

Perhaps the starkest realisation of the need to find new patterns and processes of development has come from an improved understanding of the environmental unsustainability of contemporary development. At the time of the Stockholm conference, the primary environmental problems tended to be national: 'the environmental sins of one nation did not generally impinge upon other nations, let alone upon the community of nations' (Myers and Myers, 1982: 195). Ten years later, further environmental problems which affected many nations, such as acid rain or nuclear waste, were recognised and continue to challenge groups of countries currently. For example, ash carried by local atmospheric patterns from the extensive forest fires in Indonesia in 1997 led to severe problems of air quality and impacts on health and production in neighbouring Malaysia and Singapore at an estimated cost to those economies of 2 per cent of GDP (UNDP, 1998).

However, since the 1980s, there has been increasing recognition of a series of environmental problems which now affect the global community as a whole. Whilst different societies have been adapting to and altering their local environments for millennia, in the contemporary world there is a 'rising propensity of human actions to have international and increasingly global-scale environmental impact' (Castree, 2003: 279). New global environmental issues are now recognised in two senses: firstly, those human impacts on the environment that have a 'supranational' character such as climate warming and ozone depletion through the connectedness of atmospheric systems, where change generated anywhere has potential effects around the globe. Secondly, local issues such as the loss of forest, soil erosion or accessing clean water, now occur and are repeated in numerous locations (on a worldwide scale) and pose threats to resources on which more and more people of the globe depend.

The heating up of the Earth owing to the accumulation of 'greenhouse gases' (particularly carbon dioxide, but also chlorofluorocarbons: CFCs) is probably the most well-known supranational environmental issue. The significance of emerging understanding of this issue in shaping mainstream ideas on sustainable development was seen in Chapter 1. However, it is an issue that is the focus for much debate concerning its causes, impacts and the required responses. In short, greenhouse gases in the atmosphere control the re-radiation of solar radiation back into space and thereby regulate the temperature of the Earth. These gases serve to keep the Earth some 33 degrees Celsius warmer than it would otherwise be, but the increased concentration of greenhouse gases during the past century is considered to have raised the average temperature of the Earth's surface by at least 0.5 degrees Celsius over the same period (Seitz, 2002). In 2001, the Intergovernmental Panel on Climate Change (created in 1988 by the World Meteorological Organisation and UNEP) predicted that average global temperatures will rise by 5.8 degrees Celsius by the end of the next century (IPCC, 2001).

Carbon dioxide provides the main warming or 'forcing effect' in the atmosphere and is likely to continue to do so. The major source of carbon dioxide to date has been the burning of fossil fuels, contributing approximately 75 per cent of human-caused carbon emissions since the 1980s (IPPC, 2001). But CFCs, the synthetic chemicals used in various processes and products including refrigeration and as propellants, remain active in the atmosphere for much longer periods than carbon dioxide, before being destroyed in the stratosphere by ultraviolet radiation. Therefore, although the production of CFCs declined in the 1990s (Brown, 1996), atmospheric concentrations will continue to increase for centuries.

The major effects of climate warming will relate to water resources: through the rise of sea levels as a result of the thermal expansion of the oceans, the melting of glaciers and ice-sheets, and increased precipitation via enhanced evaporation from warmer seas (Potter *et al.*, 2004). But there is tremendous uncertainty concerning how these effects will impact, as witnessed (certainly in the more developed world) by the veritable industry of activity currently attempting to link recent observed environmental events to global warming. The heatwave experienced in Europe in the summer of 2003, for example, prompted the *Observer* newspaper to look more widely at environmental experiences, as shown in Figure 2.11.

Figure 2.11 *Fire and floods worldwide*

....

- Average temperatures across Europe have been 5 degrees Celsius warmer for the past two months. Drought is costing billions of euros in crop damage.
- In India, temperatures have reached 49 degrees Celsius, resulting in more than 1,500 deaths.
- Heatwaves and flooding have killed 569 people in China during the year.
- A state of emergency has been declared in British Columbia after the worst fires in 50 years.
- Pakistan's heatwave followed by rains has left hundreds of thousands homeless and damaged 45 per cent of crops in some states.
- In Russia, hundreds of fires have devastated parts of Siberia.
- A national disaster has been declared in Portugal after fires killed 11 and destroyed 100,000 acres of forest.
- Fire has destroyed 12,300 acres of forests and olive groves in Croatia.

....

Source: *Observer*, 17.8.03.

Further extreme climatic phenomena are predicted by the IPCC report of 2001. Whilst the business of prediction is extremely complex, what is certain is that the impact of climate warming will not be distributed evenly over the globe. This third major report of the IPCC acknowledges that the nature of impacts and which of them are likely to be critical for whom and where, for example, depends on future socioeconomic conditions – the 'state of the world' – and the IPCC is now working with different scenarios describing how population, economics and political structure may evolve over coming decades (Arnwell *et al.*, 2004).

Whilst climate warming can be considered the archetypal global environmental issue through the disruption of sea levels, ocean currents and the constituent gases of the atmosphere – 'a molecule of greenhouse gases emitted anywhere becomes everyone's business' (Clayton, 1995: 110) – it has also been seen through the preceding sections of this chapter that the world's environmental challenges extend far beyond these issues of the 'global commons'. The brief detail provided as to the nature of environmental concerns between and within nations has also given some sense of the highly unequal and uneven experience and impact of environmental decline. 'It would be wrong, therefore, to assume that responses to pollution problems are globally harmonious' (2004: 147). The following sections consider a number of important challenges for the global community in terms of managing environmental change into the future that centre on difficult questions of who should be responsible and/or is able to respond, for example.

Making globalisation work for the poor

There is substantial debate concerning the relationship between globalisation and development but it is very much part of the context within which sustainable development has to be secured, as considered in Chapter 1. What is well understood is that whilst the world is becoming more global, it does not necessarily mean that it is becoming more uniform. There is much evidence in the preceding sections, for example, as to how this is not the case. As Castree (2003: 279) notes, it is apparent that as human–environment relations have become more globalised or 'stretched', 'the more spatially and temporally uneven their causes and consequences seem to be'. Furthermore, it is understood that not only are processes of globalisation uneven in their reach (as considered in Box A in Chapter 1) but they operate through existing patterns of uneven development and are creating increased differences between places (some good, some bad).

The exclusion of large sections of the world's population from the benefits of globalisation is now recognised by many major institutions in development as the major global challenge. In Chapter 1, for example, it was seen that globalisation was central to the agenda at the World Summit on Sustainable Development in Johannesburg. In 2000, the UK Department for International Development headed its second White Paper on International Development, 'Eliminating World Poverty: Making Globalisation Work for the Poor'. Making globalisation work for the poor is recognised as a moral imperative. But it is also understood as being in the common interest of all as many of world's challenges, of environmental degradation, war and conflict, refugee movements, human rights violations, international crime and terrorism, and health pandemics like HIV/Aids, are caused or exacerbated by poverty and inequality.

Economic processes of globalisation are controlled substantially by transnational enterprises (TNCs), firms which have operations in more than one other country as well as in their country of origin. Their influence comes partly from their size: many TNCs have larger sales and income than whole countries, as illustrated in Table 2.6. 'The economy of Mitsubishi is larger than that of Indonesia, the world's fourth most populous country and a land of enormous wealth' (Korten, 2001: 231). Such large corporations can now subcontract production, research and development facilities to branch plants located at great distances from the centres of demand wherever it is most favourable economically to do so. Chapter 3 considers more fully

Table 2.6 *The state and corporate power*

Country or corporation	Total GDP* or corporate sales** (millions of US$), 2001
Sweden	210,108
Exxonmobil Corporation	209,417
General Motors	177,260
BP	175,389
Saudi Arabia	173,287
Denmark	162,817
Ford Motor Company	162,412
Royal Dutch/Shell Group	135,211
General Electric	125,913
Venezuela	124,948
South Africa	113,274
Toyota Motor Corporation	108,808
Chevron Texaco Corporation	104,409
Ireland	101,185
TotalFinaElf	94,418
Singapore	92,252
Malaysia	87,540
IBM	85,866
Philippines	71,438
Chile	63,545

Sources: *World Bank (2003a); **UNCTAD (2003).

the activities and responses of transnational business in relation to the prospects for sustainable development including through the role they play in influencing international trade decisions and in terms of their environmental commitments.

The most dramatic increase in economic globalisation in recent years has taken place, not in production, but in financial speculation. For example, developments in communication technologies now enable 24-hour global trading on the world currency markets with money being switched around the globe at high speeds. Money can be placed virtually instantaneously wherever it produces the highest returns (and shifted subsequently to other locations to secure greater gains). Such financial speculation has little to do with the 'real economy', in providing capital for manufacturing, agriculture or service industries, for example. It can, however, disrupt the plans of national governments, such as those to control inflation or the movement of exchange rates, with severe short- and long-term development impacts, as was seen in the crises of many South-East Asian economies (the 'newly industrialising countries' of the 1980s) from mid-1997. The International Monetary Fund recorded 158 currency crises in the 1990s, 116 of which occurred in developing market economies (Kiely, 1998). As Willett (2001: 6) notes, 'one of the great dichotomies of globalisation . . . is its power to simultaneously integrate and fragment whole economies and communities', constituting a significant challenge as future economic development will have to be secured in what is a very volatile external environment.

The information revolution, particularly the development of the Internet, has been a fundamental characteristic of globalisation. It has been suggested that Internet technology creates new opportunities for development that were not previously available and therefore has the potential to speed development through 'bypassing previous stages'. However, Box A also identified that the global reach of such technologies is not uniform. Whilst the global economy comes to depend more and more on the Internet, it seems that those who are relatively rich are also becoming increasingly 'information rich' (Kiely and Marfleet, 1998): access to mass media still depends on relatively expensive technologies be it satellite networked televisions or mobile phones, for example. Furthermore, many of the world's population remains illiterate, so that bridging any digital divide or creating digital opportunities should not be something that comes after addressing the core development issues but rather works with them (Gourlay, 2003).

However, it should be noted that these new communication technologies have also been important in enabling alliances of individuals and formal groups ('social movements') to disseminate information, speed the circulation of news, avoid official censorship, and mobilise support towards *challenging* globalisation. Modern computer technologies have become an important tool in political struggles on behalf of, for example, the Zapatista movement (Cleaver, 1999). This movement started in one of the poorest states in Mexico, Chiapas, and was largely made up of indigenous Mayan peoples, mobilised around issues of land and agricultural developments stemming from the signing of the North American Free Trade Agreement. Over the years, it has extended to encompass many other states in Mexico, other parts of the Americas and now has alliances with many organisations around the world that are engaged in similar struggles with economic, ecological and cultural objectives (Power, 2003). The role of social movements in prompting actions towards sustainable development is also discussed more fully in Chapter 3.

Computers and communication technologies have also been central to many of the advances made in reducing the environmental impacts of extractive and manufacturing industries and for the reuse and reclamation of raw materials (Thompson, 2003). This has created optimism concerning the possibilities for extending a growing global economy whilst still preserving the environment; the 'dematerialisation' of the modern global economy, moving data instead of physical objects, has the potential to reduce energy use and pollution. However, little is still known about the real environmental costs of many of the building blocks of the information society.

In summary, understanding processes of globalisation is central to the prospects of sustainable development. Yet there is much uncertainty surrounding present and future conditions across these processes of change. In this brief analysis, it is clear that new technologies are creating new opportunities but also challenges in terms of managing natural resources. Furthermore, there are now new actors shaping investments and development opportunities worldwide. In addition, globalisation is no longer seen as an unstoppable force creating uniformity. Substantial illustration is provided in the following chapters concerning how processes of globalisation work through existing patterns of uneven development; how globalisation is being 'managed' to deliver more sustainable outcomes, and how various actors are challenging powerful interests and organisations in the global economy to change those 'inevitable' processes.

Questions of responsibility and response

The current interdependence of peoples and environments throughout the world is seen starkly in the case of supranational environmental problems. The need for a coordinated international approach to such environmental issues is self-evident. However, in the moves to determine the response to such problems, the question of responsibility is inevitably raised. If change is to be implemented, particularly where such change involves (as it usually does) expense and/or compromise of some sort, there is substantial debate as to whether these costs should be borne equally by all or whether there should be some adjustment according to relative responsibility, if this can be ascertained (and also with respect to ability to pay).

One of the most fundamental challenges for ensuring sustainable productive activities in the future stems from the fact that pollution effects are often spatially and temporally removed from the site of production, as already noted. It is therefore often extremely difficult to ascertain the responsibility for pollution. Only 7 per cent of the polluting sulphur in Norway originates in that country, for example (UNDP, 1998). Box E considers aspects of the debate which continues in respect to the responsibility for global warming. The 'battle of statistics' seen in the debate is an extremely important one, since potential solutions to the problem will be argued on different figures (and different interests fostered). The use of data is seen to be highly value-laden as two calculations using the same information are made and presented concerning 'responsibilities'.

Box E

Responsibility for global warming under debate

Based on scientific understanding of the role of carbon dioxide in particular in forcing global warming and the important role of the burning of fossil fuels in this process, there have been many attempts to establish relative responsibility internationally for environmental damage. In the main, it has been established that carbon dioxide emissions from the industrialised nations have, to date, far outweighed the contribution from the developing world in total and in terms of per capita contributions, as shown in Figure 2.12 and Table 2.7.

Figure 2.12 *Carbon dioxide emissions: share of world total*

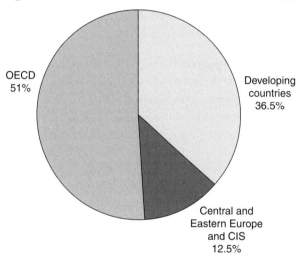

Source: UNDP (2003a).

Table 2.7 *Carbon dioxide emissions: per capita (metric tonnes)*

	1980	1999
Developing countries	1.3	1.9
Central and Eastern Europe and CIS	–	7.2
OECD	11.0	10.8
World	3.4	3.8

Source: UNDP (2003a).

However, in 1990, the World Resources Institute (the influential Washington-based research group whose environmental data are used regularly by policy-makers and other researchers) published quite different analyses concerning the contribution of individual nations to global warming, based on carbon emissions from sources beyond solely fossil fuel combustion. The conclusion was that responsibility was *evenly shared* between industrialised and developing regions, as shown in Figure 2.13a.

Figure 2.13 *Responsibility for net emissions of greenhouse gases as calculated by (a) the World Resources Institute and (b) the Centre for Science and Environment*

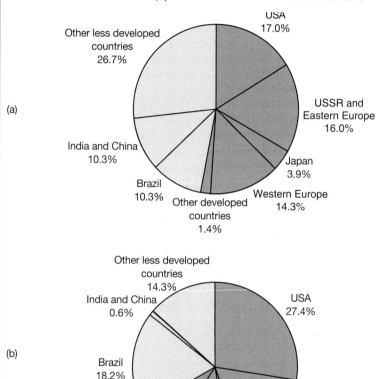

Source: Barrow (1995).

However, both the data and the way the findings have been presented by the WRI have been much criticised. For example, in calculating a single 'greenhouse index' based on one year's emissions of greenhouse gases into the atmosphere, it is asserted that the WRI is able to exaggerate the contribution of the developing countries, through choosing, for example, not to consider responsibility in terms of historical contributions to emissions. The uncertain nature of much data (such as those concerning carbon dioxide releases from land use changes) is not made explicit, nor is there any attempt within the calculations to differentiate between emissions for 'luxury' (such as vehicle use) and 'survival' purposes (as in the case of methane from paddy fields). Furthermore, the level of aggregation presented can be questioned, i.e. the choice to present emissions for whole continents rather than per person or per nation.

Figure 2.13b illustrates the divergence in terms of responsibility calculated by the WRI and an alternative suggested by the Centre for Science and Environment, based in India. Using the *same* data but an alternative methodology for calculating *net* emissions and responsibilities (fundamentally that allocates emissions and sinks on a per capita basis), just 0.6 per cent of net global greenhouse gas emissions were allocated to India and China combined, in comparison to the 10.3 per cent share calculated by the WRI. The Centre for Science and Environment argues that comparisons should be made between countries' emissions on a per capita basis, since 'every person has a moral right to air' (Barrow, 1995: 90). However, such a calculation would favour countries with large, predominantly young, populations over those with slow-growing populations (mainly the 'developed' countries).

One of the favoured mechanisms for minimising pollution is the 'polluter pays principle' (PPP), defined in Figure 2.14. However, the PPP rests on the assumption that it is possible to identify who is responsible for the production of pollution. In addition, it depends on being able to 'cost' the damage. The challenge of costing the impact of pollution is seen clearly in the case of 'acid rain', which refers to the abnormally low pH of some rainfall resulting from the concentration of primarily sulphur dioxide as a result of burning fossil fuels. Whilst it may be possible to cost the damage to trees in terms of the loss of timber resources, for example, it is much more difficult to assign a market value to the loss of diversity of flora and fauna supported by such forests, or to their decreased amenity value with regard to recreational opportunities lost for the local population as a result of acid rain. Work within the environmental justice arena regularly demonstrates that it is rarely those who contribute most to pollution that suffer the greater impacts. Mitchell and Dorling (2003), for example, considered one aspect of air pollution, nitrogen dioxide levels, and estimated the extent to which people living in each community in Britain contribute towards this pollution based on the characteristics of vehicles that they own. They found that communities that own fewest cars tend to suffer from highest levels of air pollution and those in which car ownership is greatest enjoy the cleanest air.

Even where it is clear who is responsible for pollution, as in the case of the breakdown of the nuclear reactors at Chernobyl in Ukraine in 1986, the impacts can spread far beyond national boundaries, as shown in Figure 2.15. Furthermore, the impacts of Chernobyl were experienced unevenly over space and time: 'the soil character and farming practices of Cumbria and North Wales meant that livestock have been contaminated for years; elsewhere in the United Kingdom the most obvious impacts passed in weeks' (Yearley, 1995: 156). Moreover, there is often substantial disagreement within the scientific

Figure 2.14 *The polluter pays principle (PPP)*

The principle originates from the proceedings of the UN Conference on the Human Environment in Stockholm, 1972. The principle is that the cost of preventing pollution or minimising environmental damage due to pollution should be borne by those responsible for the pollution. Measures such as taxing processes which generate pollution (for example, the use of leaded fuels) or payments for licences to emit certain levels of pollutant (such as in waste management in the European Union) are in line with the principle that the polluter should pay.

Figure 2.15 *The progress of the Chernobyl plume, 1986*

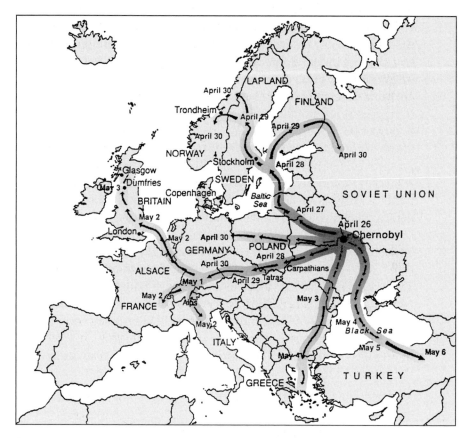

Source: Allen and Hamnett (1995).

community over the nature of the link between the pollutant and the ill health of ecosystems and humans; there is much that is not known, for example, regarding the thresholds above which nuclear wastes are hazardous to humans and concerning the length of time taken for such products to become harmless. This problem of a lack of understanding regarding the links between cause and effect in the production and impact of pollution clearly also underpins the challenge of identifying responsibilities and indeed response, so that these issues represent a major challenge for ensuring that future productive activities are sustainable.

The power to respond

It was seen above in the discussion of how understanding of poverty has changed, that people's capacity or power to make changes in their lives for the better depends on more than solely their financial assets. However, it was also seen, through various examples, that greater wealth is strongly associated with a range of improved opportunities and chances for development. Furthermore, it was evident that low-income groups share development and environment challenges that are quite different from higher-income groups and are closely related to basic survival itself in the short term. Clearly, whilst it is unrealistic to expect poor people to conserve resources for the future when they are struggling to meet primary needs such as for food and shelter, the governments of poorer nations also may have very scarce economic resources for any activities outside the provision of basic human needs. Clearly, governments themselves are responsible for determining how those limited financial resources are spent (on arms or on health, for example), but the challenge of responding to environmental management needs for a country at low levels of economic development is certainly distinct from that for those with higher incomes; the low-lying nations of both Bangladesh and the Netherlands are vulnerable to sea-level rise through global warming, but their capacities to respond are starkly different solely in terms of their financial resources. Economic and political power are closely intertwined, as illustrated in Figure 2.16 that highlights the differences in capacity to influence environmental outcomes within international trade negotiations between developing and more developed countries.

The international trade in hazardous waste is a clear illustration of where the lack of economic power on the part of developing nations constrains sustainable development. Although there are now international conventions aimed at regulating that trade (most importantly the Basel Convention which came into force in 1992), the trade continues. Fundamentally, receiving countries are so in need of income that they accept the pollutant 'without even the benefits of

Figure 2.16 *Capacities of influence in trade negotiations*

....

Developed countries have overwhelmingly the largest economic and political resources to influence policy decisions at the World Trade Organisation; they account for the greatest proportion of world trade, the headquarters of the WTO (as well as the World Bank and the International Monetary Fund) are based in developed countries, documents produced are in European languages, and developed countries can afford to support diplomatic missions at those places/in those institutions. Developing countries, in contrast, account for less trade, have weaker economic capacity and government/social structures and rely on markets in the developed countries. The costs of having diplomatic presence are prohibitive to developing countries and there are not the same strong bonds of shared culture so that developing countries often do not act as a homogeneous bloc in negotiations.

....

Source: compiled from Taylor (2003).

hosting the industrial processes which cause it' (Yearley, 1995: 165). But factors which include the varied global patterns of environmental legislation, and labour standards and wage rates, are also important in fuelling this trade. This is a clear example of environmental difference enabling processes of globalisation to occur: differences in terms of position within the capitalist economy that enable people in one part of the globe to displace their environmental problems onto other parts and save money and trouble in so doing (Yearley, 1995). Indeed, waste operators and the shipping industry, as shown in Box F, *make* money through these processes. The lack of economic power on the part of receiving countries also extends to their inability to monitor illegal trade into their country or to enforce penalties on individuals and companies that conspire to extend such trade. The worsening poverty of individuals working in that trade are also highlighted in Box F and emphasise how globalisation can lead to *enhanced* environmental difference.

It will be illustrated more fully in the following chapters that progress towards sustainable development very regularly depends on enabling individuals and local community groups to become more powerful in their control over resources and the environment. It also depends on much greater financial assistance to the developing world to assist in environmental protection. The Brundtland Commission estimated in the early 1980s that the cost for developing countries of bringing environmental legislation up to US standards was in excess of US$5 billion and the sum today would be 'considerably larger' (LeQuesne and Clarke, 1997: 171). Chapter 3 considers more fully the difficult questions for the global community of how to deliver greater financial resources for sustained development.

Box F

___

The export of hazardous waste

Already jeopardized by global environmental changes, erosion, famine, and deforestation, the Third World is currently being invaded by extensive exports and dumping of tons of hazardous waste from industrialised countries . . . For the millions of people in Third World countries, the sometimes legal, sometimes illegal importation of hazardous waste represents an unprecedented threat to their health and their environment.

(Sanchez, 1994, 137)

In the late 1980s and through the 1990s, there were a number of 'scandals' surrounding transboundary movements of toxic and hazardous materials (defined as waste which, if deposited into landfills, air or water in untreated form will be detrimental to human health or the environment). These scandals involved firms and waste brokers from the US and Western Europe 'dumping' wastes into unprotected communities in Africa, the Caribbean and Latin America. Reliable statistics on the international movement of hazardous materials are hard to come by, because of the illegal nature of much trade and the varied standards or definitions of waste used in different countries. However, 175 million tonnes of hazardous waste are thought to have been offered on formal world markets between 1986 and 1991 (*Guardian*, 1992). Factors fuelling this trade included (within the more developed countries) the increased amounts of waste being generated, the lack of land to receive these and the higher costs of treatment, disposal and storage as consumer demand pushed for cleaner industry and improved quality of local environments. Within the receiving countries, legislation and infrastructures to enforce and monitor such trade were often absent or underdeveloped, contributing to the lower costs of disposal.

The Basel Convention on the Control of Transboundary Movements of Hazardous Wastes and Their Disposal was adopted in 1989 and came into force in 1992. It called for national self-sufficiency in hazardous waste management and for the minimisation of both the generation and transboundary movement of such wastes. Where wastes were to be exported, the exporting country must have 'prior informed consent', i.e. written consent from an appropriate authority in the receiving country and an obligation on the exporter to ensure that the wastes at destination would be managed in an environmentally sound manner. The only rationales acceptable in the convention for hazardous waste exports are when a country lacks adequate technical capacity to handle/ manage those wastes domestically or the importing country requires the waste as a raw material.

In 1994, the Parties to the Convention recognised that the original obligations were not sufficient, particularly in the light of the immense economic pressures to import hazardous wastes faced by many poor countries. An amendment therefore called on all OECD countries to *ban* export of hazardous wastes to non-OECD countries. Despite requiring further ratification before it can be enforced legally, many parties are currently honouring the amendment (although others, including Canada, Australia, Japan and South Korea 'have a well known antipathy towards the Basel Ban Amendment and continue to work with the US to undermine its efficacy and entry into force' (BAN, 2002: 33)). The United States is not a signatory to the original Convention nor to its amendment. The Basel

Convention has served to limit the most obvious cases of the export of hazardous waste. However, new issues are emerging including in e-waste and shipbreaking.

E-waste encompasses a range of electronic devices and is a rapidly expanding waste stream, as identified earlier in this chapter. Much of e-waste from a scientific viewpoint is hazardous and many governments around the world tightly control its disposal and export. However, this does not prevent the widespread export of such materials: 50–80% of e-waste collected for recycling in the US for example is estimated to be exported – mostly to China.

In Guiyu town in the southern Guandon Province of China, an estimated 100,000 people are employed in processing e-waste largely from the US, but also from Japan, South Korea and Europe. Their work is based on receiving and recycling obsolete and broken computer equipment: heating printed circuit boards over charcoal burners to release possibly reusable computer chips; ripping apart printer cartridges to collect remnant traces of toner and for recyclable plastic and aluminium parts. Cathode ray tubes from televisions are also hammered open for copper yokes. Ship loads of containers come through the port of Nanhai and then hundreds of trucks depart each day to Guiyo town (BAN, 2002: Gittings, 2002). Workers in these enterprises are totally unprotected: there is no basic safety equipment, they breathe in toner fumes, and are exposed to heavy metal contaminants. Local rivers are polluted and drinking water has to be trucked in.

Whilst China is a signatory to the Basel Convention and has national legislation prohibiting imports of solid wastes that are unusable as raw materials, for example, and severely regulates imports of wastes that can be used as raw materials, the infrastructure to enforce the legislation is extremely lacking (with some additional concerns as to the political will to enforce it) (BAN, 2002). In turn, impoverished farmers are willing to take the health risks and risks of prosecution through their desperate need for money, as evidenced by the facts that such activities often take part under the cover of darkness or re-start immediately once officials leave. Corruption is also evident as officials take money from operators in the e-waste business.

The breaking up of ships past their lifespan is also creating concern amongst international NGOs like Greenpeace. Ships generally have a 25–30-year lifespan. Predominantly, they comprise steel and historically they have been sold for breakup and dismantling to recover this raw material. In the 1970s, these highly mechanised operations were concentrated in Europe, but are increasingly done now in Asia, especially India (where 60 per cent of ships are broken), but also Bangladesh, Pakistan and China (Greenpeace, 2003). Shipbreaking provides 15% of India's steel needs and the largest shipbreaking yard in the world is at Along, India. As well as recyclable steel, however, these ships contain huge amounts of hazardous materials including PCBs (thought to be carcinogenic, known to infiltrate food chains and known to cause reproductive problems in wildlife); heavy metals such as mercury and lead (mercury affects the nervous system, lead delays neurological and physical development); asbestos used widely for non-retardant properties (respiratory disease and cancer) and old diesel and oils.

In 1997, the Supreme Court of India passed an Order banning the import of hazardous waste, but companies are known to flout this order and environmental activists, including Vandana Shiva, have taken out legal proceedings against the government of India for the way in which it has violated that Order. Furthermore, Greenpeace (2003) suggest that the efforts of the Indian government will remain ineffective as they are unilateral in a global shipping industry within which 'flags of convenience' are widely used and enable ship owners to register their ships elsewhere outside their country of origin and thereby avoid laws in the home country of the ship-owners as well as to circumvent international treaties such as the Basel Convention.

In late 2003, there was substantial media attention on the prospect of two US Navy ships entering UK waters and destined for breaking in Hartlepool. A local company, Able UK, had been contracted by the US Navy to import 13 such vessels in a £11m deal. The Environment Agency (the 'concerned authority' under the Basel Convention) had given a licence to import the material, but in fact depended on the presence of a dry dock to dismantle the ships safely and planning permission for that was not forthcoming from Hartlepool Council. Strong debates ensued with some interests pointing to the jobs that would be created in this depressed region and opponents raising environmental justice arguments noting that people in the Hartlepool district had already had 'more than their fair share of pollution' and experienced some of the worst environmental conditions in the UK.

Questions of sovereignty

A recurring issue and an important challenge for environmental management in the future concerns the questions of a country's sovereignty and the right to decide how its resources (including that of its people and their labours) should be used. Clearly, such issues are also closely related to those of the location and level of power as discussed previously.

In Chapter 1, it was noted that the initial hesitancy of developing nations to participate in the environmental debates of the 1960s was due in part to concern over the loss of control over their own development. With the rise of global governance throughout the 1990s, many of these same fears, on the part of the more developed as well as developing nations, resurfaced within international negotiations to determine actions for sustainable development (such as at the WSSD in Johannesburg). As will be seen in Chapter 3, many actions towards sustainable development undertaken in recent decades by the international community have involved the setting of standards for nations to follow. The idea that national standards should be a matter for international debate is fundamentally in contradiction of the notion of a country's sovereign right to look after the environment in a manner which it assesses to be best (Cairncross, 1995). There were fierce debates, for example, at the 1997 UN climate meeting in Kyoto, Japan, as each participating nation negotiated its 'quota of pollution'. The extremely lengthy proceedings of meetings of the World Trade Organisation are also seen to be, in part, a function of the concern of member states to apply their own rules, including those of environmental standards in production. In Box F, the challenge to sustainable development of the US *not* being a signatory to Basel Convention was seen.

Fundamentally, international institutions themselves are created by states as a means of achieving 'collective objectives that could not be accomplished by acting individually' (Werksman, 1996: xii). By definition, therefore, the conservation of the global environment demands some devolution of sovereign power, and the success or otherwise of international institutions working towards this goal depends on the willingness of those states to make such investments. However, critical evaluation is still needed regarding the nature of those goals. There remain fears in the developing world in particular that global environmental objectives are being set according to the agenda of countries in the North, as considered in Chapter 1. Priority is thus still given to issues of global climate change, deforestation and species extinction, for example, which are quite different from the environmental problems of the South, which are detailed further in Chapters 4 and 5, and which concern, most regularly, basic standards of living and life itself.

Conclusion

The inequitable nature of past development processes and patterns has been seen to be the main underlying reason why they cannot be sustained into the future, morally, economically and environmentally. Not only have the benefits and costs of progress to date fallen unevenly between nations and within sectors of society, but the persistence and entrenchment of poverty mean that increasing numbers of people are denied access to the resources on which future development depends and in the process are themselves a factor in the further degradation of those essential environments. Whilst inequalities in wealth have been seen to be important in understanding the challenges of sustainable development, from delivering basic health services through to financing pollution prevention and abatement technologies, it is also clear that these challenges are not solely economic, as illustrated in the case of premature deaths of girl children in India, for example.

There are evidently substantial new challenges for international relations. Whilst some degree of collective action has been fundamental to the survival of human societies throughout the history of civilisation, people and places today are connected in many more diverse and far-reaching ways (although at various intensities) and humanity now depends on cooperative interactions which go far beyond those of original societies in terms of both number and complexity. In the immediate term, for example, the challenges of sustainable development have been seen to include many different nation states in negotiation over the sharing of water use and in the location of potentially environmentally degrading production or products. States are also negotiating within newly created international fora in an attempt to deal with the challenges of sustainable development over the longer term, such as with respect to carbon dioxide and CFC reduction targets. However, the political challenges of sustainable development extend to individuals: the choices we make concerning our own consumption levels and preferences and in our own capacity to monitor and prompt change within the institutions that represent us. In summary, sustainable development is a challenge for people across the globe rather than for particular institutions of development or for certain regions of the world in isolation.

Discussion questions

* Why are natural resources so often the focus for conflict?
* List the various ways in which low-income groups may suffer more from environmental degradation.
* What happens to your mobile phone when you update it for a fresh model?

* Select a contemporary international news item as covered in the print media. Critically consider the explanations of the cause (responsibility) and the solution (response) presented.

Further reading

Buckles, D. and Rusnak, G. (1999) 'Conflict and collaboration in natural resource management', in Buckles, D. (ed.) *Cultivating Peace: Conflict and Collaboration in Natural Resource Management*, International Development Research Centre, Canada, pp. 1–10.

Castree, N. (2003) 'Uneven development, globalisation and environmental change', in Morris, D., Freeland, J., Hinchliffe, S. & Smith, S. (eds) *Changing Environments*, Oxford University Press, Oxford, pp. 275–312.

O'Riordan, T. (ed.) (2000) *Environmental Science for Environmental Management*, second edition, Longman, London.

Satterthwaite, D., Hart, R., Levy, C., Mitlin, D., Ross, D., Smit, J. and Stephens, C. (1996) *The Environment for Children: Understanding and Acting on the Environmental Hazards that Threaten Children and Their Parents*, Earthscan, London.

World Bank (2003) *World Development Report*, Oxford University Press, Oxford.

Actors and actions in sustainable development

Summary

- Measures towards the global governance of the environment have multiplied in recent decades but the challenges of implementing these in practice, making them relevant to local needs and overcoming more narrow national interests are substantial current challenges.
- The World Bank has been a target for environmental critics, but there have also been many changes within the organisation and in its activities towards promoting more sustainable development.
- Exports of primary commodities remain the central source of finances for development in low-income countries. Reforming world trade to address poverty is now high on the political agendas within those countries and amongst many international non-governmental organisations (INGOs) in particular.
- World trade increasingly takes place through and within transnational corporations rather than countries and this trade increasingly comprises services rather than commodities or manufactured goods.
- Research is revealing that public access to information can be a powerful tool for ensuring business interests are more accountable to the environments and people that their activities impact on.
- Continued mounting debt in less developed countries has many direct and indirect impacts on the environment. Research suggests that past prescriptions to solve the crisis such as structural adjustment programmes have often made things harder for people and governments in those countries.
- Civil society organisations are now significant agents in development. The chapter explores the reasons behind their growth and provides examples of INGOs campaigning for changes at the World Bank and World Trade Organisation, of social movements undertaking direct actions on shared concerns, and of southern-based NGOs working to deliver development needs.

Introduction

Accepting the necessity and desirability of sustainable development in the future was the essential prerequisite for the global community to start taking action. Measures taken by actors at various levels with the explicit aim of moving towards sustainable development have escalated since the 1980s. In so doing, however, the real challenges of sustainable development, those of reconciling the ambitions of various interest groups, of identifying basic versus extravagant needs and of balancing present and future development aspirations, have all become clearer. Inevitably, the practice of sustainable development is proving more difficult than professing an intention, yet there are signs of progress.

Figure 3.1 illustrates the various forces and actors that interplay to affect environmental conditions. This chapter identifies some of the principal actors in sustainable development, the international institutions, the state, business and civil society, and considers the broad kinds of activities they are undertaking. In particular it identifies how they have changed what they do as understanding of the demands of sustainable development have become more clear over the last two decades. Concurrently, a number of core arenas that explicitly link the prospects for sustainable development in less developed countries with actors and activities beyond their boundaries are also investigated: those of aid, trade and debt.

International action

> Perhaps our most urgent task today is to persuade nations of the need to return to multilateralism . . . after a decade and a half of a standstill or even deterioration in global co-operation the time has come for higher expectations, for common goals pursued together, for an increased political will to address our common future.
>
> (WCED, 1987: x)

One of the primary means by which countries can confirm their cooperation within international efforts to support global environmental goals has been through their signatures to various treaties that bind international behaviour, what are termed 'multilateral environmental agreements'. 'MEAs have been among the most visible manifestations of the intergovernmental community's interest in sustainable development' (Najam, 2004: 74). Table 3.1 highlights some of the most important international agreements on the environment (in that they have the most signatories). Currently, some five hundred MEAs exist although approximately 30 per cent cover regional issues such as fisheries and therefore have a more limited number of signatories. Sixty per cent of all MEAs have been signed since the Stockholm conference of 1972 (WRI, 2003).

Figure 3.1   Forces and actors in environmental outcomes

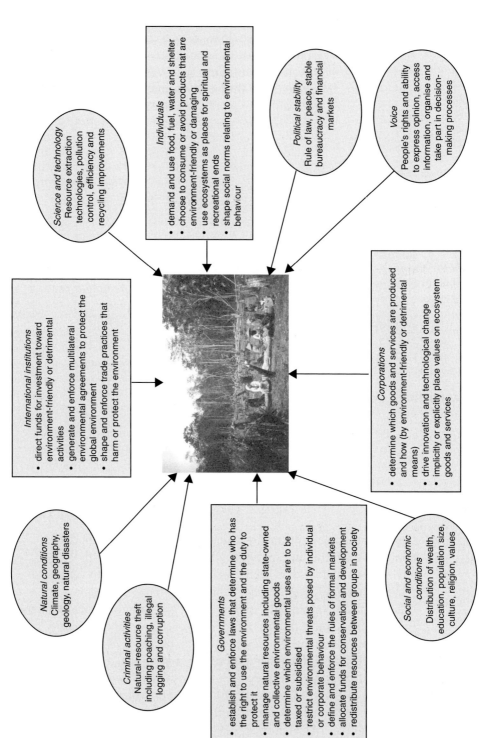

Science and technology
Resource extraction technologies, pollution control, efficiency and recycling improvements

Individuals
• demand and use food, fuel, water and shelter
• choose to consume or avoid products that are environment-friendly or damaging
• use ecosystems as places for spiritual and recreational ends
• shape social norms relating to environmental behaviour

Political stability
Rule of law, peace, stable bureaucracy and financial markets

Voice
People's rights and ability to express opinion, access information, organise and take part in decision-making processes

International institutions
• direct funds for investment toward environment-friendly or detrimental activities
• generate and enforce multilateral environmental agreements to protect the global environment
• shape and enforce trade practices that harm or protect the environment

Corporations
• determine which goods and services are produced and how (by environment-friendly or detrimental means)
• drive innovation and technological change
• implicitly or explicitly place values on ecosystem goods and services

Natural conditions
Climate, geography, geology, natural disasters

Criminal activities
Natural-resource theft including poaching, illegal logging and corruption

Governments
• establish and enforce laws that determine who has the right to use the environment and the duty to protect it
• manage natural resources including state-owned and collective environmental goods
• determine which environmental uses are to be taxed or subsidised
• restrict environmental threats posed by individual or corporate behaviour
• define and enforce the rules of formal markets
• allocate funds for conservation and development
• redistribute resources between groups in society

Social and economic conditions
Distribution of wealth, education, population size, culture, religion, values

Sources: WRI (2003); *Guardian*; photograph by Rebecca Elmhirst.

Table 3.1 *Selected Multilateral Environmental Agreements (MEAs)*

MEA	Purpose	Date adopted	Entry into force	% of world nations that are party to MEA
Ramsar Convention – Convention on Wetlands of International Importance Especially as Waterfowl Habitat	To conserve and promote the wise use of wetlands.	1971	1975	70
World Heritage Convention – Convention Concerning the Protection of the World Cultural and Natural Heritage	To establish an effective system of identification, protection, and preservation of cultural and natural heritage, and to provide emergency and long-term protection of sites of value.	1972	1975	91
CITES – Convention on International Trade in Endangered Species of Wild Fauna and Flora	To ensure that international trade in wild plants and animal species does not threaten their survival in the wild, and specifically to protect endangered species from over-exploitation.	1973	1975	84
CMS – Convention on the Conservation of Migratory Species of Wild Animals	To conserve wild animal species that migrate across or outside national boundaries by developing species-specific agreements, providing protection for endangered species, conserving habitat, and undertaking cooperative research.	1979	1983	44
UNCLOS – United Nations Convention on the Law of the Seas	To establish comprehensive legal orders to promote peaceful use of the oceans and seas, equitable and efficient utilisation of their resources, and conservation of their living resources.	1982	1994	74

Table 3.1—*continued*

MEA	Purpose	Date adopted	Entry into force	% of world nations that are party to MEA
Vienna Convention – Convention for the Protection of the Ozonc Layer	To protect human health and the environment from the effects of stratospheric ozone depletion by controlling human activities that harm the ozone layer and by cooperating in joint research.	1985	1988	96
Montreal Protocol – Protocol on Substances that Deplete the Ozone Layer (Protocol to Vienna Convention)	To reduce and eventually eliminate emissions of man-made ozone depleting substances.	1987	1989	95
Basel Convention – Convention on the Control of Transboundary Movements of Hazardous Wastes and Their Disposal	To ensure environmentally-sound management of hazardous wastes by minimising their generation, reducing their transboundary movement, and disposing of these wastes as close as possible to their source of generation.	1989	1992	82
UNFCCC – United Nations Framework Convention on Climate Change	To stabilise greenhouse gas concentrations in the atmosphere at a level preventing dangerous human-caused interference with the climate system.	1992	1994	97
CBD – Convention on Biological Diversity	To conserve biological diversity and promote its sustainable use, and to encourage the equitable sharing of the benefits arising out of the utilisation of genetic resources.	1992	1993	97

Table 3.1—*continued*

MEA	Purpose	Date adopted	Entry into force	% of world nations that are party to MEA
UNCCD – United Nations Convention to Combat Desertification	To combat desertification, particularly in Africa, in order to mitigate the effects of drought and ensure the long-term productivity of inhabited drylands.	1994	1996	97
Kyoto Protocol – Kyoto Protocol to the United Nations Framework Convention on Climate Change	To supplement the Framework Convention on Climate Change by establishing legally binding constraints on greenhouse gas emissions and encouraging economic and other incentives to reduce emissions.	1997	Not yet in force	57
Aarhus Convention – Convention on Access to Information, Public Participation in Decision-Making, and Access to Justice in Environmental Matters	To guarantee the rights of access to information, public participation in decision-making, and legal redress in environmental matters.	1998	2001	13

Note: Status as of June 2003: European Union included in count of parties and calculation of world percentage.
Source: World Resources Institute (2003).

MEAs are not static documents; rather, they are renegotiated as parties to the agreement or circumstances change. For example, in 1987, the United Nations Environment Programme (UNEP) brought government representatives together in Montreal to consider a protocol on substances that deplete the ozone layer. Governments representing two-thirds of global CFC use agreed to targets for the phasing out of such substances, and the 'Montreal Protocol' became effective in 1989. In 1992, signatory nations met again in Copenhagen to review the status of phase-out periods and committed themselves to an acceleration of reductions in the light of further scientific evidence regarding ozone loss. In 1995, the 150 parties to the protocol revised it once again to include controls on hydrochlorofluorocarbons which are being used as replacements for CFCs, but are also damaging ozone levels, as seen in Chapter 2 (Starke, 1997).

At the Earth Summit in Rio in 1992, 167 states signed the UN Framework Convention on Climate Change (UNFCC). Parties to the convention were obliged to aim to reduce their emissions of carbon dioxide by the year 2000 to levels lower than those in 1990. It was what is termed a 'soft-law' requiring voluntary commitments and also recognised 'common but differentiated' responsibilities and respective capabilities across world regions. Many of the developing countries, for example, were not required to take on obligations beyond broad reporting, whilst developed country parties committed to facilitating new funds and technologies to developing countries to assist them in meeting their commitments to the convention. The Conference of Parties has met each year since 1994, and in Kyoto in Japan in 1997, 113 parties agreed to the 'Kyoto Protocol' that extended the number of greenhouse gases encompassed in the agreement and set new, variable, targets that should be met within the period 2008–12. However, in order for the accord to be fully ratified and to become a legally binding agreement on emissions reduction, 55 countries representing 55 per cent of the world's greenhouse gas emissions needed to endorse it. The refusal in 2001 of the US (accounting for 35 per cent of the world's carbon emissions in that year) to sign the protocol on the basis that it would harm its domestic economy and that it unfairly favoured developing countries, illustrates how multilateral agreements are always threatened by more narrow national interests. Australia similarly refused to sign, such that full ratification rested on Russia (accommodating 17.4 per cent of world emissions). In November 2004, Russia agreed to sign such that the treaty is now legally binding.

International action on the environment is also encompassed through governments' commitments to internationally negotiated principles such as the Johannesburg Declaration on Sustainable Development considered in Chapter 1 and the Rio Declaration on Environment and Development that emerged from the 1992 Earth Summit. The latter was a set of twenty-seven principles for the future conduct of nations and peoples with respect to environment and development. It is not a legal agreement in the sense that governments are not required to follow each recommendation 'line by line'. However, it has been referred to as a 'collection of agreed and negotiated wisdoms as to the nature of the problems and relevant principles of the desirable and feasible paths . . . against which government and other actions can and will be compared' (Koch and Grubb, 1997: 455).

Similarly at Rio, the international community agreed to the formation of a UN Commission on Sustainable Development (CSD) as an overarching international environmental organisation. Its principal function was to monitor the implementation of Agenda 21 through reviewing all reports from relevant organisations and programmes within the UN system. A number of specialised agencies including the World Bank are also subject to monitoring under the CSD. In addition, the 53 elected members of the CSD have been specifically charged with monitoring financial and technical commitments of UN member nations. The CSD has no legal or budgetary authority, so that it is a forum for exchanging information, building partnerships and consensus (Potter *et al.*, 2004). Whilst it has been argued that the urgency and sense of commitment at Rio has generally not been sustained through the subsequent sessions of CSD (Upton, 2004), it has done much to promote dialogue and partnership between intergovernmental organisations, governments and NGOs through the hundreds of meetings that it has hosted (Dodds, 2002).

Regional groupings have also taken on the challenge of sustainable development and the need for co-coordinated actions amongst their members. For example, at the 1989 Commonwealth Heads of Government meeting in Malaysia, the 49 member countries adopted the Langkawi Declaration on the Environment as a mandate for future action. The heads of the governments of the Commonwealth resolved to 'act collectively and individually' in undertaking a 16-point programme of action. This included strengthening efforts by developing countries in forest management, affording support to low-lying and island countries for protection from sea-level rises, promotion of active programmes of environmental education and support measures to improve energy conservation. Since 1992, the Commonwealth Consultative Group on Environment (CCGE) has provided a forum for continued consultations, for assisting member states in meeting their obligations to MEAs and for promoting understanding and agreement on issues related to sustainable development. It meets regularly, typically in advance of major UN conferences, in recognition that the 'strength of the Commonwealth lies in its potential for building bridges between different groups through open and constructive dialogue on environmental problems that are of global concern, and sharing experiences and practical solutions to environmental management' (www.gm-unccd.org). In

1991, the Harare Declaration pledged further action to promote sustainable development and the alleviation of poverty and protection of the environment through respect for the principles enunciated at Langkawi. Box G details the lead that the European Union is giving to its member states in terms of principles for environmental policy. Recently, in January 2005, as part of an EU directive, the UK has implemented new rights for the public to access environmental information held by public authorities (and some private bodies, including utilities and contractors providing environmental services on behalf of public authorities). The significance of public access to information in prompting moves towards sustainability are considered in subsequent sections.

Whilst the increase in international environmental treaties and the creation of new institutions are evidence of the contemporary significance of environmental issues within the conduct of international relations, there are continued challenges in practice: in ensuring that they are relevant to local realities, for example, and that agreements are implemented and their impacts monitored. The long delays in reaching full ratification of the Kyoto Protocol also illustrate how MEAs can be threatened by narrow national interests.

Aid and the environment

Foreign aid is defined as any flow of capital to the developing nations which meets two criteria. First, its objective should be non-commercial from the point of view of the donor; second, it should be characterised by interest and repayment terms which are less stringent than those of the commercial world. Typically, what is termed overseas development assistance (ODA) comprises grants and concessional loans from individual governments as well as the international financial institutions (the World Bank and regional development banks, for example). The notion of foreign aid is that these grants and loans are broadly aimed at transferring resources from wealthy to poor nations for development or income redistribution.

There has always been substantial debate over the impact of aid on the recipient nations. Opinions range from the belief that it is an essential prerequisite for development, supplementing scarce domestic resources, to the view that aid perpetuates neo-colonial dependency relationships which will ensure that recipient nations remain

Box G

European Union Action Programmes and the environment

The European Economic Community (now known as the European Union) first formulated an Action Programme for the Environment in 1973. It established objectives to prevent and reduce pollution, to ensure sound management of resources, to guide development in accordance with quality of life concerns, to ensure environmental aspects are taken into account in town and land use planning, and to seek common solutions to environmental problems with states outside the Union and with international organisations. A number of principles were also established at that time, including that the Union and its member states must take into account in their environmental policy the interests of developing countries, and must in particular examine the repercussions of the measures on the economic development of those countries and on trade with them.

By the fifth programme, the development of which coincided with UNCED in 1992, a new reference to the concept and practice of sustainable development and a more wide-ranging environmental policy was evident. In particular, the emphasis moved away from considering environmental problems and controls in relation to particular media such as land, air and water, towards looking horizontally at all the environmental implications of the various sectors of the economy and therefore towards mainstreaming/integrating environmental policies within other EU policies. A central concept was also of the shared responsibility, between government, industry and the consumer for solving environmental problems.

In 1997, sustainable development was made one of the overriding objectives of the EU in the new Amsterdam Treaty, committing the membership to the principle that the European Union's future development must be based on the principles of sustainable development and a high level of protection of the environment. The sixth Action Programme (2001–10) was developed at a time of significant expansion of the boundaries and membership of the EC and aims to give a greater strategic direction to the Commission's environmental policy over the next few years. It recognises the complex and very varied environmental challenges of this expanded community that now includes many smaller countries from the former communist bloc that have very substantial environmental problems but an urgent economic imperative, for example. The sixth programme seeks to ensure effective implementation of existing legislation, but also the development of new and innovative instruments and solutions through more participatory approaches to policy-making and the active involvement and accountability of all sections of society. Ensuring better and more accessible information on the environment for citizens is a core priority, a commitment enshrined in the Aarhus Convention of 1998 and which Walker *et al.* (2004: 2) suggest has been significant in driving new EU laws towards ensuring 'environmental equity issues are taken more seriously than ever before'.

underdeveloped (for key areas of this debate, see, for example, Hayter, 1989; Mosley, 1995; Todaro, 1997). Certainly, there is much evidence that aid can be (and has been) environmentally damaging. In Chapter 1 it was seen that the widespread damage to environments and local peoples caused by resettlement projects, large dams and road building, particularly in Latin America, were important in shaping public environmental concern in the US. The *Ecologist* magazine was active in publicising the environmental degradation caused by iron ore extraction and highway projects in Amazonia, for example. In turn, public concern and campaigns on behalf of international NGOs were important in shaping changes in the way such projects were planned and implemented, as considered in the section below.

In 1970, the United Nations General Assembly agreed targets for ODA for the first time, urging more developed countries to allocate 0.7 per cent of GNP annually by 1975. By the year 2000, only Denmark, Norway, Sweden, the Netherlands and Luxembourg had reached the target set by the UN for aid transfers. On average, countries of the OECD gave 0.22 per cent of GDP and most gave less in 2000 than they did in 1990 (UNDP, 2002). It is estimated that official development assistance must double (from the current US$56 billion) to meet the Millennium Development Goals listed in Figure 1.12 (UNDP, 2002). However, much of the recent debate on aid impacts has shifted from preoccupation with 'supply' issues, i.e. enhancing the inflow of financial resources for development, towards 'demand' side issues, of the capacity of individuals, communities, governments and development institutions to access and effectively use those resources (Banuri and Spanger-Seigfried, 2001). The kinds of local experience that will be seen in Chapters 4 and 5, for example (in livelihood security, poverty eradication and natural resource conservation), has been important in demonstrating that support for capacity building is often more effective than provision of concessional assistance per se. Furthermore, debates concerning aid are increasingly linked to issues of debt reduction and rescheduling, as considered in subsequent sections. The amount of aid flowing to the developing countries constitutes a very small proportion of their GDP and is also dwarfed by the flows out of those countries in debt repayments, as shown in Table 3.2.

Table 3.2 *Resource flows to and from developing countries*

Type of flow	% of developing countries' GDP, 2000
Exports	26.0
Debt service	6.3
Net foreign direct investment	2.5
Aid	0.5
Net grants from NGOs	0.1

Source: UNDP (2002).

In 1997, the newly elected Labour government in Britain set sustainable development at the top of its development assistance agenda, and recognised explicitly the interdependence of aid with areas of trade and wider foreign policy, as encapsulated in its first White Paper on Development, *Eliminating World Poverty: A Challenge for the 21st Century* (DFID, 1997: 50):

> Development assistance is an important part of the way in which we can help tackle poverty. But it is not by any means the only aspect of our relationship with developing countries. Both nationally and internationally, there is a complex web of environmental trade, investment, agricultural, political, defence, security and financial issues which affect relations with developing countries. These are driven by a range of policy considerations, all of which affect the development relationships. To have a real impact on poverty we must ensure the maximum consistency between all these different policies as they affect the developing world. Otherwise, there is a risk that they will undermine development, and development assistance will only partly make up for the damage done.

However, the seriousness of this rhetoric has been questioned (as encompassed in Figure 3.2). For example, Britain's aid contributions fell from a high of 0.5 per cent of GDP in 1979 to 0.26 per cent in the late 1990s. In 2004 it rose to 0.34 per cent and recently, there has been a commitment to raise funds to the Department for International Development.

The World Bank in sustainable development

The World Bank (WB) group, which consists of the International Bank for Reconstruction and Development (IBRD), the International Development Association (IDA), the International Finance Corporation (IFC) and the Multilateral Investment Guarantee Agency (MIGA), is the major source of multilateral aid for developing countries. In 2003, gross disbursements from IBRD and IDA totalled US$28.5 billion (World Bank, 2003a). In addition, for each dollar that the World Bank lends, it can be expected that several more will also flow to these projects from other agencies, from private banks and from the recipient governments (Rich, 1994). The rhetoric and actions of the World Bank with regard to the environment are therefore crucial in determining the prospects for sustainable development.

Figure 3.2 *Questioning the UK government's commitment to fighting poverty*

Source: D. Simonds.

The World Bank (with its 'sister organisation', the International Monetary Fund, IMF) was established at the Bretton Woods Conference in 1944, and was part of a package aimed at ensuring the reconstruction and development of Europe after the Second World War. In operation, since 1950 the World Bank (WB) has lent monies increasingly to the governments of the developing nations. The IMF is primarily concerned with economic and financial stability and sets and oversees codes of economic conduct on behalf of members. To qualify for WB loans, countries must first be members of the IMF. Fundamentally, the WB as a multilateral institution has been able to borrow money on world markets and lend more cheaply than commercial banks. It raises money by selling bonds and other securities to individuals, corporations, pension funds and other banks around the world. Its securities are considered to be amongst the world's safest, ensuring that it can borrow on very favourable terms and is able to lend money at rates below commercial rates. This is because it lends to governments and has 'preferred creditor status' with those governments (that private banks do not enjoy). Any debts have to be repaid first to the World Bank so that there is little risk involved; the World Bank gets its money back from governments even if they have to take out new loans to do so. The World Bank lends to governments over 15–20-year periods. Decisions on allocating funds take place on the basis of 'one dollar–one vote', i.e. according to the financial contribution of that voting country to the bank. On this basis, 45 per cent of voting rights are held by G8 countries with developing countries typically having less than 0.1 per cent of votes (Potter *et al.*, 2004).

In 1973, an Office of Environmental Affairs was created within the bank to review prospective environmental impacts of its lending. It was not until 1987, however, that a central Environment Division (and four Regional Divisions) was created to oversee and promote environmental activities. In 1993, the World Bank announced a four-fold environmental agenda in recognition of the way in which environmental degradation was threatening the attainment of its objectives, stated as being 'to reduce poverty and promote sustainable development' (World Bank, 1994). Central to the agenda were procedures for 'greening' project lending – that section of WB lending which goes to individual governments for specific projects as identified and designed by the governments of recipient nations in collaboration with WB personnel. Environmental assessment (EA) is now a part of the World Bank project cycle: before projects are approved, they are 'screened' for environmental impacts and various levels of investigation are triggered according to the projected severity of these and before the project can proceed to approval.

The seriousness of the World Bank's commitments to environmental reforms was quickly and severely tested in the early 1990s. In 1991, the USA (the World Bank's largest contributor) threatened to withhold 25 per cent of its 1992 contribution (approximately US$70 million) in relation to its involvement in the damming of the Narmada river in India. This project started in 1987 with the construction of the Sadar Sarovar dam, although it had been at least twenty years in the planning stages. At the time, it was the world's largest hydroelectric and irrigation complex, based on 30 major, 135 medium and 3,000 minor dams to be built over fifty years. It was designed to generate an estimated 500 million megawatts of electricity, irrigate over two million hectares and bring drinking water to thousands of villages.

The Narmada scheme was mired in controversy from the outset: the dams would displace 200,000 people, submerge 2,000 sq. km of fertile land and 1,500 sq. km of prime teak and sal forest, and eliminate historic sites and rare wildlife. The scheme has been referred to as an environmental catastrophe, a technological dinosaur and an example of flagrant social injustice (Schwarz, 1991). Fierce local and international protests against the scheme led to the World Bank taking the unprecedented step of commissioning an independent review of its activities on the programme and in 1993 the decision was made to withdraw support. The Indian government is continuing with the scheme and public opposition continues. In 1998, for example, all work was stopped on the Maheshwar dam site, when 10,000 villagers who were set to lose their homes and lands if construction was completed, engaged in one of the largest peaceful sit-ins in Indian history (Vidal, 1998). Until 2000, work stalled whilst opponents of the scheme contested its continuation at the Supreme Court of India. However, the court ruled against the petition of the Narmada People's Movement (Narmada Bachao Andolan) and the go-ahead was given to raise the height of the main dam from 88 metres to 139 (NI, 2001).

A further element of the World Bank's environmental agenda has been to provide funds for projects which specifically aim to strengthen environmental management. Lending to this core environment and natural resources management (ENRM) portfolio (defined as projects with more than 65 per cent environmental content) reached a high in 1997 of over US$2 billion although it subsequently fell. Figure 3.3 illustrates that ENRM spending as a proportion of total bank lending has risen in recent years. Such projects include funds for research,

Figure 3.3 *The Environmental and Natural Resources Management lending at the World Bank*

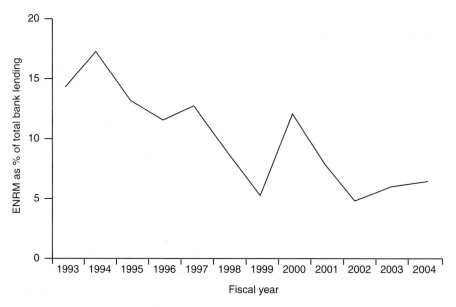

Source: *Environment Matters* (2003).

capacity building, training and monitoring, as well as direct investment in pollution prevention and treatment, the conservation of biodiversity, integrated river management and establishing national parks.

The World Bank was also integral in establishing (with UNEP and UNDP) the Global Environment Facility (GEF) in 1991. This is a programme of new monies (over and above existing ODA contributions) to assist the least developed nations in tackling explicitly global environmental problems, including the limitation and reduction of greenhouse gases, the protection of biodiversity, international water management and energy conservation. In 1994, GEF was extended from its initial pilot phase, with the World Bank acting as trustee, the UNDP providing technical assistance and preparing projects, and UNEP overseeing the integrity of projects. Current GEF projects, by thematic area, are shown in Table 3.3. It has been praised by some as an important tool for future multilateral cooperation on environmental issues, but is criticised by others for not addressing the key environmental concerns of developing countries. For example, 24 per cent of GEF projects are focused on climate change issues. Furthermore, membership of GEF is limited to those countries making a minimum contribution of US$4 million to the fund and has been dominated, 'just like the World Bank's board of executive directors', by developed countries (Werksman, 1995: 282). During the pilot phase, 80 per cent of GEF projects were linked in some way to larger ongoing World Bank projects (1995).

Table 3.3 Destination of current GEF monies by thematic area

Global environmental theme	% monies, 2004
Biodiversity	59
Climate change	24
International waters	10
Multi-sectoral	6
Ozone depletion	1

Source: World Bank (2003c).

As identified in Chapter 1, an increasing proportion of World Bank funds is now directed at broad-based policy reforms rather than to specific projects. Until the early 1980s, most lending was 'project lending', but the emerging debt crisis through the decade led to profound changes in the lending activities of the World Bank and a shift to increased 'programme' lending, i.e. the packages of macro-economic and policy reform (SAPs) that now encompass over 50 per cent of total lending (Potter *et al.*, 2004). Some of the serious concerns regarding the environmental impacts of policy lending that include pressures for 'resource-mining' and greater socioeconomic disparities are considered in subsequent sections. Whilst the World Bank remains a key target of environmental critics, it is evident that there has been substantial change in terms of its investments, its policies and the way in which it works with other institutions in development in relation to the environment. In 2001, following an independent assessment of past environmental performance, the World Bank launched a new environment strategy, *Making Sustainable Commitments* (WB, 2001). Within the strategy, the World Bank recognises that many environmental problems are best addressed by dedicated projects and is committed to disseminating best practice from these. But it also asserts that these projects are unlikely to bring lasting results in a 'distorted policy environment' so that much of their lending will continue to be to such policy reform and adjustment. The strategy commits the bank to work towards careful sequencing of policy reform and specific projects and to pay special attention to reinforcing the positive and minimising the negative outcomes of adjustment lending. Perhaps most significantly in the new environment strategy, it is recognised that change is required in the bank itself: to 'accelerate the shift from viewing the environment as a separate, freestanding concern to considering it an integral part of our development assistance' (p. xxv).

Trade and the environment

At both a global and national level, trade is an increasingly important element in development. More of what is produced is now sold in external markets around the world; between 1950 and the end of twentieth century, world merchandise trade increased almost twenty-fold, whereas merchandise production increased only six-fold (Dicken, 2003: 35). Countries worldwide also have a greater number of trading partners, a further indicator of the increasing globalisation of world trade. Trade has been responsible for a significant proportion of economic growth in recent years and further growth is required to overcome poverty, as seen in earlier chapters. However, there is concern that large parts of the developing world are cut off from the wealth generated through trade and are experiencing increased marginalisation and poverty, as seen in the discussion of 'making globalisation work for the poor' in Chapter 2. There is also evidence of pressures on the environment through processes of trade expansion.

Whilst the debate on the links between trade and the environment have tended to be rather polarised (with the truth, as suggested by Halle and Borregaard (2004), generally lying somewhere in between), reforming world trade is now high on the political agenda. For example, historic protests (the 'Battle for Seattle') by representatives of a wide range of development organisations, unions, NGOs and many individuals in 1999 led to the abandonment of the annual meeting in that city of the World Trade Organisation (the international institution charged with setting the rules and resolving disputes in the arena of international trade). Several INGOs such as Oxfam have major campaigns concerning trade reform that focus on exposing the 'double standards' and 'rigged rules' of the international trading system that they suggest work in favour of the rich and prevent the potential for trade to reduce poverty. The nature of Oxfam's concern is illustrated in Figure 3.4 and is seen to include the activities of governments, multinational business, and the World Bank as well as the WTO. Evidently actions in the arena of trade have major implications for the prospects of sustainable development.

The geography of global production and trade is complex (see Dicken, 2003). For example, whilst the value of manufactured exports

Figure 3.4 *The Oxfam 'Making Trade Fair' campaign*

- Improving market access for poor countries and ending the cycle of subsidies, agricultural over-production and export dumping by rich countries
- Ending the use of conditions attached to IMF–World Bank programmes which force poor countries to open their markets regardless of the impact on poor people
- Creating a new international commodities institution to promote diversification and end over-supply, in order to raise prices to levels consistent with a reasonable standard of living for producers, and changing corporate practices so that companies pay fair prices
- Establishing new intellectual-property rules to ensure that poor countries are able to afford new technologies and basic medicines, and that farmers are able to save, exchange and sell seeds
- Prohibiting rules that force governments to liberalise or privatise basic services that are vital for poverty reduction
- Enhancing the quality of private-sector investment and employment standards
- Democratising the WTO to give poor countries a stronger voice
- Changing national policies on health, education, and governance so that poor people can develop their capabilities, realise their potential and participate in markets on more equitable terms

Source: Oxfam (2002).

from developing countries exceeded those of food and raw materials for the first time in the 1970s, only a few such nations are significant manufacturing producers (largely the East Asian economies). Globally, the fastest growing area of trade is now in commercial services, in telecommunications, financial services, management and advertising. Again, the principal exporters of commercial services are the US and the UK, although Hong Kong, China, South Korea and Singapore are also important exporters.

In excess of two-thirds of global exports of goods and services are in the hands of transnational corporations (Dicken, 2003). Furthermore, flows of foreign direct investment (a measure of TNC activity) are expanding more rapidly than trade itself. FDI refers to investments made overseas by one firm in another for the purposes of gaining a degree of control over that firm's operations. It also includes a firm setting up a branch or subsidiary in another country. Significantly, much of the expansion in FDI in recent years (and the explanation for the recent rapid growth in number of TNCs) has been through mergers and acquisitions rather than investments in new facilities. It was seen in Box A in Chapter 1 that few developing countries are either exporters of (i.e. own TNCs) or recipients of FDI.

In short, exports remain the principal source of income for development in countries of the developing world (as seen in Table 3.2). Figure 3.5 identifies a number of options and environmental challenges associated with raising foreign exchange for developing countries that are considered in more detail in the sections below.

Figure 3.5 *Options and environmental issues in raising trade and foreign exchange*

....

● **Raising export crop production:**
   But global terms of trade for such commodities worsening . . .

● **Raising exports of primary raw materials:**
   But economic benefits are short term and resources non-renewable . . .

● **Trading in by-products of others' production:**
   But safe disposal of waste often requires high investments . . .

● **Opening economy to FDI to create industry:**
   But women often at the bottom of manufacturing supply chains, labour and health standards often low . . .

....

The World Trade Organisation and the environment

The WTO was formed in 1995. It replaced the General Agreement on Tariffs and Trade (GATT) that was established in 1947 through the same statesmanship which created the United Nations, the World Bank and the International Monetary Fund. A set of international trading rules was developed for the promotion of future economic stability and development after the era of economic crisis, heavy protectionism, mass unemployment and the Depression (which had all formed part of the backdrop to the Second World War). The WTO has the same principles of free trade and market liberalisation underpinning its rules. There are currently 148 member states of the WTO. China was one of latest to join in 2001 and negotiations for Russia's entry are currently at an advanced stage. Taiwan is still a notable absentee.

The WTO is a stronger institution than GATT in that it has legal status similar to the UN and its rulings are binding on its members. Although the WTO rulings refer strictly to international trade policy (i.e. what happens at borders), the agreements made by the organisation now have far-reaching and contested implications for economic development, peace and security and environmental protection worldwide, particularly as its scope has widened (from the original GATT activities relating to manufactured goods) to include areas such as services and patents. Significantly, to date, the WTO has remained silent on the core issue for the developing world of commodity prices. As its scope has widened, the WTO now has authority in areas formerly the preserve of national governments (like food safety). It also has the power to impose sanctions on governments through its dispute settlement system and to ensure trade policy takes precedence over other policies.

In continuity with its predecessor, the WTO has phases of greater action, known as 'rounds'. Decision-making within the WTO is based largely on consensus, with each member getting one vote (rather than being weighted according to economic contribution, as within the World Bank). In part, this system of decision-making explains the length of negotiations over its work programme: the Uruguay round took eight years to complete (1986–94) and it took a further seven years to agree even the shape of the latest round (agreed in Doha in 2001). The work programme for this round was agreed in Geneva in 2004, leaving only two years to turn this into detailed, binding agreements. Member states of the WTO agree to two fundamental principles: of 'national treatment', under which countries must treat external participants in their economies in the same way as domestic firms, and of the 'most favoured nation', which states that any concession granted by a member to any one trading partner must be extended to all.

As early as 1971, GATT had a Group on Environmental Measures and International Trade although, in practice, it never met. The new WTO has twice as many committees and councils as GATT, many aimed at providing stronger procedures for dispute resolution and enforcement and for coverage of new areas of trade. In 1995 a new Committee on Trade and the Environment (CTE) was formed, charged with identifying the relationship between trade measures and sustainable development. However, the CTE is not a policy-making body and its work to date has focused on the negative impacts of environmental measures on trade (i.e. environmental measures as distortions to free trade), rather than how trade liberalisation may aggravate or cause environmental degradation effects (Potter *et al.*, 2004). For example, it is possible under the articles of the WTO agreement for countries to regulate trade in certain products in order to protect human, animal or plant life or health. However, any such measure must be applied to domestic as well as foreign firms (i.e. be non-discriminatory) and cannot be used as a protectionist device (i.e. must be clearly for conservation ends and not for trade protection).

Critically, WTO rulings focus on the product not the processes which are involved in its production. It is possible, therefore, that a country may restrict the importation of a certain good if it will cause environmental damage. What a country cannot do is stop the importation of a good which has caused environmental damage elsewhere during the course of its production: 'the way the import is produced, if it has no effect on the product as such, is not an adequate reason to discriminate against it' (Cairncross, 1995: 227). If a country wishes to impose environmental and health standards on productive activities and passes environmental legislation (such as landfill or carbon taxes) towards that end, that country does not have a right under the WTO articles to impose those standards on other countries. As a result, it could be argued that such countries risk making their own production uncompetitive in a world market where goods produced under less environmentally friendly conditions will still be traded.

Improving environmental standards may also prove very difficult in practice, when it is considered that large transnational corporations currently control the majority of world trade (and particularly in the major products of the developing world such as tea, coffee, cotton and forestry). The economic power of such companies in relation to whole countries was noted in Chapter 2. However, WTO rulings themselves make no distinction between enterprises in terms of scale of operation or impact. Indeed, the WTO continues to assume that trade takes place between countries when evidently it does not (Halle and Borregaard, 2004). Whilst TNCs are not members of the WTO so that they have no direct power, they have huge economic and technical resources and clearly make a large contribution to particular domestic economies such as the USA and within the EU:

> this practically guarantees that their concerns will be listened to at a national level and carried forward to negotiations within the WTO. Moreover, the long-term agenda of TNCs and most governments is similar – they share a commitment to the liberal economic goals of liberalized trade and economic growth achieved through free trade. This means they share the same broad ideas and can expect the current structures of global trade to protect these.
>
> (Taylor, 2003: 209)

Furthermore, the power of developing countries to influence policy at the WTO may be reduced simply through the prohibitive costs of maintaining a diplomatic mission at the WTO, estimated to be US$900,000 a year (Taylor, 2003). Oxfam (2002) notes that eleven of the WTO members among the least developed countries are not even represented at the WTO base in Geneva, suggesting a 'façade' of a membership-driven organisation in which each country has an equal vote. In contrast, the International Chamber of Commerce (an international corporate lobby group with thousands of member companies from across the world and which is dominated by huge TNCs like General Motors, Nestlé, Novartis and Bayer) has permanent representation at the WTO (New Internationalist, 2002).

However, the role of developing countries in shaping the agenda of the WTO is considered to have reached a new height at the Doha meeting in 2001 (Potter *et al.*, 2004). For example, trade ministers from the developing world made strong representations against a number of issues that the EU wanted included in the next round of negotiations and were successful in modifying existing rules regarding trade in intellectual property rights. These are now enabling lower costs of patented medicines for treatments of HIV/Aids, for example. Further evidence for the increasing role of developing nations in influencing the negotiations came in Cancun in 2003, when a group of 20 developing countries (including Brazil, China, India and South

Africa) walked out after failing to secure commitments from the EU, Japan and US in particular, for cutting subsidies to their farmers. The round is now 'back on track', as members agreed in Geneva in August 2004 to a framework to end export subsidies on farm products and to cut import duties worldwide.

There are evidently a number of critical challenges for the WTO in future. Trade has been responsible for a significant proportion of economic growth in recent years and, clearly, further growth is required to overcome poverty. To a large extent, therefore, the new WTO will determine patterns and processes of resource exploitation and will have a considerable impact on many of the world's most pressing environmental problems. Whilst trade can encourage economies to make money in environmentally damaging ways, trade barriers can also lead to environmental damage (if, for example, they lead to such depressed world prices that the wasteful use of resources is encouraged). The revenue generated through trade (and the increased competition that comes through decreasing protectionism and freeing up trade) may enable countries (as well as provide incentives to companies) to purchase the newest, anti-pollution technologies and protect the environment. However, trade also encourages traffic of all kinds, which itself is a major cause of environmental degradation such as climate warming and ozone destruction.

The work programme now set for the WTO has certainly opened a space for a more constructive debate between the trade and sustainable development agendas (Halle and Borregaard, 2004). For the first time, the WTO within the Doha agreement recognises that the sustainable development and trade agendas can be compatible, but this needs to be ensured, including through cooperation with other bodies such as UNEP. The relationship between trade rulings and multilateral environmental agreements are also part of the agenda for work in this round for the first time. Over thirty environmental treaties place some type of restriction on international trade, thereby violating strictly the principles of the WTO. It was seen, for example, in Box F, that under the Basel Convention, parties are obliged to prevent import or export of hazardous wastes if there is reason to believe that wastes will not be treated in an environmentally sound manner on their destination. There was some fear at the WSSD in Johannesburg that MEAS could become subordinate to trade rulings. Whilst the WTO is not formally open to NGOs or other civil society representatives, there can be no doubt that their influence in shaping the debates and agenda in the area of trade is growing. The direct action mounted in

Table 3.4 *Cow power*

....

Subsidy per cow (US$)		*GNI per capita (US$)*	
Japan	2,555	Bangladesh	360
USA	1,057	Ethiopia	100
European Union	803	Honduras	920

....

Source: Adapted from The *Guardian* and
Actionaid (2003).

1999 was a significant factor in delaying and then shaping agreements for the latest round. Exposing the perversity of continued levels of subsidies to domestic farmers (Table 3.4) and the mismatch between the protectionist practices of the superpowers and the principles of free trade that they espouse (Figure 3.4) are likely to bring further support for wider trade reforms in coming years.

Greener business into the twenty-first century

As seen in the previous section, many environmentalists are fearful of the prospects of sustainable development through further trade liberalisation on a number of fronts. These are summarised in Figure 3.6 and include the dominance of TNCs in world trade, their economic size and therefore power to shape global policy and how they are accountable to a very small number of shareholders not the public (Korten, 2001). In short, TNCs are said to put profit first and hold no allegiance to any particular place, community or environment (UNRISD, 1995). There is also concern regarding the influence of business more widely over what *governments* can do; businesses are now a highly resourced and powerful pressure group. In the US for example, energy, mining and waste management industries contributed almost US$30 million to political campaigns in 1999/2000 (WRI, 2003). Furthermore, private companies worldwide are increasingly moving into sectors relating to natural resources, in energy, telecommunications, transport, water and sanitation – public services that are vital for poverty reduction and the prospects for sustainable development. Between 1990 and 2001, 132 low- and middle-income countries introduced private sector participation in these sectors (UNCHS, 2001) in the context of neo-liberalism. In Chapter 5, a specific case of water privatisation in Bolivia is discussed (Box Q). Whilst proponents focus on efficiency gains through introducing the market to these sectors, concern focuses in particular on the prospects of affordable services reaching those most in need. Furthermore, there are moral questions: not only do private companies benefit from the contracts to deliver those services, but private sector consultants from large accountancy firms and banks are commonly involved in giving technical assistance and advice towards such reform. Vast sums are earned that often come directly from aid budgets of donor countries (War on Want, 2004).

Although there are still no international binding agreements of corporate responsibility (Ainger, 2002), there are, however, a number of sources of pressure on TNCs, and also on smaller business and industry more widely to take greater account of the environmental impacts of their activities. This section considers how business is changing the ways in which it works and the sources of pressure towards greater environmental and social accountability. In short, pressures from consumer tastes, government policy and industry's own perception of its environmental responsibility have combined to move many companies to behave in a more environmentally responsible manner than previously, at least for some companies and in some sectors and countries (WRI, 2003).

Figure 3.6 *Corporate influence in global affairs*

Extent
● In 1970, approximately 7,000 corporations worldwide. Now over 60,000.

Economic power
● Account for over one-quarter of economic activity of the planet (employ < 1% of workforce).
● Of the top 100 economic units on the planet, 51 are corporations, 49 are countries.

Operations
● In 1970, 90% of all international transactions were of trade, 10% capital flows.
● In 2002, 90% of all transactions are accounted for by financial flows not directly related to trade in goods and services.
● Trade between subsidiaries within same parent corporation accounts for approximately one-third of world trade.

Shaping public policy
● Influencing courts, delaying implementation of laws, amending laws.
● Participation in consultation, expert testimony, drafting legislation.
● Economic weight, framing/sponsoring research, public relations/information campaigns.
● Representation on government committees, influencing who is in government departments, funding parties, candidates and lobby groups.

Source: compiled from *New Internationalist* (2002), no. 347.

Rising public distrust and a view of business as the primary cause of environmental problems really emerged in the US and UK in the 1970s. At the same time, many governments introduced new environmental legislation and regulatory agencies in response to this public concern. Companies responded by appointing public relations specialists and using the media to reshape public opinion. Around 30 per cent of advertising budgets of many large companies in the oil, electricity and chemical industries became directed towards environmental issues at this time (Beder, 2002). Business also engaged in all kinds of cooperative ventures, with schools, research institutes and government towards assuring the public that business interests were the same as those of the environment. In the run-up to the Rio Earth Summit, for example, 'Corporations lined up to present themselves as part of the solution, rather than the problem' (Ainger, 2002: 21); Volkswagen provided cars for use by delegates and Coca-Cola provided every school in the English-speaking world with 'Earth Summit' kits. Some consider that corporations have been so successful in these kinds of activities that they have now generated a public backlash against the Greens and cast doubt on the urgency of environmental problems (Beder, 2002; Rowell, 1996; NI, no. 347, 2002).

However, it is evident that change in consumer tastes has been a powerful factor in the greening of companies. A survey of 25,000 consumers worldwide in 1999 suggested that 20 per cent had either avoided the products or publicly criticised companies on the basis of their perceived social and environmental performance (WRI, 2003). Consumers in the more developed world are increasingly sending signals that they are willing to pay a premium for goods that are greener. Organic food sales, for example, had an estimated value of US$20 billion in 2000 and are growing annually in the US, Europe and Japan by 25 per cent. In part, this is a product of a consumer backlash against the environmental and social impacts of industrialised agriculture as discussed in Chapter 4. One of the most powerful tools for ensuring greater business transparency and accountability is proving to be public access to information that encourages and empowers civil society to join the regulatory process. West Germany was the first country to launch a government-sponsored environmental labelling scheme as a basis for more informed consumer choices in 1978. Their 'Blue Angel' endorsement now extends to over 3,500 products (WRI, 2003). Other schemes are backed by private sponsors and typically involve a coalition of stakeholders in business and public groups concerned with these issues. 'Fairtrade' labelling was created in the Netherlands in the late 1980s providing a consumer with a guaranteed label on coffee sourced from Mexico. There are now 19 organisations that run the international standard-setting and monitoring body, Fairtrade Labelling Organisations International (www.fairtrade.org). However, there are limits to the role of green consumerism in prompting corporate change. For example, it still only affects a narrow range of goods and there are tremendous problems in establishing the green credentials of a product from its origins through its use to its disposal ('life cycle analysis'). However, it should be considered that pressure for companies to behave in an environmentally responsible manner may also come from the workforce and managers themselves who wish to have an environmental record they can be proud of (Cairncross, 1995).

Historically, it has been government-imposed regulations and enforcement, inspections and penalties ('command and control') that have been very important in prompting business and industry to change. Under this approach, governments set standards, such as for minimum levels of dissolved oxygen in river water or for the amounts of nitrous oxide in the air, and then set about enforcing these standards through regional and local public servants. However, such regulatory controls also have a number of problems. To be effective they require a well-resourced and powerful regulatory infrastructure to 'police' the enforcement of the legislation. Attempts to impose tighter regulations in one country have also encouraged industry to export its hazards elsewhere (see Box F). Furthermore, in setting a ceiling on pollution, there may be little incentive for a company to invest in reducing emissions or wastes substantially below that level.

A further strategy is for governments to induce companies to undertake environmental controls through the creation of economic incentives (via the tax system) to reduce pollution. Taxes are an attempt to put a price on pollution which in theory reflects the costs that fall on society. Examples include taxing sulphur by making leaded petrols more expensive in relation to unleaded (which is done in many European countries) and the charging of higher landing fees to noisier aeroplanes, as is done in Japan, Switzerland, the Netherlands and Germany (Cairncross, 1995). Taxes raise revenues for governments without incurring the same costs as enforcement of regulatory controls, but are politically much more contentious: 'The problem with all new taxes is that somebody has to pay for them – and those who perceive themselves as hurt are usually better at campaigning than those who will benefit' (1995: 65). Figure 3.7

Figure 3.7 *Business tools for environmental accountability*

....

Government-mandated disclosure of environmental performance
- Pollution registers
- Corporate environmental reports

Voluntary corporate initiatives
- Corporate codes of conduct
- Voluntary corporate environmental reports
- Environmental management systems
- Eco-labels
- Voluntary industry–government agreements

Public action and advocacy
- Socially responsible investing
- Eco-labels/green consumption

....

Source: adapted from WRI (2003).

summarises the various tools now used by business to raise their environmental accountability.

The continued absence of an international binding agreement of corporate responsibility is a concern in the context of the increasing globalisaton of corporate activity. In 1973, the UN established a Centre for Transnational Corporations with the intention of establishing a binding code of conduct. However, this was closed down in early 1992, just before Rio summit. Instead, the Business Council for Sustainable Development was invited to compile the recommendations on industry and sustainable development themselves; 'Transnational companies had made the evolutionary leap. They were no longer entities to be managed by governments, but had mutated into "valued partners" and "stakeholders" formulating global policy on their own terms' (Ainger, 2002: 21). Friends of the Earth International continue to campaign for a legally binding treaty on TNCs that would ensure compliance with minimum criteria of human rights, environmental and labour standards, and place legal responsibility on the corporation for the impacts of their business practices. Although the campaign gathered momentum at the World Summit on Sustainable Development and was supported by many developing countries as well as the EU, it did not gain agreement in Johannesburg. However, the WSSD Plan of Implementation does suggest that such a code or Corporate Accountability Convention is still 'live'.

International debt and the environment

A further critical global issue which will test the international community's commitment towards sustainable development in action is that of international debt. Many countries in the developing world are both poor and heavily indebted, with some now owing much more than they earn, as seen in Table 3.5. The challenge of debt servicing and the key features of the 'debt crisis' in the 1980s were highlighted in Chapter 1. In the favourable global economic climate of the mid-1970s (declining real oil prices, low interest rates and buoyant world trade), heavy borrowing enabled the developing countries to achieve relatively high growth rates whilst still being able to service their debts. The benefit at the time to the developed countries was a dampening of the recession owing to increased export demand on the part of the developing world. Clearly, they also benefited from the interest repayments on loans. Figure 3.8, based on the work of Susan George (a prominent writer on the impacts of debt), questions very starkly who benefits from continued indebtedness.

The debt burdens of many developing nations have several major implications for the prospects of sustainable development. First, the need to increase short-term productivity puts pressure on countries to overexploit their natural resources. Debts have to be serviced through foreign exchange, so that they can only be met by increasing exports, decreasing imports or further borrowing. The principal exports for the majority of developing countries continue to be raw materials and

Table 3.5 *Low incomes and high indebtedness, selected countries*

	GNI 2001 (billions of dollars)	External debt as % of GNI, 2000
Angola	6.7	137
Bangladesh	49.9	20
Brazil	528.5	39
Ghana	5.7	8.1
Indonesia	144.7	96
Mexico	550.5	28
Mozambique	3.7	32
Nigeria	37.1	74
Venezuela	117.2	36
Zambia	3.3	162

Source: World Bank (2003a).

Figure 3.8 *The costs and benefits of borrowing*

From the onset of the debt crisis in 1982 through 1990, *each and every month*, for 108 months, debtor countries of the South remitted to their creditors in the North an average six billion five hundred million dollars (US$6,500,000,000) in interest payments alone.

It is estimated that flows of funds *into* the developing world, for the same 8-year period (including all bilateral and multilateral aid, direct foreign investment by private companies and trade credits), amounted to less than US$1,000 billion. Furthermore, despite the vast interest repayments made by borrowing nations, by 1990, the debtor countries as a whole were over 60 per cent more in debt than they were in 1982 and the poorest countries suffered most.

Note: emphasis added.
Source: compiled from George (1992).

primary commodities in the main, as seen above in the trade section. In the long term, this 'resource mining' raises the costs of correcting the environmental destruction inflicted now and reduces the potential for sustained development in the future of resources such as in agriculture and forestry. In an investigation of debt and deforestation through the 1980s, George (1992) established that although the links were complex, those developing countries that deforested the fastest through the decade were, in the main, the largest debtors at that time.

A second direct implication of indebtedness stems from the level of government austerity necessitated by debt servicing that reduces a government's capacity to deal with environmental protection and rehabilitation: money diverted to servicing debt is unavailable for environmental management (or indeed, wider programmes of poverty alleviation). Table 3.6 confirms that whilst debt servicing declined in some countries over the decade 1990–2000, it remains in general well above the proportion spent on education and indeed, if declined, many countries were still allocating a reduced proportion of expenditure to education in 2000 than they were in 1990.

Furthermore, there is mounting concern that the 'medicine proposed' to deal with the debt crisis, the structural adjustment programmes of the World Bank and IMF considered in Chapter 1, may be undermining the prospects of sustainable development (Reed, 1996; FOE, 1999). Even in terms of conventional macro-economic indicators, there is much debate as to what the impact of structural reform has been. There is a suggestion that neither the WB nor the IMF has been able to confirm a convincing positive relationship (Mohan *et al.*, 2000). Figure 3.9 suggests that the relationship in these terms has been clearly negative.

Table 3.6 *Government spending: education and debt servicing compared, selected low human development countries*

Country	Public expenditure on health (% of GDP)		Total debt service (% of GDP)	
	1990	*2000*	*1990*	*2001*
Cameroon	0.9	1.1	4.7	4.0
Pakistan	1.1	0.9	4.8	5.0
Kenya	2.4	1.8	9.3	4.1
Gambia	2.2	3.4	11.9	2.7
Nigeria	1.0	0.5	11.7	6.2
Mozambique	3.6	2.7	3.2	2.4
Sierra Leone	–	2.6	3.3	12.8

Source: UNDP (2003a).

Figure 3.9 *The relationship between economic growth and adjustment lending*

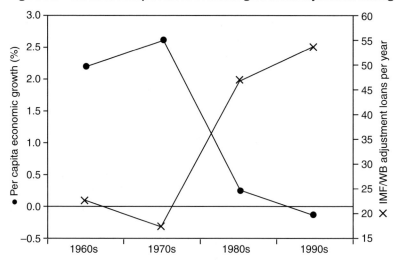

Source: adapted from *New Internationalist* (2004), no. 365.

Mohan *et al.* (2000) suggest that SAPs were 'environmentally blind' in the first ten years of implementation. Through that time, it was generally fiscal issues (i.e. the balance of payments difficulties and governments spending more than they had) that dominated, and the environment was generally not high on government or public agendas. Fundamentally, decreasing state expenditure, not increasing it through environmental protection, was the core of neo-liberal thinking encapsulated in SAPs as discussed in Chapter 1. 'In the effort to rapidly trim budget deficits, governments are forced to make choices, and inevitably, the environment loses' (FOE, 1999: 4). Not only were the budgets and staffing of environment departments regularly cut (Bryant and Bailey, 1997), weakening the ability to enforce environmental laws, but legislation may have been relaxed in order to increase foreign investment (FOE, 1999). Figure 3.10 illustrates the environmental outcomes of these pressures.

There is also evidence that structural reform has served to widen socioeconomic and gender disparities, impoverishing some of the poorest groups in society and compounding environmental degradation (Potter *et al.*, 2004). The UNICEF publication of 1987 *Adjustment with a Human Face* was particularly important for exposing the increased poverty and social polarisation (particularly the worsening fate of women and children under five) created under adjustment. It also revealed the pressure on natural resources being created by people's coping strategies under such conditions. Pressure mounted through the 1990s on the international financial institutions (IFIs) to put poverty back on the agenda and to consider the human dimensions of adjustment. In response, some adjustments were made to SAPS. For example, targeted funding became available for various 'Social Safety Nets' aimed to reduce what were considered short-term, negative impacts of adjustment on certain groups (for an overview and critique of their impacts, see Potter *et al.*, 2004).

Figure 3.10 *Pressures of adjustment on the environment*

....

- In Cameroon, the IMF-recommended export tax cuts and devaluation of the currency in 1995 led to increased incentive to export timber. The number of logging enterprises rose from 194 in 1994 to 351 in the following year. Exports of lumber grew by 50% between 1995 and 1997.
- Under SAP guidance since the mid-1980s, Guyana has implemented policies to increase large-scale, foreign-owned mining ventures. There are now 32 foreign mining companies active in the country with mining permits, covering 10% of the country.
- SAP in Tanzania resulted in rising costs of inputs for agriculture. Production increases were pursued through increased land clearing at a rate of 400,000 hectares per year. Between 1980 and 1993, a quarter of the country's forest area was lost (40% of which was to cultivation).
- In Brazil, government spending on environmental programmes was cut by two-thirds in order to meet the fiscal targets of the IMF.
- Benin, Guinea, Mali and the Central Africa Republic all established new mining codes to promote exploration and development.

....

Source: compiled from Friends of the Earth (1999).

'Poverty Reduction Strategy Papers' (PRSPs) are now the successors of Structural Adjustment Programmes (Simon, 2002). Since 1999, these are the strategic documents around which the World Bank and IMF as well as other donors coordinate their assistance to low-income countries – countries requesting support have to have one in order to obtain debt relief or concessional lending. PRSPs are written by national governments through broad participatory processes that include representatives of the World Bank and IMF but also other donors and civil society. They are required to set out coherent plans for reform focused on poverty reduction and to identify the financing needs. The World Bank also 'encourages' governments to consider environmental factors in their PRSPs, 'because of the links between environment and poverty, and because a poverty reduction strategy must be environmentally sustainable over the long term' (World Bank, 2001: 144). However, to date, there is considerable variation across countries in the extent to which such mainstreaming of the environment occurs. The World Bank recognises 'considerable room for improvement' in the quality of PRSPs (p. 145). In 2003, only 32 countries had completed a PRSP.

In the late 1980s, specific measures known as 'debt for nature swaps' (DNSs) were piloted as a way of recouping a proportion of loan debts and assisting developing countries explicitly to conserve the environment. Since the first projects in Ecuador and Bolivia, many countries have worked with donors, environmental groups and banks to establish projects, including the Philippines, Mexico and Cameroon. The DNSs take various forms, but fundamentally involve the lending agency (a government or a commercial bank) selling a portion of the debt at a discount to another donor (often an NGO), who then offers the debtor country a reprieve from that portion of debt in exchange for a commitment to a particular environmental project in the country. Another incentive to the debtor nations is that these projects can be paid for in local currency rather than foreign exchange.

The first ever 'debt for nature swap' took place in 1987, when Conservation International paid US$100,000 for US$650,000 of Bolivian debt and forgave it in return for the equivalent of US$250,000 in local currency as funds towards the Beni Biosphere Reserve (Marray, 1991). Since then, further DNSs have been implemented in only 16 countries (Rao, 2000).

Whilst the impact of these projects on overall levels of indebtedness is small (in the first decade, a total of approximately US$180 million in commercial debt was acquired: Resor, undated), the local environmental benefits of the funds acquired can be significant and further economic gains may be realised such as through eco-tourism ventures. Swaps are also occurring in other social sectors: UNICEF generated US$44 million in this way between 1989 and 1995 (Rao, 2000). However, it needs to be considered that conservation benefits are long term and where obvious markets for those resources exist (such as in logging) it is often unlikely that NGOs, multilateral banks or individual governments will be able or willing to fund such projects to a level equivalent to the earnings which could accrue over the short term from the exploitation of that resource. This leads to a moral question regarding such an attempt at long-term conservation in the light of unfulfilled short-term needs in indebted countries. Furthermore, to date, DNSs have been applied to a limited range of activities, mainly reserve establishment (Barrow, 1995), arguably reflecting 'northern' priorities in resource use rather than the needs of local people. Fundamentally, DNSs do little to change the commercial forces which perpetuate environmental degradation.

The first substantial attempt to *reduce* the external debt of the world's poorest and most indebted countries was initiated in 1996 by the WB, the IMF and a number of G8 countries. It was the first time that the debts to the WB and the IMF (the 'preferred creditors' as identified above) were included for write-off under the scheme. The aim of the Heavily Indebted Poor Countries (HIPC) initiative was to eliminate US$100 billion of the debt of the lowest income countries. The key objective was to achieve 'debt sustainability', defined as total external debts (to all creditors) below 150 per cent of annual exports. Uganda was the first country to actually receive money under the initiative. Before qualifying for HIPC, countries have to take part in IMF and WB economic reforms and engage fully with other 'traditional' debt relief mechanisms such as those available through bilateral arrangements. By 2000, only five countries had completed the qualification process. Substantially in response to widespread campaigning by INGOs, particularly the Jubilee 2000 coalition, it was agreed to 'enhance' the HIPC initiative in 1999 to provide greater levels of debt relief to more countries. Significantly, many bilateral creditors, including all G8 countries, also agreed at this time to 100 per cent cancellation of bilateral debts owed to them. The influence of civil society groups in prompting this change was important: in 1998, 70,000 people had formed a human chain encircling the Birmingham summit of G8 leaders to expose the unpayable and unjust nature of current debt levels. In 2005, the UK

Plate 3.1 *Generating awareness of HIV/Aids in Africa*

a. Zambia

Source: David Nash, University of Brighton.

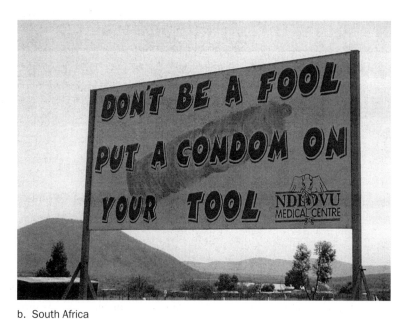

b. South Africa

Source: Bjorn-Omar Evju.

had the chair of the G8, and the British Chancellor of the Exchequer announced that he would use the year to push for further implementation of this process of bilateral and multilateral debt cancellation.

However, there remain significant concerns regarding the HIPC scheme and on which many prominent INGOs continue to campaign: in particular, the transparency of the qualification process (judgements are made entirely by the IMF and WB with no participation of the debtor government or of civil society in either debtor or creditor countries), the criteria used to determine debt sustainability (based entirely on macro-economic indicators rather than social realities or country-specific issues such as levels of expenditure on social development or particular challenges like HIV/ Aids), and the amount of relief that has actually been forthcoming. To date, only 6 countries have received any cancellation in their debt stocks under enhanced HIPC so far totalling US$17 billion and the 27 countries that have entered the process continue to pay US$700 million a year in debt payments to the IMF and WB (www.jubileeplus.org).

It is evident that issues of debt have widespread implications for the prospects of sustainable development. Perhaps most starkly, debt raises the question of intergenerational equity; debts are having to be repaid by ordinary people today in relation to loans taken on previously by governments (and in some cases, dictators). The unjust nature of continued debt is an ongoing challenge for actions toward sustainable development.

National action

Governments, as seen above, are important actors in influencing cross-boundary environmental issues, in negotiating internationally to establish multilateral agreements and trade outcomes, for example. They are also responsible for establishing the policy and regulatory and institutional framework within a country and are therefore important actors in the prospects for sustainable resource management in many wider arenas within their own boundaries. Figure 3.1 identified how governments play a key role in many economic mechanisms for environmental protection – in determining which uses are taxed and which are subsidised, for example, and for allocating funds for conservation. Governments also set mandates for many of the regional and local agencies with responsibility for environmental protection. Furthermore, political stability is a major factor in influencing resource use and environmental outcomes, as seen in Chapter 2, and it is increasingly recognised that governments have a key role in shaping the extent to which people are able to participate in political and decision-making processes that are critical in many aspects of sustainable development, as seen above, but also as investigated in more detail in Chapters 4 and 5.

The state was considered by the Brundtland Commission to have a key role in finding solutions to environmental degradation, in ensuring that the various actors in development, including business and consumers, behaved in the interests of environmental conservation. By the early 1990s, virtually every country in the world had prepared a national report of some kind on its environment (WRI, 1994), typically national conservation strategies (NCSs) or national environmental action plans (NEAPs). The Dutch National Environmental Policy Plan (NEPP) of 1989 was heralded as a significant landmark, containing 'some of the strongest language seen in an official document on the environment' (Starke, 1990: 39) and the first attempt to convert the principles of sustainable development identified by Brundtland into concrete steps for action to change both production and consumption (WRI, 1994).

In the developing world, preparation of national strategies has generally been under the guidance of and through funding from international donors, including the World Conservation Union (formerly IUCN) and the World Bank. National environmental action plans (NEAPs) continue to be supported by the World Bank. The aim is to assist developing countries in moving beyond environmental reporting and the setting of specific action plans for the environment, towards integrating environmental considerations into a nation's overall economic and social development strategy. Critically, NEAPs were to be catalysed from within the country itself rather than by the donor community and drawn up after wide consultation with working groups representing business and industry, public institutions, NGOs and the citizens themselves. However, it is recognised that the impact of NEAPs has been uneven (World Bank, 2001). In particular, whilst some have enhanced and guided both domestic and donor resources for environmental purposes, the impact on developing environmental management capacity has been less good: many were being developed simply to comply with donor requirements rather than stimulating local ownership (2001). A high level of government support has been identified as critical to the success of the NEAP process, as have strong environmental institutions (which usually need to be established from scratch) and well-motivated and qualified staff (WRI, 1994). In the new Environment Strategy of the World Bank, it is recognised that 'a remaining challenge is to build on the experience and achievements of the NEAPs in strengthening mechanisms and capacity in client countries to support sustainability in their development' (World Bank, 2001: 26).

Signatories to Agenda 21 in 1992 also committed themselves to creating national strategies for sustainable development. In the first three years after Rio, 74 countries submitted to the Commission on Sustainable Development national reports on their activities undertaken to meet the objectives set out in Agenda 21 (Lindner, 1997). In 1997, a UN Special Session of the General Assembly set 2002 as the date by which all countries should have such strategies. The WSSD Plan of Implementation also recommits governments to continue to promote coordinated frameworks for sustainable development at a national level and to begin implementation of such strategies by 2005. However, as already noted, the quality of the reports and the processes of planning and consultation on which they are based have been variable within both the developing and more developed worlds. As Bass and Dalal-Clayton (2004) note, early strategic planning efforts tended to be all-encompassing, 'perfectionist master plans', their focus was on environmental dimensions rather than integrating social and economic concerns and they were often too remote from the realities of resource use on the ground. As a result, many have been treated as 'at best checklists, or as encyclopedias of ideas, to turn to whenever the occasional policy space or financial opportunity emerges to do something "green" ' (p. 102). There is also a danger of 'strategy fever' as countries (particularly in the developing world) are required to produce so many strategies including those to secure finances, as seen in the case of PRSPs above.

Agenda 21 (and the WSSD Plan of Implementation) also commits governments worldwide to establish a framework at the local level through which local authorities would work towards implementation of Agenda 21 through the development of their own sustainable development plan. Whilst early 'Local Agenda 21' activities were confined largely to municipalities of high-income countries, Table 3.7 shows that the number in developing countries (as well as worldwide) is increasing. Box H highlights the core features of the process of planning LA21 in the Philippines and Peru. Although there are still

Table 3.7 *The number of municipalities involved in Local Agenda 21*

Region	1996	2001
Asia	87	461
Europe	1,576	5,291
Middle East and North Africa	8	98
Sub-Saharan Africa	35	133
North America	26	101
Central America and Caribbean	–	26
South America	34	93
Oceania	44	213
Developed countries	1,681	5,738
Developing countries	131	678
World	1,812	6,416

Source: Compiled from World Resources Institute (2003).

Box H

Agenda 21 planning

The Philippine Agenda 21

Three months after the UNCED conference, President Ramos set up the Philippine Council for Sustainable Development (PCSD) with the main functions of monitoring his government's compliance with official commitments made at Rio and co-coordinating the formulation of the Philippine Agenda 21 (PA21). The Council is composed of representatives from government, people's organisations, NGOs, and the labour and business sectors. The Council received assistance through the UNDP 'Capacity 21' initiative. In 1996, the Philippine Agenda 21 was launched and the PCSD became responsible for overseeing and monitoring its implementation.

Core principles outlined in PA21 include:

- Solidarity, convergence and partnerships between various stakeholders in the state, civil society and the market. In particular, the full participation of marginalised and disadvantaged sectors is required.

- Sustainable development is culturally, morally and spiritually sensitive. It thrives best in an atmosphere of unity and respect for cultural integrity, diversity and pluralism. It is important to nurture the inherent strengths of local and indigenous knowledge, beliefs and practices.

- Gender sensitivity must be the norm. Achieving full equity and equality between women and men and enhancing the participation of women in social development must be a goal.

Source: Department of Environment and Natural Resources (1995).

Local Agenda 21 in Cajamarca, Peru

In 1993, the mayor of Cajamarca initiated a LA21 effort in what was one of the poorest communities of Peru. The principal challenge was to create a substantially different, decentralised planning body through which all interests could be negotiated and local communities empowered. The city was first divided into twelve neighbourhood councils and the surrounding countryside into 64 'minor populated centres'. Each elected its own mayor and council. An Institutional Consensus Building Committee was established with representation from the province's jurisdictions, NGOs, the private sector and other key groups.

'Theme Boards' were then created to develop action proposals in the areas of education; natural resources and agricultural production; production and employment; cultural heritage and tourism; urban environment; and women's issues, family and population. Each board was charged with developing a strategic plan for its areas of work and training workshops were held to assist them in gathering local inputs.

All the plans were subsequently integrated into a Provincial Sustainable Development Plan, submitted to the provincial council in 1994 and then for public approval through a citizens' referendum. In total, the LA21 process in Cajamarca has raised more than US$21 million for activities, including providing potable water, sanitation, environmental education and rural electrification.

Source: ICLEI (1997).

concerns as to how these are being implemented and over outputs on the ground, the rising number of experiences of LA21 now within the developing world can be considered important (McGranahan *et al.*, 2004). For example, they represent concrete experiences of addressing the substantial problems of urban areas and many have made considerable achievements for the benefits of those citizens. Most are locally developed and sustained. They have also served to support and reinforce good local governance when characterised by democratic practices, accountability to citizens and partnerships between local authority, community organisations and NGOs, for example. How and why such characteristics are central to sustainability is considered in subsequent sections as well as in Chapters 4 and 5.

Clearly, there are a host of specific measures which governments can take to help clean up or prevent further environmental destruction. Figure 3.11 highlights a number of environmental taxes which are now common across many countries, including in the developing world. As seen, many countries now tax car use, for example, through levies on fuels. In France, legislation has enabled the authorities in Paris to restrict car use in the city when pollution levels reach certain thresholds. They effect the controls through allowing only cars with even-numbered registration plates to be driven into the city when pollution levels merit such action (and odd-numbered ones on the

Figure 3.11 *Examples of environmental taxes*

Tax base	Where taxed
Solid or hazardous waste generation	Australia, Austria, China, Finland, France, Netherlands, Poland, United States, many municipalities in industrial countries
Fresh water use	Australia, Belgium, Denmark, Finland, France, Germany, Ireland, Netherlands, Poland, Turkey, most former Soviet republics
Sales of fertilisers or pesticides	Austria, Finland, Norway, Sweden
Water pollution	Australia, Belgium, Canada, China, France, Germany, Netherlands, Portugal, Spain, most former Eastern bloc nations
Air pollution	China, Denmark, France, Japan, Norway, Portugal, Sweden, most former Eastern bloc nations
Production of ozone-depleting chemicals	Australia, Denmark, Singapore, United States
Carbon dioxide emissions	Netherlands, Scandinavian countries
Motor fuels sales and car ownership	almost all countries

Note: place lists are not necessarily exhaustive.
Source: Brown (1996).

next occasion). London also introduced a system of 'congestion charging' where drivers of private vehicles are charged to enter a particular zone. Similar schemes based on electronic toll cordons around city centres also exist in Norway, Singapore and Australia, for example.

These few examples of actions taken by national governments towards sustainable development in their countries illustrate that the role of the state in conservation action is both wide and challenging. There is often, for example, a tension between the state as protector of the environment and its role as developer. In Chapter 1 it was seen that in much of the developing world in the decades following independence, the state took a primary role in leading national and, particularly, industrial developments, including through the creation of large state public utilities, nationalised mining and agricultural enterprises. Yet, as discussed in Chapter 2, there is a substantial challenge in 'cleaning up' the negative environmental impacts of such developments including in the former Eastern European and Soviet states. There is the further issue that many of the most powerful groups in societies may have built up their position precisely through their control of such (environmentally damaging) activities, particularly in mining and energy generation (Bryant and Bailey, 1997). Some of these actors may be political leaders themselves, causing substantial challenges for the state in fulfilling its stewardship role. Corruption (worldwide) is an important factor in the ability of states to foster sustainable development within their borders.

There is also concern that the ability of governments to act within their territories and over their peoples towards more sustainable development is being weakened through processes of globalisation. As seen in Chapters 1 and 2, introducing the market to state activities was a central tenet of structural adjustment programmes, so that private capital increasingly shapes what is provided and who can access basic services and environmental improvements, for example. In the sections above, it has also been seen that the power of states to regulate the operation of TNCs within their boundaries is often low. In short, many of the features of the substantially liberalised world economy of the twenty-first century suggest a shift in the relative control of development processes away from states to private enterprise, with new challenges as well as opportunities for sustainable development.

Non-governmental organisations and sustainable development

NGOs are highly diverse organisations, engaged in various activities and operating at a variety of levels.

> The term non-governmental organisation encompasses all organisa-
> tions that are neither governmental nor for profit. What is left is a
> residual category that includes a vast array of organisations, many of
> which may have little in common. They can be large or small, secular
> or religious, donors or recipients of grants. Some are designed only to
> serve their own members; others serve those who need help. Some are
> concerned only with local issues; others work at the national level, and
> still others are regional or international in scope.
>
> (WRI, 1992: 216)

NGOs are one aspect of 'civil society' that has been receiving substantial interest in the literature of sustainable development (and beyond) in recent years (Edwards and Gaventa, 2001). Commonly, civil society is identified as 'an arena for association and action that is distinct and independent from both the state and the market, a voluntary, self-regulating, "third sector" sector in which citizens come together to advance their common interests (excluding business)' (Potter *et al.*, 2004: 308). This broader arena also encompasses 'social movements', the term generally used to refer to coalitions and networks of actors (some of whom may be members of more formalised NGOs), which increasingly are seen to mobilise around issues including the environment and operate transnationally. For example, in the 'Battle for Seattle' referred to in the trade section above, numerous individuals of no particular organised group joined representatives of a host of development organisations, unions and NGOs to demonstrate their shared belief in the unfair way in which world trade was being managed and the harmful effects on people and environments (Taylor, 2003). Some authors forge a distinction between social movements and NGOs on the basis that the former tend to work outside existing structures and work to present a more radical challenge to those than is the case with the latter (Ford, 1999).

NGOs are not able to sign treaties, pass legislation or set targets for emissions as governments are able to. Historically, however, they have been a strong force in lobbying for such actions to be taken, in modifying governmental activities and in contesting the operation of international institutions such as the World Bank (as seen in the example of the Narmada dams above) as well as the WTO. Increasingly, NGOs have been prominent participants in international summits as shown in Figure 3.12. Other NGOs have a long-established tradition of working in direct actions at village level around relief and welfare issues in particular. Many have moved subsequently into actions to address the underlying causes of suffering and deprivation, into promoting self-reliant development, and towards facilitating development by other organisations (Korten, 1990). The emergence of 'participatory development' as a discourse within development thinking in the early 1980s was identified in Chapter 1. 'Empowering' community and 'grassroots' organisations is now promoted by various agencies as the route to an alternative development which may be more sustainable, as well as more democratic and efficient, than previous patterns and processes (Potter *et al.*, 2004). However, the 'apparently inexorable spread' (Cook and Kothari, 2001: 3) of participation in development brings significant challenges as well as opportunities, as considered here and in subsequent chapters.

Perhaps some of the best known NGOs are international. Amnesty International, for example, has over 1.8 million members in more than 150 countries (www.amnesty.org, accessed 17.07.04). Other

Figure 3.12 *Civil society participation in environmental summits*

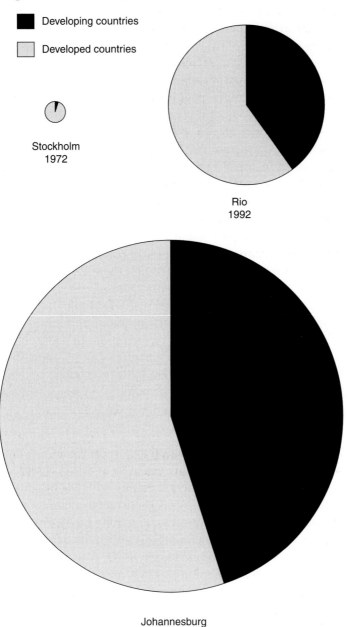

Source: WRI (2003).

organisations like Greenpeace or the World Development Movement, Oxfam and the World Wide Fund for Nature, are relatively long established, have paid professionals and tackle issues of truly global concern through lobbying, campaigning, direct action and service delivery (and often have branches in many countries). Typically, they work for public benefit rather than for that of their members. At the other end of the NGO spectrum are many more numerous, local, 'grassroots' or 'community' organisations. Particularly in the developing world, groups of people come together for all kinds of reasons to help themselves: by pooling labour, to assist in gaining credit or to enable them to purchase goods in bulk, for example. They may also form community groups in response to the failure of government to provide services such as water or sewerage to low-income housing developments as detailed in Chapter 5. At times, they are formed in response to the inadequacy and unacceptability of what governments do, for example in reaction to political repression or police brutality. It is estimated that there are over 200,000 grassroots or 'community benefit organisations' in Asia, Africa and Latin America (Thomas and Allen, 2001) although there are problems of quantifying such organisations as many are very fluid in nature and often lack formal registration. In addition, as seen in the sections below as well as in Chapters 4 and 5, the distinction between groups working for members or the public benefit is becoming more blurred in recent years, as NGOs are increasingly working together with both multilateral institutions and governments, for example.

National-level non-governmental organisations have regularly been formed to coordinate the activities of local organisations. In the Philippines, for example, there are many umbrella organisations which seek to service and support grassroots membership (people's) organisations in particular areas of activity such as health or land reform. Each people's organisation exists in its own right and is perhaps serviced by more than one NGO. Alternatively, national non-governmental organisations may have their origins in precisely those 'grassroots', community initiatives, which subsequently spread to form national movements. The Green Belt Movement in Kenya, for example, started in 1977 with a single tree nursery at a primary school and now has mini green belts and community nurseries throughout the country. Its founder (the long-time campaigner for environment, civil and women's rights and *opponent* of the government), Wangari Maathai, was elected to parliament in the first democratic elections in Kenya in 2002 and became the Assistant Minister for Environment,

Plate 3.2 *NGO–state collaboration in slum upgrading, Delhi, India*

Source: Hamish Main, Staffordshire University.

Natural Resources and Wildlife in January 2003. In October 2004, she received the Nobel Peace Prize for this work.

Part of the explanation of the recent rapid formation of NGOs in the developing regions lies in the growing size and affluence of the middle classes, their desire for cleaner environments and the advent of more democratic political regimes (Bryant and Bailey, 1997). This is particularly true in South and South-East Asia and Latin America. However, in Africa, such processes have been more restricted due to lower levels of economic development generally and by the persistence of authoritarian states resistant to autonomous local activities (1997). The pursuit of sustainable development actions has also been a primary factor in promoting the growth and importance of NGO activities and for stimulating interactions between these organisations and other institutions of development.

NGOs are considered to have a number of characteristics that are thought to make them particularly suited to effecting sustainable development including their size, their tradition of working closely with local people and their environment and their flexibility. In the following chapters, illustrations will be given of the specific actions of NGOs in rural and urban environments. The WCED recognised the key role which NGOs could have in fostering sustainable development based on their proven ability to secure popular participation in decision-making, and experience is suggesting that this can best be secured through processes of planning and action which put people's priorities first rather than those defined by outside actors and agencies (Chambers, 1983). Similarly, NGOs have traditionally shown greater flexibility and adaptability than larger and more bureaucratic government institutions and experience of sustainable resource management suggests that a local body through which people's own values and needs can be discussed, planned for and acted upon is essential. In particular, poverty, as discussed in Chapter 2, is regularly a symptom of people not having the power to control the resources on which they depend so that empowering the poorest sectors of society to become agents of their own development is a critical requirement of sustainability. NGOs have often traditionally worked with some of the poorest groups at the grassroots levels and this is a further reason for the attention paid to these institutions in current research and development.

NGOs have also proliferated as the interest in them has risen; there has been an expectation in recent years that civil society generally will be the source of responses to cure a whole host of 'social and economic ills left by failures in government or the marketplace' (Van Rooy, 2002: 489). More official aid now goes through NGOs rather than governments, for example. In 1998, over US$5 billion of ODA was channelled through NGOs, either as subsidies to their activities or via contracts with NGOs to implement donor activities (World Bank, 2001). Many new NGOs have formed in response to the increased availability of such funds, working in collaboration with these institutions through the late 1980s and 1990s, as many governments' capacity in service delivery shrank with debt and under SAPs, for example. In this way, the proliferation of NGOs can be considered in part the outcome of the neo-liberalisation of governance through the 1990s, i.e. as community participation in many instances may be being sought less for the political objectives of empowering the 'voiceless' (as will be seen in Chapter 4 in relation to reversing dominant models in rural development), but more for pragmatic reasons such as not relying on the state to provide (Bebbington, 2004; Mohan, 2002). Table 3.8 shows how collaboration between the NGOs and the World Bank has increased rapidly through the 1990s. Whilst, historically, NGOs have been vociferous opponents of the Bank, increasingly they are working with it. However, there are questions concerning the nature and extent of this collaboration: whether NGOs are merely informed, consulted at the initial stages of a project or engaged in sustained partnerships, for example. There is evidence that participation of community-based organisations is often limited to the implementation stages of World Bank projects and is therefore according to pre-identified agendas, with little shared control over development processes (Malena, 2000).

Table 3.8 *Increasing collaboration between the World Bank and NGOs*

Date	% of WB projects involving collaboration with NGOs
1993	30
1998	50
2000	71

Source: Compiled from Potter *et al.* (2004).

Although, as will be seen in subsequent chapters, NGOs have certainly been involved in many development actions which are showing signs of being more sustainable than centralised, 'top-down' initiatives, the prospects for sustainable development depend on change throughout the hierarchy of institutions discussed in this chapter. Community organisations, for example, need to move beyond actions in their traditional arena of immediate practical concerns, to engage with wider political processes to act strategically. Empowering the poor implies a very different role for the state in development and it may be unpopular and resisted at many levels. Indeed, whilst NGO is read as politically neutral in the English language, when translated into Indonesian, for example, it takes on strong anti-governmental tones which may not be conducive to developmental work at all in what is still a politically repressive country. It can also be that actions on behalf of donors towards empowering local communities serve to compromise or stultify improved capacity amongst state institutions. In Chapter 4, the recent enthusiasm amongst donors in 'finding community' in natural resource management initiatives is seen to raise questions for sustainability once external support is removed but also over how such activities may serve to remove the incentives for capacity to develop amongst local state institutions in the medium and longer term.

A challenge for NGOs themselves may be to maintain their accountability to local communities and 'watchdog' functions as more official aid is now channelled through them and they are increasingly required to operate in commercial markets in the delivery of services. It may be that the 'better organized, more acceptable or least scrupulous' (Mohan, 2002: 53) capture resources, for example. There is the prospect that the original missions of NGOs and power to control their own agendas may become compromised. In competing in the marketplace, smaller NGOs may be squeezed out, and NGOs generally may be forced to become more bureaucratic, leading to more finances being spent in those arenas rather than on their beneficiaries. As donors increasingly work through NGOs rather than governments, this may also dampen wider processes of democratisation in those countries as the pressure for governments to become more accountable and transparent is decreased. Critically, it cannot be assumed that all interests are served through 'community development efforts' (Potter *et al.*, 2004); all societies are highly differentiated including by gender, ethnicity and class, for example, that ensures that NGOs do not offer a simple panacea for sustainable development.

Conclusion

Many of the actions taken at various levels to promote sustainable development, as highlighted through this chapter, give cause for optimism. It is evident that many institutions of development are transforming what they do in operation, are modifying the ways in which they work with other organisations and are changing their internal structures. Furthermore, new institutions are being created at all levels towards the elimination of poverty and the revitalisation of economic growth, with greater weight given to environmental concerns not least through public pressure for more information, transparency and accountability. It is also clear, however, that further such changes throughout the hierarchy of institutions are required. Indeed, the capacity to generate sustainable development interventions at any level very often depends on actions at other levels. For example, community organisations require a national framework which allows local democratic processes to develop and local voices and needs to be articulated and acted upon. The effectiveness of international institutions is bounded fundamentally by national governments being willing to look beyond narrow national interests to the collective objectives that cannot be accomplished individually and by the strength of their commitments to develop the rules of behaviour and to ensure compliance where necessary within their borders. Whilst significant partnerships have certainly developed in recent years, there are substantial concerns, for example, as to how the traditionally strong characteristics of NGOs in sustainable development may be compromised through new relationships with donors, governments and international institutions. There are also concerns as to how genuine and sustained the commitments of large business interests are to environmental and social responsibility or whether their efforts are more to do with 'greenwashing' to secure larger markets. It is unclear as to whether the new partnerships announced at the World Summit on Sustainable Development will prove to weaken governments' commitments to multilateral environmental agreements and whether recent pronouncements by developed world government and multilateral institutions regarding debt relief and cancellation will be realised in practice. The following Chapters 4 and 5 consider how these changes in the operation and practices of core institutions in development have shaped outcomes for people and environments within rural and urban contexts of the developing world.

Discussion questions

* Identify the arguments for and against the World Bank now being a greener institution.
* Why are the actions of TNCs so central to the prospects for sustainable development in the future?
* Research in more depth one of the campaigns of an INGO such as Oxfam on reforming world trade or Jubileeplus on alleviating debt.

* Rehearse the links between debt and the environment. How have measures to alleviate debt to date enhanced (or otherwise) the prospects for sustainable development?
* Identify the range of ways in which civil society organisations are now working in the arena of sustainable development. What kinds of problems does this bring?

Further reading

Bigg, T. (ed.) (2004) *Survival for a Small Planet: The Sustainable Development Agenda*, Earthscan/IIED, London.

Cairncross, F. (1995) *Green Inc.: A Guide to Business and the Environment*, Earthscan, London.

George, S. (1992) *The Debt Boomerang*, Pluto Press, London.

Mohan, G., Brown, E., Milward, B. and Zack-Williams, A.B. (2000) *Structural Adjustment: Theory, Practice and Impacts*, Routledge, London.

Potter, R.B., Binns, J.A., Elliott, J.A. and Smith, D. (2004) *Geographies of Development*, second edition, Addison Wesley Longman, Harlow.

4 Sustainable rural livelihoods

Summary

- Rural areas worldwide are expected to provide a range of functions central to sustainable development.
- The chapter identifies the key but highly varied and dynamic characteristics of rural livelihoods in the developing world.
- The extension of models of industrialised agriculture has been a dominant characteristic of much rural development to date in less developed countries.
- A 'gene revolution' for world agriculture is being offered as a route to further increases in global food production, but there are many examples of opposition and resistance to, for example, the prospective detrimental impact on resource-poor farmers in the developing world.
- 'Putting Farmers First' has become a powerful narrative in rural development and has done much to guide more sustainable rural development interventions in practice. The chapter details what this means for research, for planning processes and for projects on the ground and the continued challenges revealed through these experiences.
- Women often have a close relationship with environmental resources and suffer most from degradation. Their 'interest' in environmental conservation is explained differently by ecofeminists and subscribers to the Gender and Development (GAD) school of thought. Successful sustainable rural development initiatives centre on building women's rights in resource issues but also on changing gender relations with men (within the household) and with wider authorities (such as local administrations).
- Lessons drawn from the experience of Community Based Natural Resource Management continue to be important for understanding the capacities of local institutions, the challenges of community participation in practice and for understanding the structures that influence local management outcomes.

Introduction

For the large numbers of people resident in the developing world, their basic needs in terms of both development and conservation are immediate and local; survival in the short term is their primary concern and for this they depend largely on the resources of the surrounding area. For approximately 60 per cent of the people living in the developing world, these needs are also rurally based (UNDP, 2003a). Although levels of urbanisation in the developing world are increasing, providing sustainable rural livelihoods, not just for the present population but for many billions more under projected population increase, is an urgent endeavour. It was seen in Chapter 2 that a large share of the world's most impoverished people live in some of the most 'fragile' ecological zones, in terms of slopes, soils and constraints set by aridity, for example. Through the 1990s, the impacts of processes of globalisation identified in Chapters 1 and 2, including trade liberalisation and structural reform, have often hit the rural poor hardest (Mullen, 2002). Rural people generally have weaker purchasing power and thereby suffered more as currencies were devalued, for example. The collapse of extension systems (i.e. support structures) as governments had to cut their budgets, the removal of concessional credit and subsidised inputs to agriculture and the worsening terms of trade for agricultural goods all had adverse impacts on farmers in particular.

The significance of creating sustainable rural livelihoods also emerges through the varied (public and private) functions that agriculture is now expected to deliver worldwide, as displayed in Figure 4.1. Over and above individual subsistence and food security needs, primary commodity production, for example, remains the principal source of exports and access to foreign exchange for many developing countries, as discussed in Chapter 3. The loss of the world's tropical forest ecosystems (including through the expansion of agriculture) is also a global challenge in terms of global warming, as seen in Chapter 2, and for the future conservation of biodiversity. In the UK, the role of farming in the future management of natural resources and conservation of valued landscapes (and lifestyles) is being hotly debated as public subsidies for agricultural production are being scaled down and the government moves towards banning fox-hunting. Worldwide, farming and food production by the twenty-first century

Figure 4.1 *The multi-functional role of agriculture*

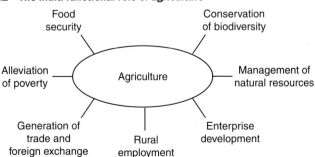

has moved from family-based production for local and national markets to being part of a complex, global 'agri-food system' where what is produced, how much, by what method and for whom is increasingly linked to the choices made by international consumers and large supermarket chains (Gwynne, 1999).

The importance of rural development in sustainable futures in the developing world stems in part from the numbers of people living in rural areas in these regions. There is, however, much diversity in this respect. On average in Latin America and the Caribbean, only 24 per cent of the total population lives in areas classified as rural. In sub-Saharan Africa, this figure is 65 per cent (UNDP, 2003). Within these regions, there are also differences between countries, as seen in Table 4.1. The significance of rural development in overall considerations of sustainable development stems also from the prevalence of poverty in the rural sector of developing countries, which in the main tends to exceed that in the urban areas, as also shown in Table 4.1. The central importance of overcoming poverty if environmental or development goals are to be met in future was detailed in Chapter 2.

Table 4.1 *Aspects of the reality of rural living*

Country	B Rural population as % of total, 2001[a]	B % people below national poverty lines[b]		B Agriculture as % of GDP[b]	% of people with sustainable access to an improved water source, 2000[a]	
		Rural	Urban		Rural	Urban
India	72	37	31	24	79	95
Zimbabwe	64	31	10	18	73	100
Indonesia	58	–	–	16	69	90
Uganda	85	–	–	42	47	80
Nigeria	55	36	30	30	49	78
Argentina	12	–	–	5	–	–
Brazil	18	33	13	8	53	95
Sri Lanka	77	–	–	19	70	98
Peru	27	65	40	8	62	87
Bangladesh	74	40	14	23	97	99
Kenya	66	46	29	21	42	88
Malaysia	42	–	–	8	94	–
Mexico	25	–	–	4	69	95

Sources: [a]UNDP (2003a); [b]World Bank (2003a).

Yet, rural areas of the developing world have often been left out of development initiatives in the past. In 1977 Michael Lipton forwarded his now classic thesis on 'urban bias' in which he argued that the major explanation of the persistence of poverty in developing countries has been the 'anti-rural' development strategies followed therein. In short, his suggestion was that the urban sector benefited disproportionately from the public allocation of resources in developing countries, in education and other services and through cheap food policies and other public subsidies, for example. Similarly, Chambers' similarly well-cited work of 1983 detailed a range of biases that have served to limit the understanding of the needs of rural communities and environments and compromised rural projects and programmes in practice. These included what he terms 'tarmac bias', referring to the way in which bureaucrats, academics and journalists the world over rarely venture into remote areas; 'person bias', resulting from the tendency to speak only to influential community leaders; and 'dry-season bias', which comes through visiting rural areas when travel is easiest. By 1998, Shepherd asserted that a new paradigm in the theory and practice of rural development could be identified based on a number of important shifts that have occurred in recent years. These included the move from an emphasis on technical fixes towards holistic approaches and sustainable solutions, the move from technocratic management to participatory developments and the shift from control by external organisations to local institutions in management. Many of the characteristics of this 'new' paradigm will be seen to underpin the progress made towards more sustainable rural development seen through this chapter. However, it will also be seen that overcoming the biases identified by Lipton and Chambers remains central to the prospects for sustainable rural development, in particular, those of changing the power relations between groups (within rural areas as much as between urban and rural) and fostering research and practice that empower the most marginal groups.

In recent years there has been a better understanding of the linkages between rural and urban sectors that shape both rural and urban landscapes and livelihoods (see Lynch, 2005, in this series). Despite this, much policy-making and agency practice continues to treat rural and urban separately (Satterthwaite and Tacoli, 2002; Momsen, 2004). However, separating people into 'rural' and 'urban' has become increasingly problematic as empirical evidence, for example, demonstrates the significance of 'fluid, fragmented and multi-location households to survival strategies' (Lynch, 2005: 11). 'Static' definitions of urban and rural cannot accommodate the significant flows of migrant populations. But migrancy is just the most visible form of the interconnecting and multi-directional flows between rural and urban that also include money, food and ideas, for example (Lynch, 2005). Very often, rural communities are closely tied to urban centres – both within the country and internationally – as markets for agricultural goods, sources of income and as centres of political power. In Chapter 5, greater consideration is given to the environmental linkages that exist between rural and urban; the urban needs that are supplied by rural resources and the impact of urban (mis)management on rural areas. Furthermore, there are sectoral interactions between rural and urban: rural sectors such as agriculture are important in urban areas and urban sectors such as manufacturing are found in rural ones. In addition, 'many households live in peri-urban areas outside the urban boundary but derive their livelihoods from work within it, while people living inside the urban boundary engage in activities such as farming, fishing, collecting wood or trading which take them to the surrounding rural areas' (Rakodi, 2002a: 33).

However, as discussed in the introduction to this text, there remain important differences between rural and urban contexts that need to be understood for the development of effective approaches to sustainability. Across these two sectors (presented separately in two chapters) it will be seen how the priority issues for low-income groups can be quite different (access to land, capital and labour to maintain productivity in rural contexts or environmental health and the lack of social and human capital to secure employment in an urban setting, for example). The characteristics of governance in those sectors can also be very different: increasingly distant in the case of many rural areas as state capacity is reduced under structural reform, but perhaps stronger in some cities with processes of decentralisation. In addition, residents of urban centres generally depend on markets to a greater extent than rural people so that security of cash incomes becomes particularly important in understanding the nature and impacts of urban poverty. As Satterthwaite and Tacoli (2002: 52) summarise,

> While the often neglected sectoral and spatial linkages and inter-dependencies between urban centres and countryside are often critical both for local economic development and for the livelihood strategies of the poor (and non-poor) groups, there are also crucial differences in the urban and rural vulnerability contexts which require careful consideration.

Making a living in rural areas

> For adequate and decent livelihoods that are sustainable, much
> depends on policies which affect agriculture.
>
> (Chambers *et al.*, 1989: xvii)

Aspects of the significance of agriculture in national economies in the
developing world are confirmed in Table 4.1. Certainly, in comparison
with the general pattern in the 'more developed' countries, agriculture
tends to be more prominent in the overall structure of production in
these regions. However, it can be seen in Table 4.1 that agricultural
production has a greater significance currently in some countries than
others. Similarly, *within* rural areas, agriculture can play a varied role
in securing livelihoods at the household level. As Rigg (1997) has
suggested, 'there is more to rural life than agriculture' (p. 197) and in
recent decades, there is evidence of the 'de-agrarianisation' of the
rural sector in many areas of the developing world (Murray, 2002).
For example, it was estimated that perhaps 20 per cent of the rural
labour force in developing countries during the 1980s had some
engagement in rural non-farm activities (Chuta and Leidholm, 1990).
By the 1990s, extensive research by Reardon (2001) suggests that on
average 40 per cent of household rural income in Latin America came
through non-farm activities including waged employment, self-
employment and migration. In sub-Saharan Africa, at the end of the
1990s, it was estimated that between 60 and 80 per cent of rural
household income came from such non-farming sources, an increase
from 40 per cent in the 1980s (Murray, 2002). Figure 4.2 identifies a
range of means for accessing products, labour and finance towards
securing adequate stocks and flows of food and cash to meet basic
needs, i.e. a livelihood in rural areas. Generally, however, and in
contrast to the situation in the industrialised world, the majority of
households of the developing world produce directly a high
proportion of their subsistence requirements.

Diversity at any one time and at all scales is one of the key features of
rural livelihood systems. In the savannah lands of Nigeria, for
example, the Hausa and Fulani societies secure their sustenance in
close proximity but through very different agricultural systems, based
on permanent cultivation and semi-nomadic pastoralism respectively.
In many parts of South-East Asia, farmers are also regularly
industrial workers, travelling perhaps a few kilometres daily or
seasonally much further, to take up waged employment, without
giving up agriculture altogether. In Latin America, generally larger
numbers of rural people secure a living through agriculture, but as

Figure 4.2 *Sources of rural livelihood*

....

- Home gardening – the exploitation of small, local micro-environments
- Common property resources – access to fuel, fodders, fauna, medicines, etc. through fishing, hunting, gathering, grazing and mining
- Processing, hawking, vending and marketing
- Share-rearing of livestock – the lending of livestock for herding in exchange for rights to some products, including offspring
- Transporting goods
- Mutual help – small loans from saving groups or borrowing from relatives and neighbours
- Contract outwork
- Casual labour or piecework
- Specialised occupations such as tailors, blacksmiths, carpenters, sex-workers
- Domestic service
- Child labour – domestic work at home in collecting fuel and fodder, herding, etc. and working away in factories, shops or other people's houses
- Craft work – basket making, carving, etc.
- Selling assets – labour, children
- Family splitting – putting children out to other families or family members
- Migration for seasonal work
- Remittances from family members employed away
- Food for work and public works relief projects
- Begging
- Theft

....

Source: compiled from Chambers (1997).

wage labour on plantation estates owned by others. Contract farming, whereby production remains in the hands of smallholders but is linked to contracts with larger enterprises (which may variously be with the state or agribusiness concerns) has also increased in recent years.

Dynamism (i.e. diversity over time) is a further key feature of rural livelihoods in the developing world. Indeed, the capacity to move the emphasis of any particular element within the livelihood system or to introduce new components has been central often to survival itself. Research into how poor households cope with food insecurity in times of drought, for example, has highlighted the varied adaptations to changing environmental and social circumstances which households can and do make (Mortimore, 1989; Devereux, 1993). A key concern, however, is whether these responses constitute movement towards more secure rural livelihoods or greater vulnerability.

Plate 4.1 *Income opportunities in rural areas outside agriculture*

a. Wage employment in
brick-making, India
Source: author.

b. Packing flowers, Kenya
Source: Hazel Barrett, Coventry University.

Plate 4.1—*continued*

c. Desert tourism, Tunisia
Source: author.

Diversity also exists within rural households. Originating in the work of Amartya Sen on famines (Sen, 1981), the concept of entitlements has been useful in understanding the variation which exists between and within rural households in terms of the command they have over food, but also other resources. This concept was referred to in Chapter 2 in terms of broadening notions of poverty beyond those which have tended to stress income levels. The basic suggestion within the idea of entitlements is that people differ, not only in the tangible assets which they have (such as land, equipment and stores), but also in their ability to access further resources for livelihoods. Figure 4.3 distinguishes the tangible assets (endowments) from the less tangible claims and access of individuals (entitlements), with particular reference to food resources in this case. A whole host of factors at various levels affect individual entitlements with respect to particular resources (see Young, 1996, for details with regard to food). In the case of access to land resources, women as a group, for example, may be denied access through elements of the legal system and/or the cultural system, which define how, when and by whom land may be held or inherited within a community.

The concept of 'agro-ecosystems' as illustrated in Figure 4.4 captures aspects of both the diversity and dynamism of rural livelihood systems. The model confirms how farming is only one option for securing basic needs for food and cash in rural areas, and that farming

Figure 4.3 *Concepts of endowment and entitlement*

....

Endowment: Refers to the assets owned and personal capacities which an individual or household can use to establish entitlement to food.

Entitlement: The relationships through which an individual or household gains access to food. These can be established through *direct entitlement* (through own production and consumption); *exchange entitlement* (command over food which is achieved by selling labour power in order to buy food); and *trade entitlement* which refers to the sale of produce to buy food.

....

Source: Crow (2000).

itself may be based on a combination of livestock (including fish) and/or cropping (including forestry) systems. Further diversity stems from the limitless number of factors shaping individual farming and livelihood systems, each farming system involving the manipulation of basic ecological processes (such as the competition between species or the predation by pests), via agricultural processes of cultivation or pest control, and led by human goals (which may be set at the individual, community, state or international levels).

Change in the agro-ecosystem may come via the full range of environmental, economic, political and social factors across this hierarchy. For example, a decline in demand for a particular handicraft item such as basketry (an economic factor) or a lack of rainfall (an environmental factor) may operate at the local level to prompt change in individual livelihoods. Further up the hierarchy, a new national government policy concerning recommended soil conservation practices or the incapacity to finance local extension services may also serve to change local cropping patterns. Decisions within the (increasingly global) economic community such as regarding agricultural subsidies now being debated at the WTO as well as within the EU, as seen in the previous chapter, impact on the profitability of cash-cropping decisions of farmers at the local scale. Box I highlights the economic and social impacts of the formation of a new regional trading block for maize farmers in Mexico. As with any 'system', change in any one element has implications for the functioning of the system as a whole. The impact may be direct or indirect, large or small, immediate or delayed. Understanding rural livelihood systems within the agro-ecosystem framework, therefore, begins to illuminate the extent and nature of the challenges for sustainable rural development.

Figure 4.4 *The hierarchy of agro-ecosystems*

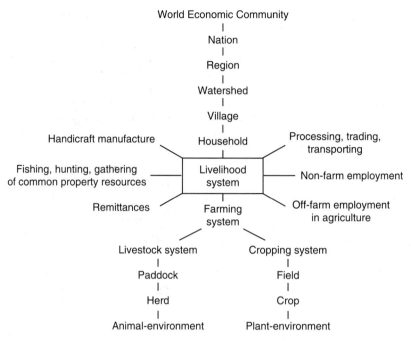

Source: adapted from Conway (1987).

Box I

The impact of free trade on maize production in Mexico

Maize is Mexico's lifeblood – the country's history and identity are entwined with it.

The domestication of maize 9,000 years ago was the basis of the development of the Mesoamerican civilisation. The Mayan people, who built one of the most remarkable cultures in human history, believed that the gods create people out of corn. Maize is at the heart of indigenous and *campesino* identity throughout the country.

When the North American Free Trade Agreement (NAFTA) was signed in 1994 between the governments of Mexico, Canada and the US, the vision was that competition would force 'uncompetitive' maize farmers in Mexico to move from farming into employment within the assembly plants that were expanding across the country. Cheap imported (heavily subsidised) maize from the US would be welcomed by urban consumers in Mexico.

However, in practice, those jobs often did not materialise or were concentrated in particular areas such as along the US border (see Box P). Imports of maize tripled, but farmers suffered a 50 per cent reduction in the prices paid for their corn. Urban consumers faced higher prices as government subsidies on staples (tortillas) were removed and agribusiness concerns increasingly took over the market.

An estimated 1.5 million farmers in Mexico have indeed left their lands: some to factory jobs but many more to work as farm labourers in the US. And ironically, many of those who remain in rural areas have opted to grow *more* corn (the opposite of what was predicted). Mexico was expected to produce record levels of corn in 2005 at record low prices. Factors underpinning this apparent blindness to market signals include the high levels of remittances from migrants back to relatives who continue to grow corn. Corn also remains the basis of *food* security for many subsistence farmers. Furthermore, large landowners in northern Mexico have expanded the areas of maize under irrigated production so that corn producers are now increasingly either very rich or very poor. Whilst maize originated in Mexico and a large diversity of varieties exist, this genetic heritage is now under threat from GM contamination. Growing genetically modified maize is illegal in Mexico, but not in the US from where 99 per cent of imported maize comes (a quarter of which is estimated to be GM).

However, these threats of free trade to Mexico's culture and food security are being resisted. A series of forums and actions are being led by *campesinos* themselves 'In Defense of Corn'. They have called for a moratorium on maize imports until it can be proven that they are not harmful to native varieties. A hundred thousand people also marched through Mexico City in an attempt to get the government to remove staples from the NAFTA agreement. The movement is also carrying out its own genetic testing and developing longer-term projects towards building local and regional capacity and autonomy. Local groups of *campesinos* have also taken on various activities such as towards reducing chemical use in production and conserving soil, water and forests, all 'In Defense of Corn' and in their commitment to continue the production of the crop of their ancestors.

Source: Compiled from Carlsen, L. (2004) in *New Internationalist*, no. 374.

The incorporation of rural areas of the developing world into the global economy

Although many residents of rural areas in the developing world continue to earn their livings as primary agricultural producers, few people or environments now remain outside the workings of the world economy. Agriculture as an economic sector and as an activity has become globalised; it is increasingly dependent on an 'economy and set of regulatory practices that are global in scope and organisation' (Knox and Marston, 1998: 337). In many places (although to varying degrees), the 'farm', which had been the core of agricultural production, is now just one part of an integrated, multi-level industrial system encompassing production, processing, marketing and distribution of food and fibre products (Redclift, 1987). Aspects of this globalisation of agriculture can be seen in simple terms, for example, in the global expansion and reach of the trade of fresh horticultural goods. These now make up approximately 5 per cent of global commodity trade (a level equivalent to the trade in crude petroleum) and the principal exporters of such produce are located widely through the developing world (Robinson, 2004). In recent years, external capital, including transnational agri-food companies and supermarket chains, has been of primary importance in bringing farmers of the developing world into the global food supply system.

Figure 4.5 summarises the principal forms (not mutually exclusive) through which developing world agriculture has been incorporated into global markets over time. The conquest of the New World and the slave trade, for example, enabled the establishment of new plantation systems of production, involving new crops and new labour processes, in countries including Brazil. British settler colonialism in sub-Saharan Africa led to the expropriation of lands from indigenous ownership and brought large areas of agricultural lands under cash crop production for external markets. But it was through taxation and the monetisation of local economies, often initiated during colonial periods, that possibly the most far-reaching impact on agriculture and rural livelihoods in the developing world occurred; land and labour almost ubiquitously came to have a monetary value, with people in rural areas of the developing world having to sell some of what they produce and buy some of their household requirements.

With the increasing globalisation of agriculture as currently observed, supplying non-staple crops (such as fresh flowers or other horticultural goods) to overseas markets almost inevitably requires farmers of the developing world entering into some kind of advance contract with a buyer (White, 1997). Some of the largest agricultural

Figure 4.5 *The major forms of incorporation of agriculture into the world economy*

Form	Example
Plantations and estates	Caribbean, Brazil
White settlements	Kenya, Rhodesia, South Africa
Taxation, rent and other levies in specified crops	Dutch East Indies
Taxation, rent and other cash levies	West Africa
Taxation, rent and other levies in labour	Dutch East Indies, much of Latin America
Creation of new cash needs to purchase imported goods	Burma, Thailand
Restriction of land area for traditional agriculture	East and West Africa

Source: Dixon (1990).

contracting schemes are in tea production (in countries including Kenya) and palm oil in the Philippines. Typically, these are joint ventures between the state, transnational companies and foreign banks (Watts, 1994). Furthermore, in recent years, agribusiness concerns that formerly owned land and employed labour directly within plantation systems, have sold land and switched to contracting out production (i.e. buying produce rather than the labour, locally). Certainly, the relationships between people in rural areas and between people and the environment have changed dramatically through all these forms of incorporation into an increasingly globalised world. Through such processes, some people have been able to make profits, expand their operations and move into non-agricultural activities (Rigg, 1997). For many people, however, and particularly small-scale peasant households, the outcome has been increased hardship and insecurity of rural livelihood, as argued by Watts (1983) in Box I.

In 1987, the WCED identified three distinct types of agriculture worldwide, effectively categorised according to the degree of incorporation into the international economy. Firstly, 'industrial' agriculture was identified as largely confined to the industrialised countries, but also as occurring in specialist enclaves of the developing world. This type of agriculture is highly productive but depends on heavy external inputs such as synthetic fertilisers and chemical insecticides. Transnational corporations have taken a lead role in agro-industrial expansion and a small number of (often the same) TNCs dominate the supply of the key inputs, for example, as shown in Table 4.2. These corporations have also established networks with research institutions, agricultural colleges and even government ministries and regulatory bodies. In the 1990s, the chemical pesticide industry increasingly bought up biotechnology, plant breeding and seed interests across the world and therefore further extended their control over world agriculture. Ten corporations now supply 33 per cent of the global seed market compared to thousands of companies twenty years ago (Actionaid, 2003). Monsanto alone bought 60 per cent of the Brazilian maize seed market in the two years 1997 to 1999. This dominance of TNCs within agribusiness generally gives cause for concern in terms of sustainability, as considered below.

Secondly, the WCED in the late 1980s identified 'green revolution' agriculture as encompassing the activities of approximately 2.5 billion people in countries of the developing world, but most widely in Asia through the 1960s and 1970s. In areas of reliable rainfall or irrigation

Plate 4.2 *Cash crops for export*

a. Large-scale tea production, Indonesia
Source: author.

b. Tobacco production, Zimbabwe
Source: author.

technologies and close to markets and sources of inputs, high-yielding varieties of wheat and rice in particular and the associated technological packages required for their production transformed pre-existing agricultural systems. India, for example, utilising these technologies has been able to raise food production at rates in excess of population growth since the 1960s (Robinson, 2004). However, the

Table 4.2 *Leading crop protection and biotechnology companies*

Company	Agrochemical sales (US$ million)	Seeds/biotech sales (US$ million)
Syngenta (USA)	5,385	938
Bayer Aventis (Germany)	6,086	192
Monsanto (USA)	3,505	1,707
DuPont (USA)	1,922	1,920
BASF (Germany)	3,114	0
Dow (USA)	2,627	215
Total	22,639	4,972

Source: Compiled from Actionaid (2003).

'euphoria' of the early stages (Atkins and Bowler, 2001) faded through the 1970s as the limitations of the package beyond those 'leading innovative regions' became clear. These included evidence of widening socioeconomic polarisation and negative environmental impacts (for further detail of the uneven and often gendered impacts see Potter *et al.*, 2004). Significant changes were made through the 1980s based on emerging understanding of both the constraints but also needs of small farmers (particularly those beyond Asia). These included a move away from the 'package' approach. This accommodated the realisation that many small farmers were using high-yielding variety (HYV) seeds but could not afford the other required expensive inputs (Atkins and Bowler, 2001). Different priorities in plant breeding were also established. HYVs are labour-intensive and did not match the local situation such as in dryland Africa where food security and labour constraints were major issues. Despite these changes, the central feature of the incorporation of agriculture into the world economy and its 'modernisation' at this time was based on a move to high external input systems of production and generally modelled the characteristics of industrial agriculture.

In contrast, the third type of agriculture, identified by the WCED as 'resource poor', supported in excess of a further 2 billion people in the developing world, but was less well integrated into the world economy and can be considered to have been generally 'forgotten' within agricultural developments including through the 'biases' identified by Lipton (1977) and Chambers (1983) above. As Pretty (1995) suggests:

> Farming systems in these areas are complex and diverse, agricultural yields are low, and rural livelihoods are often dependent on wild

> resources as well as agricultural produce. They are remote from markets and infrastructure; they are located on fragile or problem soils; and less likely to be visited by agricultural scientists and extension workers or studied in research institutions.
>
> (Pretty, 1995: 31)

It has already been established that, in ecological terms, resource-poor farmers are regularly concentrated in the world's most fragile areas, where there are significant constraints on intensive agricultural production and where people's links to land are critical for their livelihood and also for the sustainability of natural resources. In economic terms, many such farmers are utilising lands of a quality, and at an intensity of production, at which returns on their labour do not exceed the costs. Many farmers find themselves in a downward spiral of borrowing money or resources to feed themselves or to cover their costs of production in the off-season, only to have to pay these back at unfavourable rates and times in the successive season (Blaikie and Brookfield, 1987). Because of their economic position, these farmers lack the financial resources to invest in the capital equipment or inputs necessary to raise production or to implement the land use management techniques appropriate to the physical ecology of the area. Such farmers can also be referred to as marginal in a political sense; they are often uninformed, disorganised and outside any formal political system. They may also have very little political power in terms of their participation in decision-making or control over the many structures which influence their daily lives, such as local administration or the operation of markets.

These general patterns identified by the WCED have not changed substantially since the early 1990s. Indeed, Vorley and Berdegue (2001), suggest that much of global agriculture has been *further* marginalised economically in recent years and that there has been *increased* divergence between and within the rural communities of the developing world. For example, only a minority of farmers may have direct contacts through supplying agri-food manufacturing companies or through relationships with supermarkets, i.e. they are integrated in some way to the global agri-food economy. The majority are marginal to this system and struggle for food security and survival through a diverse mix of subsistence agriculture, temporary migration and off-farm work (and in the context of depleting human and natural resources). Somewhere between these extremes are a shrinking number of landed peasants and family farmers who continue to produce undifferentiated commodities with low and declining returns.

Towards sustainable rural development

Different, but related, challenges in agriculture globally

The specific challenges for sustainable agricultural development are different for each of the broad types of agriculture identified above. However, they are interdependent concerns. Fundamentally, past patterns and processes of rural incorporation and agricultural developments have been inequitable, so that despite global food availability per capita being at an all-time high (World Bank, 2003), an estimated 830 million people in that world lack adequate access to food (Pretty, 2002). Not surprisingly, hunger and poverty are closely related and it is therefore in the areas of 'resource-poor' agriculture that the major challenges for sustainable development lie. The latter sections of this chapter focus on progress towards more sustainable livelihoods in these areas. Box J highlights a range of examples where some of the poorest sectors of rural society across the developing world are becoming more impoverished and insecure in their livelihoods under contemporary patterns of agricultural and rural 'development'.

Whilst poverty and marginality are concentrated in areas of resource-poor agriculture in the developing world, this is not to deny the significance of the challenges of sustainable development of industrial agriculture where it is concerns over food health and quality that are generally dominating issues. 'Food scares' such as those surrounding the health risks of additives, pesticides, high fat, variant CJD and BSE in beef cattle are now proving powerful influences on consumer choice in the UK and USA, for example. The environmental impacts of high external input systems of agriculture are also becoming clearer, including the loss of biodiversity under mono-cropping, the pollution of groundwater through pesticides, and the water shortages and draining of wetlands that are occurring under such forms. The moral issue of the existence of food surpluses being created under these systems of industrialised agriculture and the huge state subsidies required to support these forms (i.e. the economic aspects) are also being raised, as seen in the previous chapter.

In areas of Green Revolution agriculture in the developing world, there are similar concerns regarding the health impacts associated with the expansion of 'modern' agriculture. In 1990, for example, the World Health Organisation estimated that pesticide poisoning may affect as many as 25 million agricultural workers in developing

Box J

The deterioration of rural livelihoods

The following brief examples illustrate the core challenge for sustainable rural development in the future: the combination of mounting poverty, deteriorating environments and the loss of local control over the basic resources required for agricultural production, particularly land.

In **Malawi**, the deregulation of agricultural markets required under structural adjustment programmes in the early 1980s has led to decreased subsistence security for the estimated 35 per cent of the rural population who are smallholders currently operating less than 0.7 hectares. In particular, for those in remote regions, private trading (their only option with the closure of marketing boards and depots) is unprofitable due to operating costs and the distance from storage facilities. Many people have been forced to sell their labour for food at the cost of not being able to work on their own smallholdings at critical points in the agricultural calendar (Harriss and Crow, 1992).

In **Zimbabwe**, retrenchments from industry are causing people to return to their traditional 'homes' in the Communal Areas in an attempt to make a living in agriculture. The resultant population pressure in these already degraded areas is leading to further subdivision of lands and problems for young people in accessing land for livelihood (Elliott, 1996).

In **China**, the current construction of the Three Gorges dam threatens the displacement of more than a million rural people from their lands and homes (Pearce, 1997).

In the **Sudan**, salinisation within the Gezira irrigation scheme has led to water supply problems and the loss of lands for cultivation, particularly amongst small landholders (Stock, 1995).

In **Thailand**, the very rapid expansion of golf course construction has led to substantial loss of agricultural area and water shortages. In 1994, small-scale farmers were prevented from growing a second rice crop as normal, through government restriction on water supplies and consumption. Despite this, golf courses were able to continue to pump water from reservoirs (Traisawasdichai, 1995).

In **India**, outside the fast-growing regions of the north, unemployment in rural areas has risen with the adoption of the green revolution, owing mainly to the cessation of a million petty tenancies. Per capita food output has been falling in most of the country and one-third of the total agricultural area is now declared to be drought-prone (Patnaik, 1995).

In **Kenya**, on the banks of Lake Victoria, the livelihoods of fishing communities are becoming increasingly compromised by the growth of water hyacinths which inundate the shoreline and prevent the launch of fishing boats. Fertiliser and pesticide use on neighbouring agricultural lands is a major factor in the eutrophication of the lake and the rise of algal blooms. Further loss of control over the resources essential to the livelihoods of local fishing communities is also occurring with the increased costs of boats, nets and labour, in part prompted by the rise of absentee boat owners, many of whom are Nairobi-based business people and politicians (Geheb and Binns, 1997).

In south-western districts of **Uganda**, premature deaths from Aids have led to a shortage of agricultural labour. There is evidence of households no longer growing the traditional labour-intensive crop of matoke (plantain bananas), but switching to cassava and potatoes which had only been grown as safety stocks in case of famine. The social necessity of spending several days at each funeral further limits the availability of farm labour. Nutritional standards are falling and people now sell food to pay for medicines for Aids (Dunn, 1994).

In **Guyana,** economic liberalisation has led to 80 per cent of the country's state forests being leased out to logging concerns, largely foreign-owned. In many cases, logging concessions have been given with scant regard for the pre-existing claims and titles of the indigenous Amerindian forest dwellers. Impact assessments have revealed a decline in access to traditional foods, shelter and other forest resources of local communities and even the bulldozing of crops (Colchester, 1994).

countries and account for the premature deaths of half a million people every year in the Asia–Pacific region alone. Pesticide residues have also appeared in human foods and local diets have changed so much that, even as food supply has increased, people may still suffer deficiencies in certain minerals and vitamins (Conway, 1997). Furthermore, there has been mounting evidence from research stations that previous yield increases under traditional plant breeding methods are slowing, and problems such as chemical toxicity and changing soil carbon–nitrogen ratios are necessitating further external inputs in order to maintain yields (Pretty, 1995).

At the turn of the twenty-first century, it was suggested that a 'Doubly Green Revolution' was required, one that is 'even more productive than the first Green Revolution and even more "Green" in terms of conserving natural resources and the environment' (Conway, 1997: 45). However, increasingly, this debate concerning the route for further increases in global food production has shifted from a 'Green' to a 'Gene' revolution (Atkins and Bowler, 2001). Significantly, whereas it had been public monies and charitable foundations that had funded the experimentation and research centres of the Green Revolution, commercial biotechnology companies have become the major financers of agricultural research and development and are increasingly the architects of this Gene Revolution.

Genetically modified organisms (GMOs) are those where alien genetic material is introduced artificially rather than through traditional breeding or cross-breeding from one organism to another. Proponents of the Gene Revolution (most regularly those within the industry) argue that biotechnology offers the means to feed an expanding population from a restricted land base with fewer environmental costs. Crop varieties can be (and are being) created to require less pesticide, to be herbicide tolerant, to fix their own nitrogen, to yield in very challenging conditions and to be drought resistant, all of which can reduce overall commercial energy requirements (Madeley, 2002). However, there are serious challenges emerging. For example, opponents of agricultural biotechnology (particularly in the developing world and including many civil society organisations) have substantial concerns, including the rising corporate control over the food chain encompassed by these developments (as seen in Table 4.2) and the implications for small farmers who become tied into dependence on certified seeds and external inputs (Shiva, 2000).

'The application of GM "solutions" is regarded by many as the antithesis of a sustainable option for further agricultural development' (Robinson, 2004: 196). Certainly, the characteristics of this externally and technology-led approach to sustainable agricultural development are very different from those of participatory and community-based development considered below.

Opposition to these kinds of processes of agricultural development is also evident in the more developed world. To date, the large majority of GM crops are grown in the US, whereas several other countries, including the UK, are experiencing difficulties in gaining public acceptance for both the trialling and production of such crops. Some of the principal concerns regarding genetically modified organisms in agricultural production are seen in Figure 4.6. The growth of organic farming and of Fair Trade goods, as illustrated in Figure 4.7, suggest that there is now a greater public awareness in the 'post-industrial societies' of the links between food consumption and production; consumers are increasingly choosing to make purchases on the basis of what they know of the production methods involved (i.e. rejecting the environmental and health impacts in particular of industrialised agriculture) and making choices that explicitly enhance the social and economic benefits that flow to producers.

The importance of the local context

In Chapter 1, it was noted that the theoretical necessity of focusing development on the poorest sectors of society had been recognised: the interdependence of environment and development was widely appreciated and a focus on the welfare needs of the poor was required if the goals of either future development or conservation of the environment were to be achieved. The challenge of effecting these commitments in practice is still a relatively new endeavour although

Figure 4.6 *The concerns over GMOs*

....

Environmental concerns

1 Most agricultural crops have toxic ancestors and introduced genes could switch back on ancestral genes making agricultural crops toxic.
2 Genes inserted into GMOs will spread to other non-target organisms with unknown and unpredictable consequences.
3 We do not know enough about ecological interactions to be able to predict accurately the long-term consequences of the introduction of genes into the environment.
4 It is possible that development of herbicide-resistant plants could cause changes in the patterns of herbicide use in agriculture in ways that will be more environmentally damaging than existing systems.
5 It is difficult to predict what will turn into a plant or a weed. Once an organism becomes a pest it can be difficult to eradicate.
6 A gene does not necessarily control a single trait. A gene may control several different traits in a plant and the placement of genes is a very imprecise science in many cases.
7 A gene which is safe in one country and one soil type may behave differently under changed conditions. Therefore there are problems of scaling from field trial to commercial release.
8 The majority of the new GM crops require high-quality soils, high investment in machinery and increased use of chemicals. They do not solve the food needs of the world's poorest people.
9 GMOs encourage continuous cropping and thus discourage rotations, polycultures and the conservation of biodiversity.

Socioeconomic concerns

1 Genetic engineering is leading to the patenting of life forms, genetic information and indigenous knowledge of local ecology. Such commodification or privatisation of nature and knowledge is morally wrong.
2 Corporations are concentrating research and development on the most profitable elements of biotechnology rather than the applications that best promote sustainable development.
3 The control of the global food economy by fewer large corporations is leading to more genetic uniformity in rural landscapes.
4 Competition to gain markets and hence profits is resulting in companies releasing GM crops without adequate consideration of the long-term impacts on people or the ecosystem.
5 Without adequate labelling, consumers have no choice as to whether they eat food derived from GMOs.
6 There is no conclusive evidence that GMOs are superior to conventional crops. They may divert resources from exploring more appropriate, sustainable low-technology alternatives to intensive agriculture.
7 Using GMOs to increase agricultural productivity in the North may lead to reduced imports from the South. Farmers in the South may then turn to more environmentally damaging alternatives with adverse effects on biodiversity.

....

Source: compiled from Huckle and Martin (2001).

Figure 4.7 *Aspects of the backlash against industrialised agriculture: the growth of organic farming and Fair Trade products*

....

Organic (production methods that largely exclude use of synthetic fertilisers, pesticides, feed additives and growth regulators)

- *US*: (1997) 5,021 certified growers, over 300,000 hectares in production, 0.2% total agricultural area (Robinson, 2004)
- *UK*: (2003) 4,000 organic farms, over 700,000 hectares managed organically, approximately 4% of UK farmland, UK market now third biggest in world, worth in excess of £1 billion (Soil Association)

Fair Trade (produce sourced from companies who are paying a price to producers that covers the costs of sustainable production and living and pay a premium for those producers to invest in business development or social projects)

- *US*: Fair Trade sales amounted to US$180 million in 2002, up 44% from the previous year (www.fairtradefederation.org)
- *UK*: (2004) shoppers spending £2 million per *week* on products carrying Fair Trade mark, compared with £2.7 million in entire year in 1994 (www.fairtrade.org.uk)

....

many institutions are changing the way they work, as illustrated in Chapters 2 and 3.

Individuals ultimately make the land use decisions upon which sustainable agricultural development depends. They do so, however, within the context of a variety of natural (environmental and ecological) and structural (including the world economy) forces, as identified in the hierarchy of agro-ecosystems above (Figure 4.5) and as seen in Boxes K and I. Through these illustrations it is seen that whilst the range of options in decision-making regarding natural resource use may depend closely on factors of finance, access to technology and political power, it can also be suggested that behaviour is not fully determined, even amongst the poorest farmers:

> Political, social and economic forces do operate; but when they are dissected, sooner or later we come to individual people who are acting, feeling and perceiving . . . all are to some degree capable of changing what they do . . . the sum of small actions makes great movements.
>
> (Chambers, 1983: 191–2)

Whilst this 'populist' stance can be criticised for underestimating the broader context of individual livelihoods (see Bebbington, 2004), i.e. the political, economic and social structures and processes that underlie land use decisions and practices leading to resource degradation (the focus of political ecologists referred to in Chapter 2),

Box K

Coping with drought: improved security or increased vulnerability?

> If you change a man's way of life, you had better have something of value with
> which to replace it.
>
> (Kikuyu proverb)

Drought is not a new phenomenon in many areas of the developing world. What is new is the level of suffering with which drought has become associated. As Stock (1995) comments with respect to Africa, 'from the late 1960s to the early 1990s, hardly a year has passed without reports of famine in some part' (p. 178). Drought is not a sufficient condition for famine, but it is often the final trigger prompting large-scale starvation and death. Since drought has undoubtedly been an important factor around which rural communities in the developing world have had to adjust their activities for many centuries, research is now focused increasingly on understanding why it is only recently that people, in such large numbers, have been unable to cope with it.

Such research has shown that there are many adjustments that individuals and communities can and do make to reduce the impact of factors such as drought on their food supply. For example, as shown in Figure 4.8, where food production is insufficient, coping strategies may involve a range of actions to secure food through other entitlements or to reduce demand for food within the household. Specific actions include economic strategies such as sales and exchanges in formal markets. However, it is increasingly recognised that non-market transfers such as of gifts of food or loans of cattle may be very important for survival in times of hardship (Adams, 1993). These strategies trade on the social relationships at various levels: between families, through lineage groups or clan membership and amongst neighbours. Assistance may be found through these institutions in terms of gifts of food, loans of cash or even the temporary support of members of one household within another. Such assistance between members of communities is usually based on reciprocity: it may represent repayment of past kindness or a commitment to help in the future.

Such coping strategies amongst communities living in harsh environments have developed over many years and evidence suggests that additional strategies are evolving as the physical, political-economic and social environments change for these people. However, there is much debate as to whether these coping strategies constitute a source of optimism and a basis for future development, or a 'cop out' for development planners (see for example, Davies, 1993).

Watts (1983) argues that peasant households have become more vulnerable to food insecurity with integration into the market economy (starting with colonialism). Specifically, he details how the 'colonial triad' of taxes, cash crops and monetarisation has increased socio-economic inequalities within communities and eroded the 'moral economy' which had provided a degree of security for communities living in harsh environments. The breakdown of traditional coping strategies has left large numbers of people increasingly vulnerable, not just to natural events, such as climatic drought, but also to crises associated with their incorporation into the market economy, such as the fluctuations in cash crop prices. Whilst one set of values, which had regulated successfully the relationship between people and the environment, has been eroded, another effective set has yet to be incorporated. Famine may itself disrupt precisely the social institutions and mechanisms which gave people a degree of support and ability to cope over time, such as when people move to emergency relief centres, breaking traditional networks of communication.

Figure 4.8 *Responses to food deficit*

Trigger event (production)	Behavioural category (consumption)	Strategy (generic)	Response (specific)
	Protect consumption	Purchase grain (market exchange)	– sell non-food crops – use off-farm income – sell assets (e.g. animals) – borrow cash – postpone debt repayment – reduce non-food spending
		Receive grain (non-market transfers)	– remittances – charity – begging – food aid
Grain production deficit	*Modify consumption*	Reduce consumption (ration)	– smaller portions – fewer meals per day – fewer snack foods
		Diversify consumption (change diet)	– less preferred varieties – wild foods – less nutritious diet (no meat or fish)
		Reduce consumers (change household size)	– wife returns to father – children sent to relatives – male temporary migration – betroth daughter

Source: Devereux (1993).

there is much evidence from analyses of apparently sustainable agricultural development that the local level is a key arena for success. For example, Pretty (1995) has documented cases of agriculture delivering economic and environmental benefits across the broad spectrum of the three categories of agriculture identified by the WCED. Whilst the technologies and specific practices may vary, they share three common elements: the use of locally adapted resource-conserving technologies, coordinated actions at the local level and supportive external institutions. The types of resource-conserving technologies which are delivering favourable changes to several components of the farming system simultaneously are highlighted in Figure 4.9. Techniques such as intercropping and agro-forestry demand a close understanding of the specifics of local ecological and environmental conditions, substantial management skills and access to information and often significant levels of investment and cost adjustment. Coordinated actions at the local level are necessary to ensure that the sustainable development measures of one person or section of the community are not to be compromised by the actions of others.

In 1988 Chambers put forward five interdependent prerequisites for sustainable rural development on the basis of analysis of apparently successful and sustainable projects in the developing world. These principles, as listed in Figure 4.10, have come to inform much rural development research and practice in areas within and beyond agriculture. The importance of the local level is again confirmed, for example, in prioritising local people's issues and concerns but also through the specifics of the values and commitments of staff. However, the more detailed analysis of these five requirements encompassed in the following sections indicates that the conditions for sustainability extend also beyond the local level. They will include international trading rules that widen access to commodity markets on behalf of poorer nations and national systems of tenure which promote security and encourage long-term investments. Similarly, research and planning institutions that encourage and give value to community voices are needed at all levels. However, further experience is suggesting (as illustrated through the remainder of the chapter) that the challenges of sustainable rural development often lie in the relation between these levels of action: in how women are empowered to address strategic needs that tackle gender relations rather than 'simply' their practical, immediate needs as defined by existing gender roles (Pearson, 2001), and how local rural people's organisations articulate with donor organisations and state institutions (Bebbington, 2004).

Figure 4.9 *Agricultural technologies with high potential sustainability*

....

Intercropping	The growing of two or more crops simultaneously on the same piece of land. Benefits arise because crops exploit different resources, or interact with one another. If one crop is a legume it may provide nutrients for the other. The interactions may also serve to control pests and weeds.
Rotations	The growing of two or more crops in sequence on the same piece of land. Benefits are similar to those arising from intercropping.
Agro-forestry	A form of intercropping in which annual herbaceous crops are grown interspersed with perennial trees or shrubs. The deeper-rooted trees can often exploit water and nutrients not available to the herbs. The trees may also provide shade and mulch, while the ground cover of herbs reduces weeds and prevents erosion.
Sylvo-pasture	Similar to agro-forestry, but combining trees with grassland and other fodder species on which livestock graze. The mixture of browse, grass and herbs often supports mixed livestock.
Green manuring	The growing of legumes and other plants in order to fix nitrogen and then incorporating them in the soil for the following crop. Commonly used green manures are *Sesbania* and the fern *Azolla*, which contains nitrogen-fixing, blue-green algae.
Conservation tillage	Systems of minimum tillage or no-tillage, in which the seed is placed directly in the soil with little or no preparatory cultivation. This reduces the amount of soil disturbance and so lessens run-off and loss of sediments and nutrients.
Biological control	The use of natural enemies, parasites or predators, to control pests. If the pest is exotic these enemies may be imported from the country of origin of the pest; if indigenous, various techniques are used to augment the numbers of the existing natural enemies.
Integrated pest management	The use of all appropriate techniques of controlling pests in an integrated manner that enhances rather than destroys natural controls. If pesticides are part of the programme, they are used sparingly and selectively, so as not to interfere with natural enemies.

....

Source: Conway (1997).

Plate 4.3 *Harnessing scarce water resources for agricultural production in Tunisia*

a. Tabia and jessour irrigation

Source: author.

b. Water control in the El Guettar oasis

Source: author.

Figure 4.10 *Lessons for the achievement of sustainable rural livelihoods*

....

1 A learning-process approach

2 People's priorities first

3 Secure rights and gains

4 Sustainability through self-help

5 Staff calibre, commitment and continuity.

....

Source: Chambers (1988).

A learning-process approach to planning

The basic model for agricultural development encompassed within both the Gene and Green Revolutions encapsulates what has been termed a 'blueprint' approach to planning: in short, new technological packages are developed in research stations and laboratories for transfer via extension systems to farmers. Over the years, criticism of this approach was important in generating the call for 'another' or 'alternative' development (as seen in Chapter 1) that prioritises people's needs, ecological soundness and popular empowerment. In direct contrast to the packaged, blueprint approach, a 'Farmer-First' one (Chambers *et al.*, 1989) to agricultural development is based on a 'learning-process approach' where projects are continually modified rather than being held to a rigid set of aims and procedures. Changes are made in response to dialogue between all interested parties and the experience gained during the course of the operation of the project. A learning-process approach has widespread implications for how projects are defined, the value of particular kinds of 'expertise' and the systems of communication, for example. The key features and contrasts of the two approaches are identified in Figure 4.11.

The continual modification of 'the project' as it proceeds is illustrated in the case of Yatenga in Burkina Faso (Reij *et al.*, 1996). What started as a forestry project in the early 1980s quickly evolved into an initiative focusing on soil and water conservation in response to farmers' priorities. Initially, a system of earth bunds or contour banks was developed and tried, but in practice farmers preferred rock bunds. In conditions of low and erratic rainfall, the farmers' priority was to keep water on their fields rather than to control the movement of water across their plots. Rock bunds are not damaged by run-off and therefore this reduces maintenance; they are permeable, so that crops and therefore yields can be increased; and they encourage the infiltration of water, so raising the effectiveness of the limited rainfall

Figure 4.11   *The contrasting 'blueprint' and 'learning process' approaches to rural development*

	Blueprint	Learning process
Idea originates in	capital city	village
First steps	data collection and plan	awareness and action
Design	static, by experts	evolving, people involved
Supporting organisation	existing, or built top-down	built bottom-up, with lateral spread
Main resources	central funds and technicians	local people and their assets
Staff training and development	classroom, didactic	field-based learning through action
Implementation	rapid, widespread	gradual, local, at people's pace
Management focus	spending budgets, completing projects on time	sustained improvement and performance
Content of action	standardised	diverse
Communication	vertical: orders down, reports up	lateral: mutual learning and sharing experience
Leadership	positional, changing	personal, sustained
Evaluation	external, intermittent	internal, continuous
Error	buried	embraced
Effects	dependency creating	empowering
Associated with	normal professionalism	new professionalism

Source: Chambers (1993).

in the area. With such changes, the adoption of bunding increased and, in conjunction with the use of organic manures and improved traditional planting pits, this led to the reclamation of degraded and abandoned lands in the region, so enabling the expansion of the cultivated area in conditions of high population pressure. Yields increased significantly in the short term, which encouraged more and more farmers to adopt the technology. Over time, the level of external subsidy to the project has been reduced and farmer-to-farmer visits have widened the adoption of the techniques to include areas of neighbouring Niger.

Understanding and valuing local priorities

Putting people's priorities first in the design of projects, rather than those of 'externally' based professionals (be they overseas or within cities, for example), is proving to be a further requirement for sustainability, but has often not been the case in rural development. Indeed, as already discussed, resource-poor agriculture has generally not been the focus of research and development, yet farmers' and scientists' priorities may differ in a number of core respects, as shown in Figure 4.12. Chambers (1983, 1993) has been influential in detailing the powerful forces which tend to perpetuate 'first' ('scientist' or 'outsider') priorities, those which start with 'economies not people', with the 'view from the office not the field' and lead to centralised, standard prescriptions for change, rather than the priorities of the 'last' (i.e. farmers). Aid agency bureaucracy, for example, can lead to pressure to produce a portfolio of projects quickly and to spend budgets by deadlines, giving little time within the project process to be open to changing conditions and experience from practice or for projects to evolve. Too often, in the past, 'outsiders' have assumed that

Figure 4.12 *Where farmers' priorities might diverge from those of scientists*

	Priorities	
	Scientists	*Resource-poor farmers*
Crops	– yield	– flavour
	– compatible with machine harvesting	– local marketability
	– single variety	– multiple variety cropping
Cropping systems	– mono-cropping	– diverse cropping
	– high external input	– low external input
	– high yield	– yield less important
Management	– maximise production	– minimise risk
	– maximise growth	– livelihood security
Use of labour	– minimise labour input	– use all family labour
Constraints	– meeting demands of scientific community	– meeting traditional obligations
	– project cycles	– maintaining good community relations
	– meeting demands of donors	

they knew what poor people wanted when, in practice, the priorities of farmers and of different groups within the local community would vary quite widely.

Accomplishing this requirement to put farmers first requires a substantial number of 'reversals' in 'normal' research and development learning and practice. To understand and learn from indigenous technologies and to build research and extension activities to combine these with 'conventional' science is of paramount importance, as discussed in Box L. This was a central element also for Conway (1997) in defining his 'Doubly Green Revolution':

> Whilst the first Green Revolution took as its starting point the biological challenge inherent in producing new high-yielding food crops and then looked to determine how the benefits could reach the poor, this new revolution has to reverse the chain of logic, *starting with the socio-economic demands of poor households* and then seeking to identify appropriate research priorities. Success will not be achieved either by applying modern science and technology, on the one hand, or by implementing economic and social reform on the other, but *through a combination of these that is innovative and imaginative.*
>
> (Conway, 1997: 42, emphasis added)

Since the 1990s, many methods (rooted in the philosophy of 'Farmer First') have been developed to explore local issues and realities and to give greater voice to a wider set of local interests. These include a greater reliance on qualitative techniques (interviews rather than surveys, for example) but also oral and visual methods rather than written accounts. 'Participatory Learning and Action' is now the umbrella term used to refer to the tools and ways of working that have done much to move understanding forward of the knowledge, values and priorities within local communities and the 'complex, diverse and risk-prone environments of resource-poor people' (Scoones and Thompson, 1994: 4). PLA is centred on trying to see the world from the point of view of those directly affected by development interventions (Mohan, 2002). Through the type of research tools and approaches identified in Figure 4.13, originally in rural areas and now extended more widely (Rakodi and Lloyd-Jones, 2002), more appropriate research priorities and entry points for development interventions are being realised.

However, despite substantial progress, there are continued challenges and changes required in the way that research and development is carried out. For example, Guijt and Shah (1998: 4) suggest that the 'frenzied levels of global interest in participatory methodologies'

Box L

The value of indigenous technologies

> Rural people's knowledge and scientific knowledge are complementary in their strengths and weaknesses. Combined they may achieve what neither would alone.
>
> (Chambers, 1983: 75)

During the 1950s and 1960s, there was tremendous optimism for the role of western science in raising agricultural production throughout the world, encapsulated in the research and extension activities associated with the 'green revolution'. The locus of research was the experimental station and the challenge was to transfer the new technology to the farmers' fields. When it subsequently became clear that farmers were unable to gain yields on their own farms comparable to those achieved at experimental stations, the 'blame' was passed between 'ignorant farmers' and 'poor extension services'.

It is now appreciated more widely that rarely do farmers fail, through ignorance, to effect land use decisions which will raise productivity or conserve resources. Rather their behaviour is, more regularly, rational in the light of their political-economic, social and environmental circumstances. It is now thought that research conducted at experimental stations has limitations for solving the 'real-life' problems of the farmer (particularly the resource-poor farmer). Scientists have an important role to play in conducting research *about* a problem, for example how potatoes grow. But for *solving* a problem, such as how to grow potatoes, it is thought that farmers in fact have a lot to teach scientists (Chambers *et al.*, 1989). The problem for research and extension activities, therefore, becomes not how to transfer technology from research station to farmer but how to close the gap between the two so that insights from both can be shared and built upon.

The value of indigenous technology and the benefits of closer links between scientist and farmer can be seen in the example of a technology for potato storage. The success of research into 'diffused light storage' is regularly attributed to the International Potato Centre in Peru (Chambers *et al.*, 1989). However, the basis of the technique was first observed by scientists amongst farmers in Kenya and Nepal. This led to testing and refinement at the research centre and the technique was then passed back to the farmers. However, an investigation into the uptake of the technique in several countries found that only in 2 per cent of 4,000 cases was this technology adopted according to the full recommendations. More regularly, farmers experimented with the technology, selected elements of it and adapted them to suit their own constantly changing circumstances (including financial and social considerations).

However, as more has become known regarding the ways in which farmers learn and experiment, often in very contrasting ways to modern science, it has also become clear that there are differences amongst rural people in terms of their knowledge and power. 'The issue is not just "whose knowledge counts?", but "who knows who has access to what knowledge?" and "who can generate new knowledge, and how?" ' (Chambers, 1994: xv). Not only, therefore, are there substantial and continued challenges in instilling changes in attitudes, behaviour and methods in the work of institutions and extension agents, but new insights are required into how those who are variously excluded at the local level can be 'strengthened in their own observations, experiments and analysis to generate and enhance their own knowledge; how they can better seek, demand, draw down, own and use information; how they can share and spread knowledge among themselves; and how they can influence formal agricultural research priorities'.

(Chambers, 1994: xv)

Figure 4.13 *The major components of participatory learning and action*

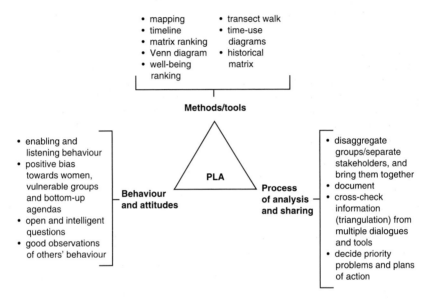

Source: Neefjes (2000).

through the 1990s stimulated the production of so many handbooks, guides and courses that a 'manual and method-oriented mania' has emerged. They point to the paradox of the situation given that the original ideals (of the philosophy of Farmer First, for example) were about *challenging* the standardised approaches and solutions of so much development work in the past. Clearly, understanding and valuing local knowledge and practices (as well as adopting the learning-process approach in planning and development practice considered in the section above) depend on the participation of communities. Whilst 'participation' has long appeared as an objective within many development efforts, as discussed in Chapter 3, the empowerment of individuals and communities so that they can become agents of their own development (Craig and Mayo, 1995) is now a widespread policy goal amongst many different institutions in development. As 'participatory processes' have frequently become a condition for funding, there is a concern that many are engaging with participatory methods 'despite a superficial understanding of the underlying empowerment principles that were at the root of much pioneering work' (Guijt and Shah, 1998: 5). Evidently, further critical reflection on the complexities of power and power relations in the tools and processes of 'community participation' are required (Cooke and Kothari, 2001).

Secure rights and gains

Ensuring that individual land users and communities have secure rights to resources and the benefits from investments is a further condition of sustainable rural development, as seen in Figure 4.10. This condition is based on the continued high dependence of the poorest rural households in particular on natural resources (despite the processes of de-agrarianisation considered above) and the need to take a long-term view of resource use. When people are sure, for example, that they have the rights to the products from trees that they plant, invest in and manage, they plant many more than they do when there are restrictions on the use or appropriation of such resources. Because of the centrality of agricultural production in rural livelihoods, issues of land ownership and tenure are central to the question of security of rights to resources and benefits. As well as being the foundation for economic opportunity, land is also regularly a major correlate of social prestige and political power in rural societies of the developing world. Yet substantial inequality in the distribution of landholdings is a widespread, entrenched and worsening feature of many developing countries despite decades of land reform programmes (see Potter *et al.*, 2004). Currently in India, for example, 9 per cent of the population owns 44 per cent of agricultural land (Halweil, 2002). Furthermore, many people (particularly in Asia) are engaged in agricultural production under systems of tenure including share-cropping arrangements, which deliver the major benefits to the landlord rather than the tenant (see Bernstein *et al.*, 1992). The limited autonomy of farmers under many forms of contract farming is also a concern, when not only does the contractor control many of the on-farm operations, but farmers can ultimately be evicted from lands if leases are contravened (Watts, 1994).

For Middleton *et al.* (1993), land reform is one of two 'inseparable starting points in any fight for sustainable agriculture' (p. 124), the other being the rights of women. It is estimated that 80 per cent of food in sub-Saharan Africa is produced by women (Middleton *et al.*, 1993: 124). In Asia, the figure is between 50 and 60 per cent, and it is approximately 30 per cent in North Africa, the Middle East and Latin

America. Twice as many women as men currently work in agriculture-related activity in developing countries (Momsen, 2004). Yet, women own less than 2 per cent of the world's total agricultural area. Clearly, these patterns illustrate that questions of security of rights and gains include not only 'ownership' of resources (as encompassed in formal land laws, for example), but rights to control the products of labour that are defined by gender relations. In many parts of the developing world, women receive rights to land through their husbands on marriage, but may have few rights to decide what is cultivated or marketed or how any profits made are spent. Gender divisions of labour are clearly not equivalent to gender divisions of responsibility or control over income. Furthermore, there is often a gender bias in terms of access to training (such as technical assistance from extension workers) and access to modern inputs to agriculture, that ensures that many agricultural development interventions have very different impacts on women and men (Momsen, 2004).

The role of women in conservation

Throughout the 1980s and into the 1990s, it was widely argued that women were the key to sustainable development: 'the achievement of sustainable development is inextricably bound up with the establishment of women's equality' (WRI, 1994: 43). In the 1950s and 1960s, work had focused on women's role in the domestic sphere and on bringing women into development through programmes addressing 'women's areas' such as family planning and nutrition (understood as the 'Women in Development' school of thought, WID). Through this, a better understanding of women's additional roles in agricultural production and wider productive activities, such as fuelwood and water collection and management, developed. Women were considered to have a 'substantial interest' (Braidotti et al., 1994) in environmental resources, as illustrated in Figure 4.14. Ecofeminists took these notions further to suggest that women have a natural affinity with nature aligned to their child-bearing qualities that men do not have. Authors such as Vandana Shiva (1989), for example, have contrasted what they consider women's essential features of caring and empathy with the controlling, manipulative position of men, to argue that women may be the key to new and more sustainable ways of living and social relations, if these 'feminine principles' could be sufficiently recovered.

Figure 4.14 *Women's substantial interest in the environment*

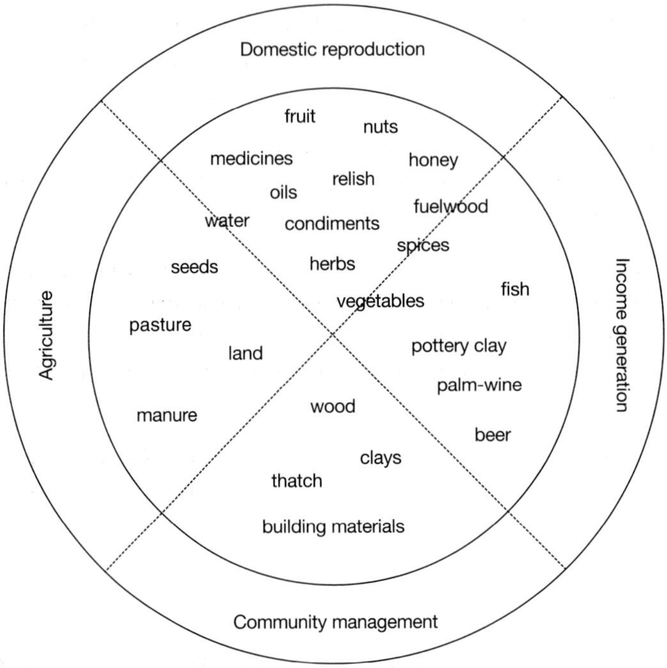

Source: Barrett and Browne (1995).

Certainly, some of the most successful examples of sustainable development to date have been built on women's initiatives. For example, the Chipko movement in India started with a small group of women presenting non-violent resistance to the contract felling of trees in their local area. The principles and practices of this original group have since spread to hundreds of local autonomous initiatives for the protection of forests. Subsequently, many projects have worked with women, building on their existing roles as managers of natural resources and an understanding of women as 'privileged environmental managers' (Braidotti *et al.*, 1994) due to their knowledge of local environments accumulated in the process of their daily activities as detailed in Figure 4.15.

However, there have also been substantial emergent problems. For example, the suggested relationship between women and the environment whereby they are the main 'users' and 'managers' of natural resources at the local level (Pearson, 2001) is now seen by many as reflecting accepted gender roles and a lack of alternative opportunities for women rather than any chosen or inherent empathy with conservation and natural resources. Through the gendered

Figure 4.15 *Women organising to manage environmental resources*

....

● Women on the Yatenga plateau in Burkina Faso became frustrated at men's inactivity concerning building a dam to capture rains. Women were unwilling to carry water over great distances any longer, so organised to build the dam themselves.

● In Khirakot village in Uttar Pradesh in northern India, local women took responsibility for managing a community woodlot. When it was threatened by a mining interest, they protested in court and got the mines closed.

● In Andhra Pradesh, India, village-level women's organisations developed the idea of collectively leasing and managing lands which had become degraded. Although many banks declined to assist the women, they eventually found loans through the Deccan Development Society and have returned over 280 hectares to production through projects which now involve 400 women in 20 villages.

● In Katheka community in Kenya, twelve, mostly female, self-help groups have formed to collectively construct extensive terraces and check dams to control erosion and enable production in a densely populated, arid land.

....

Source: WRI (1992, 1994).

division of labour (whereby women take primary responsibility for collecting and managing the energy and water needs of the household), women's immediate 'practical gender needs' (see Pearson, 2001) regularly centred on accessing environmental resources and environmental degradation was seen to affect women most (Dankelman and Davidson, 1988). Accepted gender roles also structure how women tend to take greater responsibility for maintaining communal services such as schools, health posts (and community woodlots and wells) and generally often provide the 'glue' between the elements and activities of the community (such as organising weddings). The outcome of many 'Women, Environment and Development' (WED) project interventions was that conservation became the 'fourth burden' on women to add to their gendered responsibilities in production, in the reproduction of the household and in community management, particularly through the way that they assumed that women had the spare time to undertake these projects.

Current work within the 'gender and development' (GAD) school of thought now considers that it is not sufficient to work only with women or to assume that women's relationships with the environment are undifferentiated. Gender divisions of labour are not uniform or static (Jackson, 1995); nor are gender relations. Furthermore, women

Plate 4.4 *Women in environmental management*

a. Fuelwood
collection,
Zimbabwe
Source: author.

b. Organising the community: a Lampungese wedding
Source: Becky Elmhirst, University of Brighton.

Plate 4.4—*continued*

c. Preparing fields for agriculture, The Gambia
Source: Hazel Barrett, Coventry University.

are not an undifferentiated or homogeneous group. Relations between men and women may vary, including with class or other social divisions and are continually 'struggled over'. Box M illustrates the importance of working for women's needs in resource management and the kinds of resistance met, but also the importance of changing relations between women and men and between local villagers (men and women) and wider political structures for the sustained development of core resources in the livelihoods of the poor.

Assuring and securing rights to resources for women and confronting fundamental gender inequalities are continued challenges for sustainable development. Women may not necessarily be the source of solutions to environmental problems: groups of women as well as men may act in environmentally damaging ways and women's apparent 'closeness' to nature may stem more from their lack of opportunities outside the household and the social relations in society than their biological makeup. Sustainable development, therefore, depends on removing women's subordination and oppression as well as their poverty, not simply 'grafting on women as a group' or 'lumping' women's varied interests together (Middleton *et al.*, 1993).

Box M

Building women's rights in sustainable water management

The Self-Employed Women's Association (SEWA) is a trade union of over 300,000 women in India. It was formed in 1972 and is both an organisation and a movement in that it aims to empower poor, illiterate and vulnerable women through ensuring full employment and working towards income, food and social security. An estimated 200,000 of its members are poor, self-employed women working in the informal sector in the rural districts of Gujarat state.

In Gujarat (home to the Narmada river and the Sardar Sarover dam), rainfall is low and erratic and the majority of villages have no reliable source of fresh water – many relying on mobile water tankers that may or may not arrive. Women typically spend up to six hours a day collecting water. Agricultural productivity and pastoral production are compromised by drought and increasing salinity and there is substantial 'distress migration' of people during the summer months.

As a trade union, SEWA's work is mandated by the members themselves. It has a national executive formed of representatives of 'local associations' from the districts. At the village level women are organised into unions and cooperatives, often according to the different occupations that they are involved in.

In 1986, the State Water Board in Gujarat was aware of the failings of centralised management of local water resources in the districts. It approached SEWA knowing their expertise in grassroots development, to look into involving local communities in building, operating and managing a water supply system. On the basis of its previous experiences, SEWA understood that it would be easier to recruit members into water development activities if these could be linked to economic improvement. SEWA mobilised women around eight economic activities ranging from embroidery to anti-desertification measures. By 2000, nearly 200 groups have been formed under the 'Development of Women and Children in Rural Areas Programme' – a joint initiative of the Indian government and UNICEF.

Historically, water infrastructure such as bore holes and dams was regarded as male territory, and many women were therefore often reluctant to come forward into this area and men were widely critical of women entering this public domain. Despite this, many of the water user committees established in Gujarat (*pani samities*) were all women or at least equal in number to male members.

SEWA has initiated many different types of activities amongst the water committees in various districts. These included visits to other functioning cooperatives to see how democratic frameworks operate and meetings with water engineers to understand water supply systems. Much of their work has involved assisting women to understand and negotiate their way through the maze that is India's system of governance of water resources. There are seven bodies solely at the national level, for example, that have some authority and responsibility over water. This gets more complex as it moves to district and sub-district and then to local *panchayat* levels.

In order to take steps to restore traditional sources of water, women had to learn about the roles of different agencies, decide which to approach and how. SEWA assisted in bringing engineers from the Minor Irrigation Departments together with the villages to plan, design, source and pay for materials.

The continual training, support for women to deal with the technical, institutional (and social and cultural demands) of water related activities has been fundamental to SEWA's success in securing the sustained participation of villagers. It has also been of paramount importance for institutionalising grassroots governance in the water sector whereby new institutions dominated by women have been created with strong links to existing governing institutions at wider levels. A shift in attitudes towards women has also been identified: they have earned respect within their families and their communities for their knowledge and abilities and mainstream institutions are now willing to accept illiterate women on their training programmes, for example. There have also been cases of districts abandoning contracts with private sector companies (India is increasingly privatising the water sector) in favour of local organisations.

Source: Compiled from WRI (2003).

The capacity of local institutions and the role of outsiders

When people have secure rights to resources and gains from investments, it has been found that they also have a perceived self-interest in project development and implementation, itself a further lesson for the achievement of sustainable rural livelihoods identified by Chambers in 1988 (Figure 4.10). It appears from experience that when people participate for the reason that they have seen success achieved and have become enthusiastic enough to work towards achieving it for themselves, projects tend to be more relevant, to spread more quickly and encourage innovation on the part of the people. This was certainly seen in the case of Yatenga above. Furthermore, as Pretty and Ward (2001) suggest, 'for as long as people have managed natural resources, they have engaged in forms of collective action' (p. 209). Such collaboration is evidenced in a huge variety of local associations such as work teams, burial societies and credit groups and in the varied rules of behaviour and values guiding the association between individuals that shape resource management. Together these comprise the 'institutions' that are now the focus of much of the development theory and practice seen in earlier chapters. In recent years, many rural development interventions have recognised the importance of strong local institutions for their potential to foster sustainable development but also through understanding that it can be the breakdown of such institutions that is part of the explanation for environmental degradation. The work on social capital is also emphasising the value of social bonds and norms of behaviour within local institutions for facilitating actions for mutual advantage such as are required in many conservation efforts.

Some of the wider forces prompting this emphasis on the role of civil society in development were identified in Chapter 3, including the widening desires for democracy on behalf of citizens of the developing world themselves. It was also seen that NGOs as one component of civil society have become more prominent in development thinking and active in development practice. Their tradition of working at the local scale, with people and unique environments, and their less bureaucratic nature, for example, were some of the characteristics that it is suggested make them particularly suited for working towards sustainable development. The 'quality' of their staff, historically recruited for 'sensitivity, insight and competence' and where the 'reversals of normal values are often most at home' (Chambers, 1988: 13), has been a further lesson for better practice in sustainable rural development (Figure 4.10). However, NGOs themselves are subject to many forces of change which may alter their capacity to work according to these required values, as also seen in Chapter 3.

Pretty and Ward (2001) estimate that over 400,000 new community-based groups worldwide may have been formed since the 1990s in natural resource sectors (involving between 8.2 and 14.3 million people, largely in the developing world). Examples of programmes established in specific countries are shown in Figure 4.16. These groups may be formed as new associations between different actors (such as between the state and community groups in joint forestry management), to build on existing community groups (women's associations becoming more formalised in the context of micro-finance projects, for example) or through identifying and strengthening existing informal institutions (such as enhancing traditional community organisations operating to manage common property resources like grazing lands). Clearly, the existence of new institutions does not ensure sustainable resource management although there has been much success in terms of farmers organised into groups performing better than those who are not in particular natural resource-based project interventions (Pretty and Ward, 2001).

In recent years, substantial optimism has been expressed concerning 'Community Based Natural Resource Management' (CBNRM) initiatives (Campbell *et al.*, 2001). A host of international institutions and donors have 'found community' (and provided substantial amounts of money) in conservation (Agrawal and Gibson, 1999). CBNRM encompasses a breadth of policies and programmes in practice, but typically involves one of three kinds of experiences: some

Figure 4.16 *Social capital formation in natural resource management, selected countries*

Watershed and catchment groups
- *India*: programmes of state governments and NGOs in Rajasthan, Gujarat, Karnataka, Tamil Nadu, Maharashtra, Andhra Pradesh
- *Brazil*: 275,000 farmers in three southern states adopted zero-tillage and conservation farming as part of watershed groups
- *Kenya*: Ministry of Agriculture catchment approach to soil and water conservation
- *Honduras/Guatemala*: NGO programmes for soil and water conservation and sustainable agriculture
- *Burkina Faso/Niger*: water harvesting programmes

Irrigation water users' groups
- *Sri Lanka*: Gal Oya and Mahaweli authority programmes
- *Nepal*: water users' groups as part of government programmes
- *India*: participatory irrigation management in Gujarat, Maharashtra, Tamil Nadu and Orissa
- *Philippines*: National Irrigation Administration turned over 12 million hectares to local management groups
- *Pakistan*: water users' associations in Punjab and Sindh

Microfinance institutions
- *Bangladesh*: Grameen Bank nationwide
- *Pakistan*: Aga Khan Rural Support Programme in Northern Areas
- *Nepal, India, Sri Lanka, Vietnam, China, Philippines, Fiji, Tonga, Solomon Islands, Papua New Guinea, Indonesia and Malaysia* have a wide variety of bank and NGO programmes

Joint and participatory forest management
- *India*: joint forest management and forest protection committees in all states
- *Nepal*: forest users' groups

Integrated pest management
- *Indonesia*: 1 million graduates trained in rice and vegetable IPM programme
- *Vietnam, Bangladesh, Sri Lanka, China, Philippines, India:* a further 8,000 trained

Farmers' groups for research and experimentation
- *Kenya*: organic farming groups
- *Columbia*: farmer research committees

Source: compiled from Pretty and Ward (2001).

kind of joint or collaborative management involving local communities in the management of (typically) previously defined 'state' resources, those that look to decentralise authority to (usually newly created) local/community institutions, and those that work to strengthen the traditional, local institutions and controls that are already in place (Elliott, 2002). CBNRM initiatives are being undertaken for various reasons and can encompass quite divergent ideas about conservation:

> At one extreme fall existing conservation projects (e.g. conventional protected areas) that belatedly make minor efforts to draw in local people . . . at the other extreme lie initiatives aimed specifically at the development of particular (often 'sustainable') uses of natural resources by local people who are given full tenure over those resources . . . The first is based on the idea that conservation has to do with concern for 'wild' species and their associations (ecosystems and habitats) . . . the second is based on the idea of conservation as the sustainable management of renewable resources.
>
> (Adams and Hulme, 2001: 14)

Box N details a specific example of 'community conservation' in Uganda that aimed to raise both benefits to local communities and for wildlife conservation within and around a national park. It is a model that is increasingly being used around protected areas in Africa and elsewhere, and it illustrates a number of the continued challenges that are being revealed with experience of CBNRM that Campbell *et al.* (2001) suggest is tempering some of the enthusiasm shown in theory. Emergent problems include issues of sustainability where such high levels of donor support are involved (and the negative impact this may have, for example, on incentives for the development of local and national capacity). Furthermore, many traditional institutions in resource management are being broken down through processes of resource scarcity, immigration and a decline in authority of traditional leadership, for example. Perhaps most fundamentally, many CBNRM initiatives have assumed distinct 'communities' exist, whereas they are in fact highly diverse and dynamic, contain many different interests and environmental priorities within them and have very varied abilities or power to negotiate and make change (Elliott, 2002). But working to accommodate the internal differences and dynamics within communities presents substantial challenges as Gubbel (cited in Reij *et al.*, 1996: 10) suggests:

> 'Putting farmers first' is striking, resonant rhetoric, but not easy to put into practice. It requires deciding *which* category of farmers should come first. *Not* deciding inevitably means that local elites come first. Indeed, to achieve goals such as promoting self-reliance, peasant organization and community environmental management, outside intervention is often not able to avoid working with rural power structures and may have to compromise on equity issues.

Box N

Community conservation in Lake Mburu National Park, Uganda

Lake Mburu National Park is in south central Uganda. It comprises 260 square kilometres of open and wooded savanna and wetlands. It was designated as a National Park in 1980, but was historically an area reserved for the herds of the king of the Banyankole people and has had a number of formally recognised designations in between. In 1980, National Park status declared residence within the boundaries illegal so that up to an estimated 25,000 people and 45,000 cattle were evicted (often with substantial violence) from the area. In 1985, many of these people went back into the park encouraged by the National Resistance Army of Museveni.

Although Museveni, on coming to power, subsequently expressed a strong personal interest in the future of the park, setting up a task force for research and action, its recent history has been characterised by a number of problems. These include disputes over the precise boundaries, local communities pushing for a return of the park to landless farmers and for pastoralism, and a lack of morale amongst officers of the Uganda National Parks service. Whilst some households (including those basing their livelihoods on fishing, farming and pastoralism) were given permission to remain in the park until land could be provided for them elsewhere, the lack of clarity over the legal status of these people (who perceive themselves as residents and have invested in clearing new lands and establishing schools, for example), combined with further in-migration to the park, has been a source of conflict and poor relations between park staff and community members.

In the early 1990s, visiting international conservation workers identified that park–people relationships were so poor and support for the park so weak, that the future of the park (with a remit to conserve biodiversity and encourage sustainable use of resources) was threatened if new ways of working with the community were not found (and financial support was not forthcoming). In response, the Lake Mburu Community Conservation Project was formed with finance from the African Wildlife Foundation and the Swedish International Development Agency. In 1991, the Community Conservation Unit (CCU) was formed, appointing the first Community Conservation Warden in Uganda and a number of extension rangers. Their first task was to improve relationships with the park's neighbours and other stakeholders. This included changing local perceptions within surrounding communities of park staff as enemies, changing the behaviour of the park's enforcement officers, encouraging consultations (rather than confrontations) between squatters and park management and undertaking research to understand and define the park's neighbours.

As park–people relationships stabilised, further activities were undertaken. Although visitor numbers to the park had risen to over 8,000 by the mid-1990s, it was recognised that few economic opportunities (i.e. jobs in the tourist sector) would flow to local people, so that ways had to be found to channel funds directly to communities. A system for revenue sharing was established whereby 20 per cent of gate royalties are now used to fund community projects. The CCU works directly with local people to identify projects and there are transparent criteria identified with the park administration for deciding where, for what and for whom monies are allocated. Projects that have been supported have included tree nurseries, bee farms, an aid post and dispensary, well digging, road improvement, women's groups and a school, some of which have been important in encouraging further visitors to the park.

One of the principal concerns of the park administration has been the control of illegal grazing in the park. The CCU has initiated research into the role of grazing for habitat management and has enabled the identification of 'water access corridors' in recognition of the importance of the River Ruizi as a dry-season source of water for pastoralists. Some legal rights on behalf of local residents to fishing in lakes and for access to medicinal plants have also been established. The CCU also attempts to deal promptly and sympathetically with incidences of wild animal incursions that have been a problem for local farmers. The CCU has also been very important in securing further funding such as matched grants for the community projects and finances for compensating 'squatters' who have now been resettled out of the park. These experiences at Lake Mburu in providing benefits to local communities and in strengthening structures for flows of information as well as benefits are considered to be successful. In 1995, USAID initiated the Community Conservation for Uganda Wildlife Authority Project towards extending this experience to the national level in Uganda.

Source: Compiled from Hulme and Infield (2001).

Conclusion

For too long, the debates about both the environment and development have been dominated by the interests and values of the rich rather than the poor, men rather than women, and the urban rather than the rural. The challenges of reversing these priorities have been seen within this chapter to be wide and substantial, yet integral to the prospects of sustainable rural development. Whilst individual farmers ultimately make many of the land use decisions in rural areas, ensuring that these are sustainable depends evidently on many broader factors. The continued high dependence of many developing economies on agricultural commodities for exports brings a level of vulnerability to fluctuations in world markets which it could be argued is being accentuated by current processes of globalisation. The capacity of national governments to influence these outcomes (and shape their impact on people and environments within their jurisdiction) such as via national policies in agriculture has probably declined in recent years. Although no single scale of production is inherently more or less sustainable than another, past emphasis on the large-scale production of export crops in the more favoured locations of the developing world has been shown to be unsustainable in terms not only of the practices employed but also of the people it excluded.

Making the rural poor the starting point in research and development has been seen to have benefits for the environment and development.

But there are also substantial remaining challenges. Whilst there is evidence to suggest a new paradigm in rural development and of local successes towards more sustainable rural development policies and practices, community participation, for example, remains 'conflictual' (Mohan, 2002: 51). It challenges existing structures of power ranging from the legal authority of state institutions to accepted norms of behaviour such as gender roles and relations within the household (both seen in Box M). Furthermore, there is the potential that 'the emphasis on grassroots civil society can leave important structures untouched' (Mohan, 2002: 53) in that many processes affecting individual lives cannot be tackled at the local level. However, the long-term benefits of providing secure rural livelihoods for the rural poor will also fall to the wider communities: rural insecurity is a major factor in maintaining high fertility rates and in prompting rural to urban migration. Improving rural livelihood security will help to relieve population pressure on resources as well as to slow the demand for employment and shelter in urban areas, which are currently two key demands on the limited financial resources for urban planning in the developing world.

Discussion questions

* How and why is agriculture only one (and in places, a declining) aspect of rural livelihoods?
* Identify the principal differences between the 'green' and 'gene' revolutions in world agriculture.
* How and why does Robert Chambers' work in rural development suggest that the realities of local farmers have not been understood in much planning and practice to date?
* Do women hold the key to sustainable rural development?
* Review the benefits and challenges of 'finding community' in programmes for natural resource conservation.

Further reading

Conroy, C. and Litvinoff, C. (1988) *The Greening of Aid: Sustainable Livelihoods in Practice*, Earthscan, London.

Conway, G.R. (1997) *The Doubly Green Revolution: Food for All in the 21st Century*, Penguin, London.

Lynch, K. (2005) *Rural–Urban Interactions in the Developing World*, Routledge, London.

Momsen, J.H. (2004) *Gender and Development*, second edition, Routledge, London.

Robinson, G.M. (2004) *Geographies of Agriculture: Globalisation, Restructuring and Sustainability*, Pearson Education, Harlow.

Scoones, I. and Thompson, J. (eds) (1994) *Beyond Farmer First: Rural People's Knowledge, Agricultural Research and Extension Practice*, Intermediate Publications, London.

5 Sustainable urban livelihoods

Summary

- The rising concentration of the world's population in urban centres presents opportunities as well as challenges for sustainable development. Questions of urban sustainability are different from those in rural areas, but not unrelated.
- Urban residents are more dependent on markets for food, basic needs and services than their rural counterparts and therefore any threats to income have more profound impacts on poverty than within rural areas. Yet there are many aspects of urban deprivation that relate more to political systems than they do to income.
- Low-income groups in developing world cities face substantial environmental health risks in the course of basic activities of living and working but are mediated through class and gender differences, for example. Immediate local issues of inadequate sanitation and water supplies, of poor housing and cramped living conditions are at the centre of the environmental agendas of these cities.
- Processes of decentralisation of authority and decision-making from the state to city level and of privatisation of many basic services within cities of the developing world are two key features of contemporary urban development with key implications for sustainability.
- The capacity, accountability and transparency of local authorities is a key factor in the prospects for sustainable development, but this also demands working in new ways with NGOs and citizen groups. More sustainable urban development interventions are being generated where local people are empowered to renegotiate their relationship with such wider state apparatuses.

Introduction

The proportion of people living in urban areas of the globe is increasing, and particularly in the developing world. Whilst in 1800 only 3 per cent of the total world population lived in towns and cities, the world, is now almost 50 per cent urban (UNCHS, 2001). The majority of the world's urban population is now in the developing world, as shown in Table 5.1. Almost half of the world's urban population live in Asia (although, as seen in the previous chapter, the majority of the population of these regions remain based in rural areas). Although a greater proportion of the population of the more developed world currently live in cities, i.e. these regions are more urbanised, as shown in Figure 5.1, the number of people in cities and towns is much larger in the developing world and is predicted to increase further. On the basis of average annual population increases in cities of the developing world since the 1990s, 64 million more people each year are added to this total, half through natural increase and half through rural–urban shifts (UNHCS, 2001). It is suggested that 93 per cent of the urban growth worldwide to the year 2020 will occur in the developing world.

In 1987, the World Commission on Environment and Development suggested that the urban challenge lay 'firmly in the developing countries' (WCED, 1987: 237), due in the main to the unprecedented growth rates being observed and the challenge of meeting the immediate needs of an expanding urban poor. In that year, for example, the World Bank had estimated that approximately one-quarter of the developing world's absolute poor were living in urban areas (World Bank, 1990). In 2001, it was estimated that the number of urban poor will treble to 1,500 million by 2025 (UNCHS, 2001). However, there are substantial challenges for *all* cities in managing the environmental implications of economic growth, in meeting the needs of their residents and in protecting the environmental resources on which they depend into the future. City-based production currently accounts for the majority of resource consumption and waste

Figure 5.1 *Levels of urbanisation and predicted change*

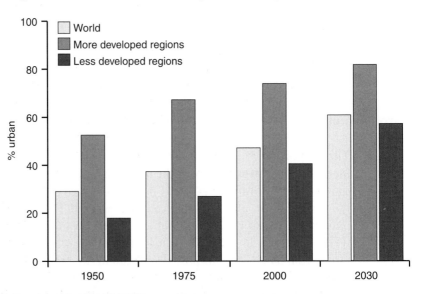

Source: compiled from UN (2003).

generation worldwide (WRI, 1996); throughout history, cities have been a driving force in development processes and, as cities grow, productive activities tend to concentrate in urban centres. Furthermore, with rising affluence, the environmental burden of cities tends to fall increasingly at the global scale (and on the future generations) as shown, for example, in the higher per capita emissions of carbon dioxide and levels of waste generation from cities of the more developed world (McGranahan and Satterthwaite, 2002).

The focus of this chapter is the cities in the developing world and the particular environmental challenges therein that to a large extent are not key concerns in wealthier cities. Box O describes and contrasts what have been termed the 'Green' and 'Brown' agendas for the most affluent and more impoverished cities respectively. The level of affluence is not the only factor affecting the environmental burden of cities, as will become clear through this chapter. Furthermore, the differences identified in Box O should not distort the common, global challenges of sustainable urban development nor should the multiple deprivations of urban poverty illustrated in this chapter deflect from the fundamental pattern that affluence creates more pollution than poverty, but those impacts will tend to be felt largely by successive rather than current generations. In addition, whilst the Brown Agenda is the priority for low-income countries but a substantially 'old' issue for the more developed countries, the local and immediate problems in the developing world are bound up with 'new economic, social and ecological processes many of which are global in scale' (McGranahan et al., 2001: 6) and will require actions beyond that scale, as seen in subsequent sections.

Cities are central to attempts at meeting the goals of sustainable development in the sense that this is where the majority of the world's population will soon be located, with all the associated physical demands (such as for food and shelter) and the political, social and cultural requirements associated with the adoption of urban values. However, cities also provide opportunities for more sustainable development. The large numbers and concentration of people and activities provide opportunities for economies of scale (lower unit costs) in providing services such as piped water, roads, electricity, and can reduce the costs of providing emergency services, for example. The risks from natural disasters can also be reduced more cheaply and effectively in urban centres through measures such as drainage to reduce the risk of flooding and improved buildings to better withstand flooding when it does occur. Opportunities for sustainable development in urban centres also include the potential to reduce

Box O

Green and Brown environmental agendas

The term 'Green environmental agenda' as shown in Figure 5.2, encompasses issues such -
as the depletion of water and forest resources. These concerns are most relevant to cities
of the more developed world, to future generations and natural ecological systems. In
contrast, the Brown Agenda encompasses issues of access to basic water supplies,
sanitation and housing; the 'pollution' of urban poverty that is most relevant to poor
urban residents of today and to human health.

Figure 5.2 *The Green and Brown urban environmental agendas*

Features of problems on the agenda	The Brown Agenda	The Green Agenda
Principal impact	Human health	Ecosystem health
Timing	Immediate	Delayed
Scale	Local	Regional and global
Worst affected		Future generations
Aspects emphasised in relation to		
Water	Inadequate access and poor quality	Overuse; need to protect water sources
Air	High human exposure to hazardous pollutants	Acid precipitation and greenhouse gas emissions
Solid waste	Inadequate provision for collection and removal	Excessive generation
Land	Inadequate access for low-income groups for housing	Loss of natural habitats and agricultural land to urban development
Human wastes	Inadequate provision for safely removing faecal material (and water) from living environment	Loss of nutrients in sewage and damage to water bodies from its release of sewage into waterways

Source: adapted/compiled from McGranahan and Satterthwaite (2002).

Whilst affluent cities can be considered to have performed better in terms of meeting the
needs of their current populations, historically these have been met by displacing the
environmental burdens over space (elsewhere) and time (delayed). For example, sewers have
been put in to take human waste out of the city and goods whose production may have been
resource intensive or damaging have been imported. The burden of dealing with the

levels of waste generated or high levels of fossil fuel combustion will fall on the next generations through their contribution to global warming, for example. In wealthier cities, the key challenges for action lie in reducing excessive consumption of natural resources and the burden of wastes on the global environment (WRI, 1996).

The environmental burdens in low-income cities are much more generally falling now and within the city, where particularly the most impoverished groups suffer ill-health, vulnerable and shortened lives. 'As we move into the twenty-first century . . . the importance of the "brown" agenda is undiminished . . . economic change is outpacing urban environmental management and the achievement of social justice. Moreover, there is a serious danger that as new "green" concerns are added to the environmental agenda, the "brown" concerns will be neglected or misrepresented' (McGranahan *et al.*, 2001: 10).

fossil fuel consumption through the increased provision and use of public transport rather than private motor vehicles and the enhanced scope for recycling and reuse presented where large numbers of people live in close proximity. The concentration of people in cities can also facilitate their involvement in local district and city level politics and partnerships; and in the same way, it is easier for authorities to collect charges and taxes for public services and to fund environmental management. But close investigation is needed to consider where these opportunities fall – to governments, private enterprises or particular groups, for example, and who is excluded or unable to access such benefits. For Satterthwaite (2002a: 264), city authorities have a key role to play in these respects: 'realizing these potential advantages of urban concentrations requires competent city governments that are accountable to their populations'.

In the twenty-first century, the nature and direction of urban change in any city or country is now more dependent on the global economy than ever before. Processes of globalisation are producing a far more integrated and interdependent world economy today and whilst globalisation has been seen in the previous chapter to affect rural areas, many of the global forces (examined in Chapter 2) are concentrated in cities and it is here where many of the major impacts are seen. Cities across the globe are experiencing change, not solely in terms of their size, but also in respect of the activities they host and the function they play in the world's economic, trading and political systems (Hamnett, 1995) as they compete for investment and resources in this global marketplace. Certain cities, termed 'world cities', including New York, London and Paris, but also Singapore, Hong Kong, Shanghai and Johannesburg (among others) are now considered the nodal points through and within which processes of global capitalism are focused and sustained (Friedmann, 1995; Knox, 2002; Potter *et al.*, 2004). But cities more widely are also growing in economic and political influence within their national borders, for example, as many countries implement decentralisation policies that seek to devolve greater authority, decision-making and finances to city and local levels.

This chapter details the primary characteristics of these processes of change and patterns of urban development in the developing world in order to illustrate more fully the specific nature of the challenges and opportunities of sustainable development in this sector. It is understood that there are many processes of change currently that make rigid distinctions of urban and rural problematic, as seen in the previous chapter. Just as large numbers of rural people now engage in non-agricultural activities and indeed may commute seasonally or daily to urban areas, large sections of the population of 'urban' areas also work in agricultural enterprises or in industries that serve rural demand. The substantial flows of goods, income, capital, information as well as people between rural and urban need to be understood (Satterthwaite, 2002a). Cities also have significant environmental linkages with rural areas – through the resources they draw on (such as in agriculture and in energy supply) and the pollution they generate (influencing air and water qualities in surrounding areas, for example). In addition, some cities such as Jakarta and Mumbai are growing very quickly with economic activities spreading outwards and effectively merging with other urban areas to form 'extended metropolitan regions' (Potter *et al.*, 2004) that further question the utility of the separate consideration of urban from rural. However, in continuity with the arguments made in the previous chapter, there are differences between these sectors that continue to be important in understanding the demands and prospects of sustainable development. For example, the influence of good (or bad) governance on shaping poverty outcomes is more significant in urban than rural areas, where the influence of rules and regulations, both formal and informal, can determine access to jobs and basic services to a much greater extent, for example (Satterthwaite and Tacoli, 2002).

Patterns and processes of urban change in the developing world

Whilst the general trend across the developing world, as seen in Figure 5.1, is for increasing levels of urbanisation, there are significant differences between regions and countries in the patterns of change. For example, it can be seen in Table 5.1 that whilst Africa has relatively small numbers of people currently residing in urban centres,

Table 5.1 *Actual and predicted distribution of the world's urban population, by region*

Region	Millions (2003)	% of world total, 2003	Predicted annual rate of change (%), 2000–30
Africa	329	10.8	3.10
Asia	1,483	48.7	2.22
Europe	530	17.4	0.10
Latin America and Caribbean	417	13.7	1.42
North America	261	8.6	1.16
Oceania	24	0.8	1.07
Total	3,044	100	

Source: Compiled from United Nations (2003).

Table 5.2 *Historical distribution of the world's 100 largest cities*

Region	1800	1900	1950	1990
Africa	4	2	3	6
Asia	64	22	32	44
Latin America and Caribbean	3	5	8	16
Rest of the world	29	71	57	34

Source: Compiled from Hardoy et al. (2001).

it is also where the most rapid change in the near future is predicted to occur. However, it is in Asia that the largest numbers of people currently reside in urban areas and where the greatest future expansion in terms of additional urban residents will occur. Countries such as India have very large urban (as well as total) populations, for example. Indian cities such as Calcutta and Mumbai are amongst the largest centres in Asia and indeed the world (see Figure 5.3). Whilst most of the largest cities are now in developing world, this is, however, a recent phenomenon, as shown in Table 5.2.

Some caution is also needed when considering projections of urban change. The rates of increase identified for Africa, for example, are expansions over a small base and growth is occurring more widely across many smaller and intermediate urban centres than is the case in Latin America. Some of the fastest increases in Africa were after independence that heralded the removal of colonial restrictions on the rights of local African people to live and work in cities. Projections are

Figure 5.3 *The world's largest urban agglomerations in 2000*

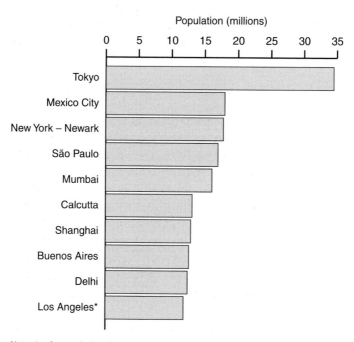

Note: * refers to the Los Angeles–Long Beach–Santa Ana urbanised area.
Source: compiled from UN (2004).

also based on the historic association between economic growth and urbanisation, yet many countries (particularly in Africa) are not experiencing steady economic growth. Furthermore, some cities are expanding through contemporary influxes of refugees that may constitute temporary growth. Certainly, the growth rates predicted for some of the largest cities in the developing world in the 1970s did not materialise in subsequent decades. For example, in 1980 it was predicted that Mexico City would have 31 million people by 2000, yet in fact only reached 18 million (Satterthwaite, 2002b). A number of factors explain this mismatch between predicted and actual growth: economic growth slowed, so fewer people moved to these larger cities, but decentralisation policies in many countries have also made more resources available to smaller cities and therefore encouraged the growth of smaller centres. Advances in transport and communication technologies have also lessened the advantage for business to concentrate in bigger cities providing an impetus to the growth of these smaller centres. In short, although there is a growing number of urban centres of unprecedented size, something under 5 per cent of the global population live in mega-cities, i.e. with populations over 10 million (UNCHS, 1996) and certainly, the world's largest cities are not the fastest growing (Hardoy *et al.*, 2001). New kinds of urban systems are developing worldwide, which include networks of very dynamic, although smaller, cities (see Potter *et al.*, 2004) and it is perhaps in these rapidly expanding smaller centres that some of the largest challenges for sustainable urban development lie.

The key processes of urban change in the developing world are certainly without historical precedent. 'Contemporary urban growth and rural–urban shifts in the South are occurring in a context of far higher absolute population growth, at much lower income levels, with much less institutional and financial capacity, and with considerably fewer opportunities to expand into new frontiers, foreign or domestic' (UNCHS, 2001: 3). In nineteenth-century Europe, people migrated to the towns and cities in search of employment and economic advancement. The industrial activities located in those areas depended on this process of migration to raise output and generate wealth. Urbanisation, industrialisation and 'modernisation' (the adoption of urban values) were processes which occurred simultaneously in the cities of Europe and were mutually reinforcing. This has not been the case in the developing world. Table 5.3 highlights the cases of a number of Latin American countries in the 1960s (a period of relatively rapid industrial development), where it is seen that employment growth lagged substantially behind that in manufacturing output. Such 'jobless growth' continued to be a feature of urban change in the developing world into the 1990s and most recently is seen in the decoupling of urbanisation from economic growth in Africa as illustrated above.

Table 5.3 *Industrialisation and employment in selected Latin American countries, 1963–9*

Country	Manufacturing annual output growth (%)	Manufacturing employment growth (%)
Brazil	6.5	1.1
Colombia	5.9	2.8
Costa Rica	8.9	2.8
Dominican Republic	1.7	−3.3
Ecuador	11.4	6.0
Panama	12.9	7.4

Source: Todaro (1997).

Plate 5.1 *Urban informal income opportunities*

a. Door-to-door welding, Harare, Zimbabwe
Source: author.

b. Garment production, Kairouan, Tunisia
Source: author.

Clearly, in urban areas, employment is critical to securing a livelihood and avoiding impoverishment and for sustained development. Todaro (1997) has suggested that one of the most 'obvious failures' of the development process over the past few decades has been 'the failure of modern urban industries to generate a significant number of employment opportunities' (p. 247). Few of the urban poor can afford

Plate 5.1—*continued*

c. Food trading/transport, Calcutta, India
Source: author.

to be unemployed for any length of time. Many, in fact, will be under-employed; either they are working less than they would like or are doing so at such low rates of production that their labour could be withdrawn with very little impact on overall output. In recent years, structural adjustment programmes have also led to contraction in formal sector employment opportunities in the cities of the developing world, through the loss of jobs in the public sector and the denationalisation of industries, for example. In response to a lack of employment opportunities within this 'formal' sector, many urban residents in the developing world look to a wide variety of both legitimate and illegitimate income opportunities available within the 'informal' economy. This term is commonly used to refer to small-scale, unregulated, semi-legal economic activities which often rely on local, internal resources, family labour and traditional technology. The host of activities encompassed within this sector is illustrated in Figure 5.4. Whilst there are some problems with quality data, it is estimated that the sector provides employment, goods and services for as much as 60 per cent of the urban population. Certainly, 'the extent and impact of poverty on urban populations, as well as on urban and national economies would be much greater were it not for the informal sector' (UNCHS, 2001: 212). It is also now appreciated that the informal sector is better integrated with and recognised by the

Figure 5.4 *Informal sector activities*

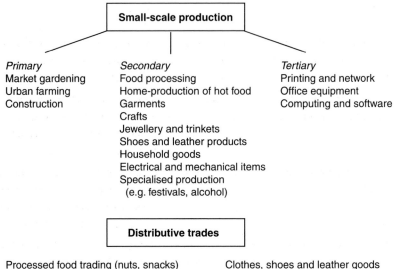

Small-scale production

Primary
Market gardening
Urban farming
Construction

Secondary
Food processing
Home-production of hot food
Garments
Crafts
Jewellery and trinkets
Shoes and leather products
Household goods
Electrical and mechanical items
Specialised production
   (e.g. festivals, alcohol)

Tertiary
Printing and network
Office equipment
Computing and software

Distributive trades

Processed food trading (nuts, snacks)
Unprocessed produce (fruit and vegetables)
Commercial food trading (Chiclet, Coca-Cola)
Suitcase trading (imported items)
Hot food and drinks

Clothes, shoes and leather goods
Jewellery and cosmetics
Newspapers
Household items
Music and electrical items

Tertiary services

Laundry
Domestic
Shoe cleaning and repair
Hardware repair
Motor vehicle servicing
Taxi-driving and transport
Maintenance and gardening
Odd jobs (e.g. car cleaning)
Bottle and waste collecting

Specialised services

Tourist guides
Car park attendants
Car, home rentals
Residential lodgings
Secretarial, clerical
Legal and medical
Beauty services/hairdressing
Distribution/storage
Begging
Protection

Source: compiled from Potter and Lloyd-Evans (1998); Drakakis-Smith (2000).

formal sector than the term suggests (UNCHS, 2001). However, there are a number of challenges as well as benefits of employment within the informal sector, as shown in Figure 5.5.

Poor people in poor environments

It was seen in Chapter 4 that the proportion of people estimated to be below poverty lines is generally higher in rural than urban areas of the developing world. However, the absolute numbers of people living at

Figure 5.5 *Opportunities and challenges of informal sector employment*

....

Advantages	*Limitations*
More buoyant and elastic in generating jobs for an increasing urban labour force than the formal sector	Low productivity of sector and its lack of bargaining power means incomes generally lower than in formal sector
Small scale of operations and low levels of capital required lowers costs of creating employment	Nature of employment means that earnings tend to be more intermittent and erratic, making access to formal credit mechanisms by households difficult
Produces jobs that require fewer skills and less training than the formal sector	Irregular and often illegal nature of many activities makes operators in the informal sector vulnerable to official and non-official harassment and persecution
Lack of regulation and control and ease of entry makes informal sector well suited to absorption of migrants and other newcomers to the urban labour market	Unregulated nature of informal sector makes it difficult for people to obtain access to services and supports necessary for increasing earnings and moving out of poverty
Provides a safety net in times of economic crisis for those made redundant	Informal nature makes it difficult to protect those who are engaged in them, whether as paid workers or as unpaid family members, against child labour abuses or against hazards in the workplace, for example.
	Informal sector jobs don't produce government revenues to support welfare policies, social safety net programmes

....

Source: compiled from UNCHS (2001).

or below subsistence levels in the latter are much larger and are likely to grow under predicted rates of urbanisation. Furthermore, trends suggest that, although still small in many countries, the contribution of urban to overall poverty generally *grew* in the 1980s and 1990s (Rakodi, 2002b). Income inequalities are often more entrenched and apparent in cities than in the countryside (WRI, 1996) and the cost of living in urban centres is also higher.

Generally, urban dwellers have to purchase many items which can be accessed freely or more cheaply in rural areas, such as fuel and building materials. Urban consumers typically pay 30 per cent more for their food than their rural counterparts (UNCHS, 2001). Goods and services are more commercialised in urban centres, and urban residents are more reliant on cash income to secure these, which also brings a certain vulnerability to price rises and any drop in income. An understanding of urban poverty has become even more important in recent years as many basic services and housing, for example, are

Plate 5.2 *Low-income housing*

a. Bangkok squatter settlement
Source: David W. Smith, Liverpool University.

b. Public housing, Harare
Source: author.

Plate 5.2—*continued*

c. Tenement blocks, Calcutta
Source: author.

often no longer provided by the public sector but have to be accessed in the marketplace where people's ability to pay is critical. There is now mounting evidence that privatisation of public utilities such as water and electricity has led to increased tariffs and charges to consumers to levels where poor families can no longer afford sufficient quantities to secure their most basic needs (War On Want, 2004).

In continuity with the discussions of poverty in Chapters 2 and 4, the extent of urban poverty is unlikely to be captured by indicators based on income alone. Thinking only in terms of income can hide other aspects of deprivation such as poor quality housing or people's capacity to challenge detrimental changes in their local environments. Figure 5.6 displays the multiple aspects of urban poverty and some of the wider factors underpinning these dimensions. Through this chapter, some detail of how these aspects of poverty impact on the prospects for sustainable development will be highlighted: the inadequacy of basic services and their links to good health and

Figure 5.6 *The deprivations associated with urban poverty*

Incompetent or ineffective government limiting land supplies (eg inappropriate land-use controls)

Homes built on illegal and often dangerous sites; better quality housing and serviced lots too expensive

No credit available to low-income groups to support land purchase and house building or improvement

No organisation providing survival income if income source is lost or falls; no insurance for assets (lost to disaster) or to cover health-care costs

Poor quality and often insecure, hazardous and overcrowded housing

Lack of infrastructure and services causing very large health burden

Households living in illegal settlements where utilities or service providers refuse to operate

Service providers unaccountable and/or uninfluenced by democratic pressures

Debt repayments reducing available income

Limited or no safety net

Dangerous jobs undertaken because of higher incomes – high risks of injury, illness or premature death

Inadequate and often unstable income

Poorer groups' voicelessness and powerlessness within political systems and bureaucratic structures

POVERTY IN URBAN AREAS

Inefficiency or incapacity of utilities or service providers, increasing gap between what is provided and what low-income households can afford

Income lost to illness and injury (and treatment costs)

Economy producing little opportunity for better incomes

Incompetent, ineffective or anti-poor police force

High levels of violence and other crimes

Health risks from malnutrition and use of cheaper (poor quality) foods, fuels and water

High prices paid for many necessities

Inadequate protection of poorer groups' rights through the operation of the law (including protection from discrimination)

Absence of 'rule of law' and support for poor realising their civil and political rights and entitlements

High/rising prices for necessities (food, water, rent, transport, toilets, school fees...)

Inadequate unstable or risky asset base

Discrimination faced by particular groups with regard to access to income, housing, credit and services on the basis of gender, age, nationality, class/caste and ethnic group

Short-term survival limiting asset building (eg capacity to save, children taken out of school to earn/collect water)

Asset base constantly eroded as it copes with illnesses, injuries and other stresses/shocks; limits of community reciprocity

No collateral for accessing credit to allow house or plot purchase, or to pay regularisation costs or connection charges

Source: Mitlin and Satterthwaite (2004).

education, for example, and the significance of representative, democratic and accountable local authorities for ensuring people's rights to organise and for their protection against eviction will be seen. As Mitlin and Satterthwaite (2004: 12) state, 'of the multiple deprivations that most of the urban poor face, many of these deprivations have little or no direct link to income levels, while many relate much more to political systems and bureaucratic structures that are unwilling or unable to act effectively to address these deprivations'.

Because of their poverty, many residents of cities in the developing world live in locations and settlements which are hazardous and detrimental to their own well-being. This is not substantially different from the situation in the more developed world, as illustrated in the work now regarding environmental justice. In addition, as noted in Chapter 2, as poverty becomes more concentrated into certain locations, often those of high ecological vulnerability, the urban poor may degrade these environments further in the course of securing their basic needs. Fundamentally, the poor are unable to afford the locations that are more desirable in terms of the inherent or acquired characteristics of the land. Wherever the urban poor are concentrated in cities of the developing world, it is commonly at high densities in areas of low rent. Poor groups do not live here in ignorance of the dangers; they choose such sites because they meet more immediate and pressing needs. Such sites are often the only places where they can build their own houses or rent accommodation. The sites remain cheap because they are dangerous (Hardoy *et al.*, 2001).

Regularly such locations are close to hazardous installations, such as chemical factories, and suffer continuous air and water pollution as well as the prospect of sudden fire or explosion. But critically for the urban poor, these locations may be close to jobs. As Gupta (1998) revealed, it was the high concentration of low-income people around the Union Carbide Factory in Bhopal which caused so many to be killed or permanently injured (over 3,000 dead and approximately 100,000 seriously injured). In Caracas, the capital city of Venezuela, the occurrence of slope failures has been increasing in recent decades. The maps of where these slope failures occur and those of the areas of low-income housing are almost entirely the same (Potter *et al.*, 2004). Caracas grew rapidly in the second half of the twentieth century with the development of the oil industry and much of the expanded population were housed in self-built *barrios*, the majority of which are located on the steep slopes of the narrow east–west valley in which the city is located. Significantly, whereas earthquakes were the trigger for past landslides, it is now heavy rains that regularly present a hazard to the vulnerable populations of the *barrios*. In 1999, many of those who died in catastrophic floods were low-income households living on unstable hill-slopes (Hardoy *et al.*, 2001). Box P highlights the relationship of poverty and vulnerability to hazard and ill-health, in situations where families live on and around solid waste dumps. An estimated 20,000 people in Calcutta, 12,000 in Manila, and 15,000 in Mexico City, for example, live on municipal dumps (Medina, 2000). Box P also considers how policies towards scavengers and waste collection more widely in cities of the developing world are changing.

Box P

Poverty and the environment within informal waste management activities

The recovery of materials from waste is an important survival strategy for low-income populations throughout the developing world. An estimated 2 per cent of the population of Asian and Latin American cities, for example, survive by scavenging waste (Medina, 2000). Fuelled by factors including chronic poverty, high unemployment, industrial demand for recyclables and a lack of safety nets for the poor, it is likely that scavenging will continue to exist.

Scavengers operate in extremely hostile physical and social environments and are likely also to be amongst the most politically marginalised groups. As Beall (1997: 74) suggests, 'everywhere, people involved in waste work, be it street cleaning, waste collection or scavenging, do it because they have little choice and are stigmatised by virtue of the dirty work they do. They are often marginalised groups such as ethnic or religious minorities, or are rural migrants who compete for urban livelihoods'.

Whilst many businesses, especially in steel, paper and glass production, depend on recycled raw materials supplied through informal recycling chains, it is poverty which drives the majority of waste collection in the cities of the developing world; gathering waste from the streets and dumps provides for many the only access to the resources they need for clothing, housing, fuel and work. Often it is women and children who work long hours in unhealthy conditions for the meagre returns (Momsen, 2004). There are many direct environmental hazards associated with waste picking: the materials may include hospital and toxic industrial waste, may be contaminated with faeces, and also may contain sharp objects (Hunt, 1996). In the developing world, municipal waste forms a much larger part of overall urban waste and is itself composed of greater quantities of organic waste and dust, cinders and ashes than in cities of the more developed world (Beall, 1997). The build-up of methane gases as a result of high levels of organic waste regularly causes fire and the risk of smoke inhalation and burns for waste pickers. Waste pickers are also exposed to further hazards including harassment, social ostracism and even murder.

Children may face greater health risks through factors including their relative lack of judgement and experience in collection, their inherent vulnerability to air-borne pollution hazard, their potential greater number of years in the activity (starting such work at an early age) and through the long-term impacts on their personality development (Hunt, 1996). In an intensive study of 100 child waste pickers in Bangalore in India, the health status of those children involved in this activity was found to be significantly worse than that of children who were not, as shown in Figure 5.7. The greater worm infestation is likely to be due to the contact with faecal materials. Respiratory tract infections are commonly related to the home environment (poor ventilation and close living), but may be worsened by physical work and also infection from contact with wastes. Lymph node enlargement is usually caused by minor infections, but signs of tuberculosis were also found amongst the waste-picking children.

Figure 5.7 *The health status of waste pickers in Bangalore in relation to non-pickers*

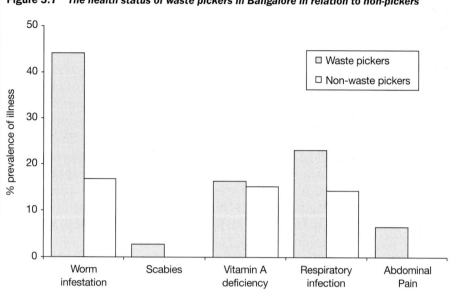

Source: Hunt (1996).

Whereas once Bangalore was known as the 'Garden City' of India, it is now known as the 'Garbage City' (Beall, 1997) due to its declining urban services.

Historically, much public policy towards scavenging has been extremely negative and repressive based on the view of scavengers as a nuisance, an embarrassment to city authorities and as a symbol of backwardness. As such, scavenging has been declared illegal and punished in many cities of the developing world (Medina, 2000). However, it is increasingly recognised that conventional models for refuse collection and disposal (as utilised in high-income countries) is too expensive and inappropriate for many urban districts of the developing world (Hardoy *et al.*, 2001) and there are now many examples of NGOs in particular, supporting locally developed solutions to match local needs and opportunities (including supporting grassroots community development).

One of the most successful and dynamic scavenger cooperative movements is in Columbia where the NGO, the 'Fundacion Social', has assisted the formation of over 100 cooperatives since the mid-1980s through its National Recycling Programme (Medina, 2000). The foundation awards grants, but also makes legal, administrative and business assistance available to cooperatives who engage in a wide variety of recycling activities including from dumps, along city streets, in source separation programmes and sometimes under formal contracts to commercial establishments and small industries. Cooperatives have been assisted in forming regional marketing associations enabling them to accumulate and sell in greater volumes and achieve higher prices. 'In total, Columbian scavengers recover and sell over 300,000 tons of recyclables each year, mostly paper, glass, scrap metals, plastics and organics. Cooperative members report a higher standard of living, as well as improvements in self-esteem and self-reliance compared with when they worked independently and on their own' (Medina, 2000: 61).

Accessing affordable and quality housing is a considerable challenge
for the urban poor. Certainly, the demand for housing far outweighs
the supply of formal housing units. For example, it is estimated that
just one formal housing unit was added to the total urban housing
stock for every nine new households in the developing world during
the 1980s (Hardoy and Satterthwaite, 1989) and the situation is likely
to have worsened in recent decades. The majority of the urban
population in such cities is housed in unauthorised informal
settlements (variously termed *barrios*, *kampungs*, *favelas*, *bustees*,
etc.), and in slums or tenements ('legal' developments which become
decayed and degraded through overcrowding and poor upkeep).
Possibly as much as one-quarter of the housing stock of urban centres
of the developing world consists of non-permanent structures and
one-third do not comply with local building regulations (UNCHS,
2001). Stark inequalities in access to land within cities are illustrated in
Surabaya, Indonesia, where 63 per cent of the population live in
kampungs that cover only 7 per cent of the city's area (Hardoy *et al.*,
2001). More than 40 per cent of the population of Metro Manila,
Philippines, live in illegal or informal settlements that cover less than
6 per cent of the land area (2001). Figure 5.8 highlights the range of
low-income options for housing and some of the key features of the
various forms. In addition to the millions of people for whom
accommodation is very insecure or temporary, there are also those
who have no home at all, but live on the streets. Although data for
cities of the developing world are sparse, it is known that there are
over 250,000 pavement dwellers in Mumbai, for example, and it is
likely that the problem is growing generally with the increasing
commercialisation of land markets in such cities.

There is a range of serious disadvantages to living in illegal
settlements. For example, in the 1960s and 1970s, many city
authorities had policies of slum or squatter clearance, where
inhabitants had no defence in the law against eviction (Hardoy and
Satterthwaite, 1989). Every year, it is estimated that several million
people are evicted from their homes as a result of public works or
government redevelopment programmes (UNCHS, 1996: xxviii).
Furthermore, because settlements are illegal, they lack basic or
emergency public services. Residents may also be ineligible for loans
to improve their housing or employment conditions (their illegal
shelter or land site being unacceptable as collateral), or indeed, for
government subsidies such as in education (for which an authorised
address may be required to register children). Fundamentally, the
cramped and overcrowded conditions exacerbate the transmission of

Figure 5.8 *The different kinds of rental and 'owner occupation' housing for low-income groups in cities of the developing world*

....

Type	Characteristics
Rented room in subdivided inner-city tenement building	Usually very overcrowded and in poor state of repair
Rented room in custom-built tenement building	Usually host many more families than built for. Often poorly maintained
Rented room, bed or bed hours in boarding house, cheap hotel or pension	Tend to be poorly maintained with a lack of facilities
Rented room or bed in illegal settlement	Share problems associated with illegality. Extra problems of insecurity of tenure
Rented land plot on which a shack is built	Highly insecure tenure; owner may require them to move at short notice
Rented room in house or flat in lower- or middle-income area of the city	Quality may be relatively good. May be located far from jobs
Employer-housing for low-paid workers	Quality often poor. Regularly rules against families living there
Public housing unit	Many small in relation to numbers living there. Inadequate maintenance
Renting space to sleep at work	Usually total lack of facilities for washing/ cooking. Lack of security
Renting a space to sleep in public buildings	Total lack of security/facilities. Payments to protection gangs or local officials
Building a house or shack in squatter settlement	Insecure tenure. Lack of public services. Dangerous locations etc.
Building a house or shack in an illegal subdivision	Sites are purchased and have degree of security. Some infrastructure. Often expensive
Building a house or shack on a legal land subdivision on the city periphery	Affordable plots on legal subdivisions often far from jobs
Invading empty houses or apartments or public buildings	Occupation illegal. Usually no services
Building a house or shack in government site and service or core housing scheme	Often far from jobs. Restrictions on employment activities from home. Eligibility criteria
Building a shack or house in a temporary camp	Often government's response to disaster situation. Infrastructure and services inadequate

....

Source: extracted from UNCHS (1996), but based originally on Hardoy and Satterthwaite (1989).

Plate 5.3 *Making a living through waste, Indonesia*

Source: author.

infectious diseases and risks of accidents and are very much part of the brown environmental agenda identified in Figure 5.2.

The urban environmental challenge

The level of economic development and affluence has been seen to be one factor influencing the nature of environmental problems facing particular cities. With higher levels of economic development, industrial and energy-related pollution become more problematic, as does the inability to deal with wastes (including toxic) as seen in Box O. Clearly, the nature of environmental problems in particular cities will also be influenced by the rate and scale of urbanisation itself and the degree of concentration of such growth. Fast-growing cities may provide particular challenges for planning and management but serious environmental problems can also occur in declining industrial centres and stagnant smaller towns, for example (UNCHS, 1996). The geographical location of cities is a further factor shaping the nature of the environmental challenge: cities in cold climates consume greater levels of fossil fuels for domestic heating, for example. Mexico City is a widely cited case where altitude and topology (the city being surrounded on three sides by mountains) combine to present particular challenges for the dispersal of atmospheric pollutants, especially from industry and the motor car. Coastal ecosystems (where some of the highest rates of urban growth are currently occurring) also have particular characteristics which are distinct from those further inland, with implications for the nature of environmental problems in cities located on such sites.

However, it is important to move beyond such broad patterns to understand the nature of the environmental burden of cities and how cities are responding to these. Wealth differences occur within cities (not just between them) and it is suggested that more competent, accountable city governments can lessen environmental burdens 'irrespective of levels of economic development' (McGranahan and Satterthwaite, 2002). It is important not to underestimate the significance of these economic and political dimensions to sustainable urban development. In Figure 5.6 it was seen that many of the dimensions of poverty in urban areas relate to factors beyond income to include aspects of people's participation and voice within political systems and the protection of their rights in law, for example, and there are many external influences that shape local environmental concerns and the prospects for sustainable urban change in future. Indeed, Hardoy *et al.* (2001: 382) suggest that 'it can even be misleading to refer to many of the most pressing environmental problems as "environmental" since they arise not from some particular shortage of an environmental resource (e.g. land or fresh water) but from economic or political factors that prevent poorer groups from obtaining them and from organising to defend them'. To further understand the nature of the challenges and opportunities for sustainable urban development and to consider how the various contributing factors interact in specific locations, substantial insight can be gained through a consideration of environment and development concerns at different scales.

The household and community level

In poor neighbourhoods of cities in the developing world, many of the most threatening environmental problems are found close to home.

Regularly, poorer households use their homes as centres for income generation, their homes also functioning as workshops, as stores for goods for sale, as shops or as bars or cafés. The environmental risks are often greater for women and children because of the longer hours spent at home and in the immediate vicinity. Women, for example, may combine in the same space and time, piece-work for income with domestic duties such as child care. The environmental problems related to such activities in the home are diverse, but include the hazards to health associated with poor ventilation, inadequate light, the use of toxic or flammable chemicals and the lack of protective clothing. A high proportion of disablement and serious injury in cities of the developing world is caused by household accidents and these are strongly aligned to poor-quality, overcrowded conditions. Many low-income urban dwellings are constructed of flammable materials like wood and cardboard and accidental fires are more common where families often live in one room and where it is difficult to provide protection from open fires or kerosene heaters (UNCHS, 1996).

Indoor air pollution is also aggravated by the burning of low-quality fuels such as charcoal for domestic heating and lighting. The major impacts are on respiratory health, whereby irritant fumes cause respiratory tract inflammation, repeated exposure leading to the onset of chronic obstructive lung disease. Urban indoor pollution is currently a major cause of premature death in the developing world, as shown in Table 5.4. Young children, who may be strapped to their mothers' backs during the course of cooking suffer more as their smaller lungs are less able to cope with pollutants. In combination with malnutrition, smoke inhalation may further retard infant growth and raise susceptibility of children to other infections. It is suggested that acute respiratory infection may now be a bigger killer than diarrhoea amongst children (McGranahan and Murray, 2003).

The most critical determinant of human health (wherever people live) is access to adequate supplies of clean water. In 1980, the WHO estimated that 80 per cent of all sickness and disease worldwide was related to inadequate water (in terms of quantity and quality) and sanitation (services to collect and

Table 5.4 Urban deaths from indoor air pollution

Region	Deaths per year in cities (thousands)
India	93
Sub-Saharan Africa	32
China	53
Rest of Asia	40
Latin America	113
Industrialised countries	32
Total	363

Source: Extracted from Potter et al. (2004).

dispose of solid and liquid wastes). Since then, where environmental improvements have been made in the quality of available water and in the disposal of excreta, illness and the burden of disease have been dramatically reduced and the impact on mortality has been even greater (World Bank, 1992). However, as many as 250 million urban residents currently have no ready access to safe piped water (UNCHS, 2001) and halving this figure is one of the Millennium Development Goals as seen in Chapter 2. Table 5.5 illustrates the challenge of extending improved drinking water and sanitation facilities in selected countries.

There are, however, acknowledged problems of data quality in respect of water supply: the tendency is towards overestimation of national levels and 'adequacy' that often do not match with research within cities that reveals substantial local difficulties (see Satterthwaite, 2002a; Hardoy *et al.*, 2001). Many governments, for example, classify adequate water provision as a tap within 100 metres of the house (WRI, 1996), yet in practice, it is common for between two and five hundred people to share access to a single public standpipe (UNCHS, 2001). In many cases, the situation may be much worse, as seen in Table 5.6a. There are further questions concerning the length of time

Table 5.5 *Proportion of urban population with improved water sources and sanitation facilities, selected countries, 2000*

Country	% of urban population with access to improved drinking water	% of urban population with access to improved sanitation facilities
Afghanistan	19	25
Angola	34	70
Bangladesh	99	71
Brazil	95	84
Chad	31	81
Gambia	80	41
India	95	61
Indonesia	90	69
Mexico	95	88
Nigeria	78	66
Peru	87	79
Uganda	80	93

Source: Compiled from United Nations Statistics Division www.unstats.un.org

water is supplied each day when considering the adequacy of provision to ensure sufficient quantities of water at the household level or to secure the health benefits within a community (Table 5.6b).

Table 5.6 *Questioning environmental improvement*

(a) the adequacy of service

City	Numbers sharing public standpipe
Dakar, Senegal	1,513
Noukchott, Mauritania	2,500
Luanda, Angola	600–1,000

(b) the consistency of household supply (survey of 50 cities in Asia and Pacific in the mid-1990s officially stated as having 24-hour access to piped home supply)

City	Reported supply (hours per day)
Chennai	4
Karachi	4
Mumbai	5
Bandung	6
Kathmandu	6
Faisalabad	7

Source: Compiled from UNCHS (2001).

When access to water is restricted in these ways, the time taken in queuing and transporting water back to homes serves to limit the amount of water used. For many low-income urban residents, the option is either to draw water from surface sources (often, in effect, open sewers) or to purchase water (of unknown quality) from vendors. In the mid-1980s, it was estimated that, for the urban population of the developing world as a whole, 20 to 30 per cent depended on water vendors for their supply and it is likely that in many places this proportion has increased (Hardoy *et al.* 2001). The costs of such water may be anything from four to one hundred times higher than the cost of water from a piped supply (WRI, 1996: 20) and it is not unusual for poorer households to spend between 5 and 10 per cent of their household income on water. This further limits the amounts of water used at the household level and is therefore an important determinant of environmental health.

Whilst poor residents of urban centres are paying for water and struggling to access sufficient quantities and qualities of this basic good, as much as half of total water supplies may be being lost through leakages and through illegal connections/corruption (UNCHS, 2001). Such inequality and inefficiency around such a fundamental right as water lead to an increased likelihood of conflict. Furthermore, as the pressure for privatisation of public water services is increasing worldwide, with proponents arguing that the poor will benefit from properly financed utilities (and save reliance on water vendors, for example), broad-based coalitions are also increasingly challenging the involvement of particularly transnational companies in these areas, as seen in Box Q. There is mounting evidence that privatisation is leading to higher tariffs for basic services and is failing to reach the poorest communities and those who have no access. Inevitably, the private sector picks off the most lucrative contracts and public authorities (whose capacities may also have been reduced under policies of structural reform considered in Chapter 3) are left with the most difficult cases (War On Want, 2004).

The inadequacy of urban water supplies serves substantially to explain the endemic nature of many debilitating and preventable diseases in cities of the developing world. Vulnerability to infection

---

Box Q

The Cochabamba water wars, Bolivia

Cochabamba is a city in Bolivia with a population of over half a million, living typically on less than US$100 per month. In 2000, it was proposed (substantially promoted by the World Bank) to sell control of its public water system to a multinational consortium of private companies (Aguas del Tunari) with the prospect of water supply rates rising to US$20 per month. A new organisation, Coordinadora de Defensa del Agua (Coordinators in Defence of the Water) formed and a four-day strike shut down the city. When the government failed to respond, a public protest was called and a coalition of peasant unions, student groups and working-class unions as well as segments of the national security forces joined in the public protest against the privatisation. Riot police clashed with protestors and this resulted in more than 175 injured civilians as the public call for the cancellation of the contract rose. The support of a peasants' union that was fighting a parallel struggle against the privatisation of water provision in rural areas was gained. It organised road blocks extending into six of Bolivia's nine regions beyond the city. City residents stormed the local city hall where talks were being held resulting in the arrest of 15 leaders of the Coordinadora. Subsequent demonstrations led to the release of the protest leaders, a reported cancellation of the contract and then denial on the part of the government and ultimately a declaration of a state of emergency and the suspension of rights to strike and legitimisation of the use of the army to prevent civilian unrest.

Rather than quell the discontent, the state of emergency fuelled further protests in Cochabamba and widespread discontent throughout the country to include university students, rural teachers and miners' unions, for example. Eventually, Aguas del Tunari itself withdrew from the deal and as it became clear that the privatisation of water provision in Cochabamba would not occur, Coordinadora called off the strikes. Whilst the immediate cause of the unrest has been removed, many residents of Cochabamba and more widely remain concerned as to the growing pressures to privatise public resources in the country.

Source: compiled from UNCHS (2001).

amongst low-income households is also enhanced by the inadequacies of urban facilities for the hygienic disposal of excreta or household garbage. In continuity with data concerning water provision, accurate data is hard to come by, but an estimated 400 million urban residents do not have adequate sanitation, i.e. have no means of disposing of excreta or waste water (UNCHS, 2001). Table 5.5 illustrates this challenge in particular countries. Even many large cities have no sewers at all. For households with no provision for individual or shared sanitation within their homes, defecating within ditches, streams, parks or other open spaces or into some container which is then thrown away ('wrap and throw') are often the only options. The lack of secluded space creates substantial problems for women and young girls. Provision of public toilets is often non-existent or of poor quality and often use of public toilets involves a fee which people cannot afford. Research has also shown that many people may not use such facilities because they do not have the time to accompany their children and young girls to them or they are too far from their homes to use after dark (UNCHS, 2001). Adult women may feel too ashamed to use a public latrine in front of men during daylight hours and run the risk of rape when using such facilities after dark (Huggler, 2004). Such poor sanitation leads to dangers for the widest community of direct exposure to faeces near homes and the contamination of drinking water. The cramped housing conditions of many informal settlements also aggravate the rapid transmission of disease between individuals, such as pneumonia and tuberculosis. Furthermore, where waste is collected, in 90 per cent of cases it is then discharged untreated and directly into rivers, lakes and coastal waters (Bartone *et al.*, 1994), compounding local environmental burdens.

In summary, the analysis of urban environmental problems at this level has revealed a number of important and substantial challenges for sustainable development in future. Primarily, it has given a sense of the extent of the environmental challenge in terms of the numbers of people still to be reached by essential improvements if their basic needs of health and livelihoods are to be met and environments conserved. Such understanding points further to the huge economic costs of implementing change, as well as to how sustainable urban development is a long-term and ongoing challenge. This level of analysis also provides an understanding of the reality of urban living, the detail of the Brown Agenda, which is essential for effecting change as considered in later sections.

The city and the wider region

Although for the majority of urban residents of poor cities it is the environmental issues closest to home which directly influence their well-being, there are a number of city-wide and regional environmental problems which are mounting, particularly in the rapidly industrialising cities of the developing world, and present further challenges and opportunities for sustainability.

Cities themselves involve the dramatic conversion of land use. Although on a global scale only around 1 per cent of the total land surface is under urban use (Hardoy *et al.*, 2001), urban developments worldwide are encroaching on some of the last remaining and most-valued reserves of natural vegetation, including mangrove swamps, protected wetlands, prime agricultural lands and forests. Urban sprawl is also impacting on existing human activities, such as in eastern Calcutta, where 4,000 hectares of inland lagoons have been filled to provide homes for middle-class families at the expense of the tenant families who formerly made a livelihood based on aquaculture in the region (WRI, 1996). Environmental degradation in peri-urban areas is also occurring through the expansion of unplanned, squatter settlements into areas susceptible to flooding or landslides, as identified in Chapter 2 (Figure 2.8). Simply providing water for industrial and domestic uses is a substantial problem for many cities. Mexico City, for example, has sunk 10 metres since the 1930s as a result of excessive withdrawal of groundwater sources (UNCHS, 2001).

Although 'urban primacy' may be less marked currently than in former times, there is still a tendency for industrial developments to be concentrated in a small number of urban centres. Regularly, in the developing world, such developments are not subject to effective planning or pollution control. It was seen in Chapter 3 that the lack of stringent pollution control legislation generally in the developing world has been an important factor in attracting industrial production facilities (often transnational enterprises) to cities in these regions. Furthermore, many countries have established export processing zones (EPZs) through the 1990s, where manufacturing activities, often using transnational capital, are by definition encouraged and concentrated (before products are exported). In response to processes of globalisation, including the need to raise foreign exchange earnings to service debts and to open up their economies and attract foreign investment, EPZs have been a popular policy for governments of developing countries. TNCs are attracted to such zones by the tax exemptions and incentives offered and the typically low labour costs (Gwynne, 2002).

The types of environmental problems which flow from the concentrated location of industry have been seen in the case of the city of Cubatão, close to Rio de Janeiro in Brazil. This area has been named the 'valley of death' because of its large collection of Brazilian industrial companies and transnational firms, the high levels of air pollution and of respiratory infection, and the numbers of babies still-born or deformed, all substantially above those of surrounding regions (Hardoy *et al.*, 2001). Water sources and vegetation in and around the city have also been affected by the high concentrations of industry and lack of environmental control; toxic wastes contaminated the major river to the extent that fish were no longer found in it and vegetation had deteriorated from the effects of acid rain. As a result, soils become unstable and residents became vulnerable to further hazards including landslips, often leading to serious loss of life. Whilst improvements were made in the late 1990s principally through enforcement of environmental controls prompted by a strong citizen movement and the actions of some progressive individuals within the state government's environmental protection agency (Hardoy *et al.*, 2001), for many people who have lost family members or are permanently disabled, the actions were too late and the longer-term impact of pollutants already in rivers and soils remains uncertain (2001). Box R identifies a number of environmental challenges of industrial developments at the Mexican border with the United States (one of the largest zones of EPZs in the world).

Problems of air pollution have long been associated with cities, although there is currently much diversity worldwide in the relative importance of particular pollutants. Pollution levels can also vary substantially by season. In the developing world, sulphur dioxide pollution and the concentration of suspended particulates are the major causes of urban air pollution, resulting in the main from industrial production and the burning of coal, oil and biomass fuels. In most cities of the more developed regions, tighter environmental regulations, measures to promote more efficient fuel use and the greater use of the least polluting fuels (such as natural gas for domestic and industrial use) have reduced pollution from these 'traditional sources'. However, city-wide environmental problems also stem from activities other than industrial production. Congested roads and poorly maintained vehicles, for example, are a growing source of 'photochemical' (particularly lead and carbon monoxide)

Box R

Maquila developments on the Mexico–United States border

In the mid-1960s, the government of Mexico initiated a programme to promote industrialisation in the previously underdeveloped northern border region through creating EPZs incorporating 13 towns (Gwynne, 2002). Mexican and foreign factories were enabled to import machinery and inputs without paying tariffs on the condition that goods were re-exported. US companies were able to take advantage of cheap Mexican labour as well as US tariff regulations. The expansion of export-only assembly factories ('maquiladoras') substantially altered the distribution of population and urban development in Mexico. For example, the population of the 36 municipalities that adjoin the United States increased from 0.28 million in 1930 to 4 million by 1990 (UNCHS, 1996: 50). The great majority of workers initially employed were unskilled and were women, contributing to social tensions in the male-dominated structures of Mexican migrant families (Gwynne, 2002). Since 1989, maquila industries were also allowed to sell products in the domestic markets, which, coupled with the devaluation of the Mexican currency against the US dollar through the 1990s, led to further urban growth in cities such as Ciudad Juarez and Tijuana (as well as in their 'partner' cities across the border of El Paso and San Diego respectively).

By 1996, there were over 2,000 industrial plants employing more than 600,000 people. However, the expansion of employment has often been at substantial cost to the local environment: 'the fact is that Mexican border towns have become garbage dumps for millions of barrels of benzene solvents, pesticides, raw sewage and battery acid spewed out by foreign-owned maquiladoras' (Johnston-Hernandez, 1993: 10). The health impacts of such inadequate disposal of toxic wastes and chemical sludge are profound in urban developments where large proportions of the population depend on open water courses for their drinking water, for example. In the eastern border town of Matamoros, the rate of anencephaly (babies born without brains) was four times the national average, with tissues taken from the mothers of such babies showing the presence of pesticides, several of which have been banned in the United States (Johnston-Hernandez, 1993).

Since the implementation of the North American Free Trade Area (NAFTA) between the USA, Mexico and Canada in 1994, aspects of the former 'enclave nature' of the border towns have started to be broken down (Gwynne, 2002). The specific advantages for TNC investment within the EPZs have been reduced in relation to other locations further away from the border and many of the old maquilas based on unskilled, low-wage and non-unionised labour are now relocating further south to benefit from cheaper labour costs.

pollution in the developing world as motor vehicle use per capita rises. Whilst it is difficult to attribute the precise health impact of air pollutants, it is considered that air pollution is now eroding many of the previously gained health improvements in cities, particularly in Asia and Latin America (McGranahan and Murray, 2003) and could account for between 2 and 5 per cent of all deaths in these regions (Potter *et al.*, 2004).

Plate 5.4 *Vehicular pollution, Calcutta*

Source: author.

In order to support the resident populations and productive activities therein, cities depend substantially on inputs of raw materials and goods of various natures from the surrounding region. Whilst wealthy (powerful) cities have long had the capacity to draw resources from far beyond their immediate region, this capacity has greatly increased in recent decades, particularly as the relative cost of transportation has declined. Increasingly, food, fuel and material goods are drawn into cities from all over the nation and indeed the world (Potter *et al.*, 2004). As already suggested, the larger and more prosperous cities make greater demands, as consumption per head rises. However, cities have many further indirect impacts on surrounding regions through, for example, the commercialisation of land and agricultural markets. This can lead to changes in the type of crops grown in rural areas, the economic viability of particular productive activities and even to the expulsion of peasant farmers from their lands. Rural to urban migration can have positive impacts on rural economies through wage remittances, but often it also has detrimental consequences in terms of the supply of labour at key points in the agricultural calendar and the loss of entrepreneurial skills, as seen in Chapter 4 (see also Lynch, 2005, in this series). Such processes are often linked to environmental decline in the surrounding rural areas.

Clearly, these types of processes illustrate some of the limitations of the dualist distinction of 'urban' and 'rural' referred to above. This is confirmed, for example, in the case of urban demand for fuelwood resources, where the supply necessarily comes from forested surrounding areas and, in many instances, pre-empts their use by rural residents; sources once available to rural inhabitants become unavailable to them as urban demand rises. This occurs through either deforestation per se or the commercialisation of fuelwood, which makes wood a commodity to be paid for rather than a resource to be collected from communal lands. Such regional environmental effects may be felt at considerable distance from the centre of demand (the city). For example, research has shown that fuelwood for the urban population of Bangalore comes typically from over 150 km away and from over 700 km in the case of Delhi (Hardoy et al., 2001). In the case of water supply for domestic and industrial use, again, water supplies are often sourced from the wider region and, indeed, the country; Johannesburg, for example, draws its water supply from 600 km away in Lesotho (UNCHS, 2001). Extraction of groundwater to serve Jakarta's water needs has led to saltwater intrusions extending 15 km inland (Hardoy et al., 2001). Electrification brings further environmental impacts to rural areas, where large hydroelectric dams, for example, lead to the loss of agricultural area and the displacement of rural people, with the benefits falling largely to urban consumers, as seen in the case of the Narmada dam-building scheme in Chapter 3.

Further regional environmental problems associated with city-based activities are linked to the inadequate provision for the safe disposal and dispersal of industrial and domestic waste. In consequence, water, for example, is often returned to sources at far lower qualities than when supplied. According to Hardoy et al. (2001: 109) 'most rivers running through cities in low and middle-income countries are literally large open sewers'. They cite the case of the Yamuna river in India that is the source of drinking water for 57 million people including the population of Delhi. Yet 1,700 million litres of untreated sewage flow into that river each day from the city (as well as the industrial waste from 20 large, 25 medium and approximately 93,000 small-scale industries). The result is that the 500-kilometre section of the river below Delhi is virtually devoid of oxygen (eutrophicated) with serious implications for the contamination of domestic water sources, the undermining of agricultural production and the decline of fishing stocks.

In summary, the urban environmental challenge in the developing world is substantial in terms of extent and scope. Industrial developments and rising consumption in urban centres have been seen to be important factors in the degradation of urban environments, but it is also evident that for many low-income households, poverty and a lack of development closely define their core environmental challenges of daily living and working (i.e. the nature of the Brown Agenda). However, it has also been seen that some urban environmental problems diminish as cities become more productive and economically advanced, confirming that there are also opportunities that cities offer for more sustained development. In part as a result of the density of urban living, cities are places where a great variety of local initiatives and actions develop, outside the formal or monetarised sectors, such as within citizens' groups, residents' associations, and youth clubs which are increasingly recognised to be essential for 'healthy' cities worldwide and a key resource for sustainable urban development actions.

Towards sustainable urban development

Figure 5.9 summarises the meaning of sustainable development as applied to cities. The various needs of urban residents and of the environment on which livelihoods depend are highlighted. It is evident that reconciling immediate and future needs as listed is a substantial challenge for action. Indeed, as Bartone *et al.* acknowledge:

> Reversing the deterioration of the urban environment without slowing economic development will require an environmental policy strategy that takes into account a wide range of actors, difficult political and economic trade-offs, and a complex set of natural, social, and economic relationships.
>
> (Bartone *et al.*, 1994: 8)

In continuity with the progress shown towards sustainable rural development, if the needs of urban residents worldwide are to be met without compromising the ability of future generations to meet their own needs, change is required throughout the hierarchy of levels of action considered in Chapter 3. For example, one of the most valuable resources available for sustainable urban development is now considered to be the capacity of citizens' groups to 'identify local problems and their causes, to organise and manage community-based initiatives and to monitor the effectiveness of external agencies working in their locality' (UNCHS, 1996: 427). However, the realisation of this capacity depends substantially on what happens at the city authority level, particularly in terms of the establishment of an effective system through which local people (including business

Figure 5.9 *The meaning of sustainable development as applied to urban centres*

....

Meeting the needs of the present . . .

● Economic needs: include access to an adequate livelihood or productive assets; also economic security when unemployed, ill, disabled or otherwise unable to secure a livelihood.

● Social, cultural and environmental health needs: include a shelter which is healthy, safe, affordable and secure, within a neighbourhood with provision for piped water, sanitation, drainage, transport, health care, education and child development. Also a home, workplace and living environment protected from environmental hazards, including chemical pollution. Also important are needs related to people's choice and control – including homes and neighbourhoods which they value and where their social and cultural priorities are met. Shelters and services must meet the specific needs of children and of adults responsible for most child-rearing (usually women). Achieving this implies a more equitable distribution of income between nations, and in most, within nations.

● Political needs: includes freedom to participate in national and local politics and in decisions regarding management and development of one's home and neighbourhood – within a broader framework which ensures respect for civil and political rights and the implementation of environmental legislation.

. . . without compromising the ability of future generations to meet their own needs

● Minimising use or waste of non-renewable resources: including minimising the consumption of fossil fuels in housing, commerce, industry and transport plus substituting renewable sources where feasible. Also, minimising waste of scarce mineral resources (reduce use, re-use, recycle, reclaim). There are also cultural, historical and natural assets within cities that are irreplaceable and thus non-renewable – for instance, historic districts and parks and natural landscapes which provide space for play, recreation and access to nature.

● Sustainable use of renewable resources: cities drawing on freshwater resources at levels which can be sustained; keeping to a sustainable ecological footprint in terms of land area on which producers and consumers in any city draw for agricultural crops, wood products and biomass fuels.

● Wastes from cities keeping within absorptive capacity of local and global sinks: including renewable sinks (e.g. capacity of river to break down biodegradable wastes) and non-renewable sinks (for persistent chemicals; includes greenhouse gases, stratospheric ozone-depleting chemicals and many pesticides).

....

Source: Hardoy *et al.* (2001).

interests) can participate in decision-making. In turn, city authorities remain responsible (despite increasing privatisation) for many functions which are critical to improving urban environments but are widely constrained in the developing world in part through the inadequate transfer of national finances to this level. Yet there are also many issues, such as the reduction of greenhouse gas emissions or promoting more sustainable international trade practices and other essential elements of sustainable urban development, that require actions on behalf of institutions beyond the city level.

The effectiveness of city authorities

Lessons drawn from 40 years' experience of national or international agencies demonstrate that most local problems need local institutions. Outside agencies, whether national ministries or international agencies, often misunderstand the nature of the problem and the range of options from which to choose the most appropriate solutions. They also fail to appreciate local resources and capacities.

(Hardoy *et al.*, 2001: 384–5)

City authorities worldwide are responsible for a range of urban management tasks including regulating building and land use, providing systems of water supply, sanitation and garbage collection, controlling pollution, managing traffic, delivering emergency services, and providing health care and education. They may not be directly responsible for all these tasks (the increased privatisation of service provision has been referred to above and in Box Q), but national and city authorities are responsible for providing the framework within which private as well as community-based developers operate, including the political context in which markets and local democracy work. The political nature of sustainable urban development should not be underestimated. As Satterthwaite (2002b: 264) suggests, 'in all cities, environmental management is an intensely political task, as different interests compete for the most advantageous locations, for the ownership or use of resources and waste sinks, and for publicly provided infrastructure and services'.

Issues of the capacity and responsiveness of local and sectoral institutions are an important determinant of the quality of the environment in a city. Yet many city governments in the developing world are seriously constrained in terms of the finances and professional and technical competencies necessary to provide the investments, services and pollution control central to healthy urban environments. In many developing countries, local governments depend on central governments for financial assistance to a much greater degree than in more developed countries. If local authorities are to address their challenges of environmental management more effectively, there is a need to devolve more responsibility for initiating, determining the rate of, and administering systems of local taxation.

Until relatively recently, however, most governments of the developing world were centralised, often authoritarian regimes which had sought to consolidate their power through the establishment of (and the concentration of financial resources within) national urban development corporations and national housing authorities, for example. The result was often the construction of large, expensive infrastructural developments in urban centres, but inadequate financial resources at the local authority level to operate and maintain them.

However, starting in the late 1980s and early 1990s, many countries throughout the world have been implementing policies of decentralisation whereby central governments are relinquishing some of their management responsibilities and powers to subnational levels, local governments and community institutions. This has been seen in the UK, with devolution given to Scotland and Wales and the creation of regional development agencies in England, for example. In the developing world, governments (often under the pressure of structural adjustment programmes) have sought to cut their budgets and find new ways to fund service delivery, health care and education (as well as natural resource management, as seen in Chapter 4). Some 95 per cent of democracies now have elected regional and local governments according to the World Resources Institute (2003). However, a further legacy of the general failure of central government to transfer management responsibilities to local authorities in the past can be a current lack of trained personnel at this level.

But perhaps the most fundamental challenge for city authorities in the developing world in the future lies in the way they will work with other organisations at the local level. It was seen in the analysis of the nature of the environmental agenda at the household level, for example, that the extent of the problems and the shortfall in delivering environmental improvements are likely to remain beyond the capacity of local authorities alone to address. New partnerships are therefore essential to overcome this 'backlog' but may require significant changes amongst all involved institutions. 'The fact that capital is limited demands a more profound knowledge of the nature of environmental problems and their causes to allow limited resources to be used to best effect . . . potential solutions will need to be discussed locally and influenced by local citizens' own needs and priorities' (Hardoy et al., 2001: 398).

The analysis of the nature of the Brown Agenda above also highlighted how the environmental concerns of the poor are intricately linked in the same space and time to economic and social goals. However, the traditional sectoral policies of urban authorities may be ill-equipped to balance such concerns:

> Most environmental problems are multidimensional, interconnected, interactive and dynamic which makes appropriate actions difficult for conventional government structures. The architects, planners and engineers who work for departments of housing or public works know very little about the environmental health problems faced by those they are meant to serve.
>
> (Hardoy *et al.*, 2001: 400)

In continuity with the analysis presented in Chapter 4 in relation to sustainable rural development, it is now understood that there has often been a mismatch between 'conventional professionally led urban development strategies and the realities of urban development as experienced by the poor' (Mitlin and Satterthwaite, 2004: 270). Whilst there have been many 'self-help' approaches in urban development, particularly in relation to housing, many have not enhanced community participation or empowerment. For sustainable urban development, there is a need to support the strategies that emerge from people's own activities to better meet the needs of urban poor, but with new relationships between professionals/the state and local residents that 'enable both parties to contribute to new solutions in urban development' (2004: 271).

Establishing new alliances and partnerships and tapping into the knowledge and capacities of the local urban population are two core (interrelated) characteristics of 'good city governance' which is now regularly forwarded as a critical condition for sustainable urban development. The failure to develop representative administrative and political systems at the local level is considered to be a primary cause of much environmental degradation to date and good governance is now acknowledged to bring major economic and social gains as well as less environmental degradation in the future (UNCHS, 1996). In Figure 5.6, for example, it was seen that many aspects of urban poverty are linked to the limited capacity of local government agencies and departments to meet their responsibilities. Since the 1980s, much progress has come through wider moves towards national democracy as well as from citizen and community pressure for more effective and accountable city authorities. However, good urban governance is also about how citizens' groups, NGOs, and efforts of community organisations are encouraged and supported at the municipal level. As Mitlin and Satterthwaite suggest,

Virtually all of the deprivations that make up poverty in any particular urban setting can be (somewhat) reduced or increased by local organizations . . . This is not to claim that the underlying causes of poverty are local – as many are obviously linked to national and international factors . . . What we argue is that many of the deprivations can be reduced through solutions that are developed and implemented locally.

(2004: 246–7)

Utilising the potential of community organisations and local innovation

There are plenty of examples of communities in urban centres of the developing world over the last decades taking actions to improve their living conditions. Indeed, the total investment by individuals and groups in their homes and neighbourhoods has greatly exceeded that made by city authorities (UNCHS, 1996). 'Often through no choice of their own, low-income households are *de facto* managers of the local environment' (WRI, 1996: 134). But it is only relatively recently that international institutions, aid agencies and national governments have recognised such initiatives as valuable. In the 1950s and 1960s, for example, many national governments (with international backing) engaged in policies of squatter settlement destruction and removal. During this period, self-help housing, for example, was viewed with 'alarm and pessimism' (Potter and Lloyd-Evans, 1998: 144) and was seen as part of the problem of underdevelopment (thus necessitating clearance) rather than a reflection of poverty or even part of a solution. Just as with local rural development initiatives which are showing signs of sustainability, understanding is now emerging not only of the value of local initiatives per se, but of the preconditions which enable successful urban environmental management based on community organisations to be generated more widely.

In the late 1980s, Conroy and Litvinoff presented five core lessons for successful sustainable urban development (as listed in Figure 5.10) on the basis of the work of NGOs and community organisations across twenty human settlement projects. In continuity with the lessons of sustainable rural development in Chapter 4, they encapsulated often very wide-ranging changes in research and development which were built on throughout the 1990s. In short, a principal prerequisite for sustainable urban development was to recognise that housing was not only a problem for central government, local authorities or the private sector but also a concern for communities themselves and '*given a chance*, poor communities hold the key to the solution of their own problems' (Conroy and Litvinoff, 1988: 252). The nature of that chance and the type of support communities have received has been varied. One of the most obvious forms of support in terms of housing improvement was in accessing land, finance and materials. For example, in a low-income district of Cali (Colombia's second largest city), an NGO, the Carvajal Foundation, assisted residents by building a warehouse in the middle of the 'squatter settlement' to provide space for manufacturers to sell construction materials directly to residents at wholesale prices (WRI, 1996). Until that time, a major factor in the inability of residents to build and improve houses had been the cost of construction materials which they had had to buy from retailers at some distance from the settlement. Once people had access to the construction materials, they were given further support such as in design and construction. Critically, the foundation played an important part in convincing the city authorities to approve the building plans and to set up a small office in the neighbourhood: 'Having preapproved building plans and easily obtainable permits was a valuable incentive for residents to build legal, affordable structures' (WRI, 1996: 138).

Figure 5.10 *Common characteristics of sustainable urban development*

....

1 Housing is also a people's problem
2 The need for building communities
3 The need for organising the community
4 The importance of outsiders
5 The importance of external funding.

....

Source: Conroy and Litvinoff (1988).

The experience in Cali also confirms that securing support from government authorities was important in giving a sense of security in a community (essential for encouraging innovation) where the legal right to occupy land was still lacking. Experience of sustainable housing projects also confirmed that a more holistic view of human settlements was required that was broader than the physical structure and included the critical issue of social organisation ('building the community' in Figure 5.10). Enabling communities to be stronger and better organised was essential for solving the immediate problems and for long-term benefits in the future. Just as with sustainable rural developments, community development in an urban context is something 'more than participation': it requires working with the poorest and most excluded groups, understanding and addressing their priorities in urban environmental management, as well as bringing together 'different voices' in the community.

Involving women in community development can bring substantial urban improvements. In low-income communities, women regularly take responsibility for providing not only individual consumption needs within the family, but also needs of a more collective nature at the community level, for example in the provision of basic collective services such as health care, water and education (McGranahan *et al.*, 2001; Momsen, 2004). As such, they regularly engage in community mobilisation activities to ensure that such needs are met. In Guayaquil in Ecuador, low-income settlements are concentrated in the tidal, swampland area of the south and west of the city. Although individual families were able to build houses without major difficulties, accessing basic infrastructural developments required substantial lobbying of municipal authorities over time, activities in which women's efforts were critical (Moser, 1995). Women urged their neighbours to form a committee to protest against their appalling living conditions. Whilst both men and women became members, women took responsibility for much of the day-to-day work of the committee and were the most regular and reliable participants. The women themselves saw it as their responsibility to improve the living conditions of their families through participation in community-level mobilisation. But they also saw themselves as the key beneficiaries of the improvements that were made, in acquiring a piped water system or access roads, for example, since many of the domestic tasks such as water collection were undertaken primarily by them (1995). However, there were costs for the women: time spent in mobilisation activities often meant compromises had to be made in other domestic and productive activities in order to participate.

> Involving women does not mean that the whole burden of community management should be placed on them. Governments, planners, and even NGOs often make unrealistic assumptions about how much energy, time, and money women can spend in communal or individual self-help programs to improve their environment. Many other case studies of communal housing projects confirm that women who are the sole income earners and childcare providers, for example, may not have the time, skills, or money to invest substantially in community management.
>
> (WRI, 1996: 137)

Experience of more successful sustainable urban development, including within housing projects as seen in Figure 5.10, but also more widely, confirms the importance of 'outsiders' for enabling communities to improve their own environments. Often it has been NGOs which have been central in acting as support, advisory or action groups for community initiatives (or in securing these functions from other agencies on the community's behalf). Box S highlights the role of a regional NGO in India, the Society for the Promotion of

Area Resources Centre (SPARC) and the ways in which it is working with other institutions including the World Bank, the municipal authorities and local community groups to foster improvements in sanitation and living conditions. As seen in the previous section, it is regularly the relationship between community and local authorities which is critical for capturing the potential of community organisation and local innovation. NGOs have often enabled communities through adoption of a mediating role with local and central governments. In Lusaka in Zambia, a national NGO, Human Settlements of Zambia (HUZA), has acted as a go-between for settlers and public authorities at many stages in a programme of squatter upgrading. The outputs of the programme have included reducing costs of house building, promoting informal activities, and nutrition and health improvements within the community (Conroy and Litvinoff, 1988). Clearly, such external support requires funding directly in terms of salaries for NGO staff and for the physical and development work that upgrading implies.

Critically, NGOs have had a significant role in recent examples of projects that successfully address the needs of low-income residents in cities of the developing world through acting in the role of support and facilitation rather than taking on what community organisations can do on their own, i.e. working *with* rather than replacing existing institutions. Again in continuity with the experience in rural development, important factors in sustainability have been the quality of the relationships between community groups and NGOs. Interventions have been based on the priorities defined by the urban poor themselves and external agencies are engaged in a process of continuous support (rather than adopting a more piecemeal, project approach); lessons are learnt from the success of one initiative, for example, to build and stimulate further projects (Mitlin and Satterthwaite, 2004). As Mitlin and Satterthwaite summarise, local NGOs recognise from the outset that poverty reduction requires more than an official recognition of the poor's needs: 'it has to include strengthening an accountable people's movement that is able to renegotiate the relationship between the urban poor and the state (and its political and bureaucratic apparatus at district, city and higher levels), and also between the urban poor and other stakeholders' (2004: 282). Furthermore, whilst low-income households may have limited financial assets, experience is suggesting that there are ways of ensuring that those with limited incomes do get better quality and more secure housing, infrastructure and services. In addition, the limited financial capacities of low-income households need not be a

Box S

The Society for the Promotion of Area Resources Centre (SPARC) in Mumbai

Community toilets

Mumbai (formerly known as Bombay) is the commercial capital of India, and a city of 12 million people. Since the mid-1990s, the World Bank has been involved in a large-scale sewer and sewerage treatment project with the Indian government. Significantly, the Bombay Municipal Corporation negotiated with the World Bank to include a smaller project to provide community toilets to 1 million people living in slum areas (initially those living on municipal land). In contrast to previous practice whereby the city organised the construction of public toilets, paid contractors to build them and municipal departments maintained them, the Bombay municipal Slum Sanitation Programme sought to involve communities in the process of design, construction, management and maintenance. The municipal authority successfully persuaded the World Bank to agree to change the funding and tendering arrangements to enable more community management and NGO involvement. One of India's leading urban NGOs, the SPARC was able to bid successfully to provide toilets in 14 wards of Mumbai.

Local people were involved in the design and construction of the toilets, supported by engineers and architects from SPARC. There were significant differences in the design of the toilet blocks over conventional government models: they were bright and well ventilated, were better constructed allowing easier cleaning and maintenance, had large water storage tanks enabling water for bathing as well; each block had separate entrances for women and men giving women more privacy and saving time in queuing, and a block for children was included. Toilet blocks also included a room where a caretaker lived that meant that lower wages needed to be paid for maintenance. The cost of the toilet blocks was 5 per cent less than the municipal corporation's costing and by mid-2003, 180 community toilet blocks had been completed.

Railway dwellers managing their own resettlement

An estimated 24,000 families have lived since the 1980s alongside heavily used railway tracks into and around the city. In order to improve the city's transportation system and to improve the lives of these people, resettlement was required. To represent civil society in the resettlement plan, the Maharashtra government sought the participation of SPARC, the National Slum Dwellers' Federation (that included a unit comprising the families who would have to move for the railway project) and a savings cooperative of women slum and pavement dwellers. By 2001, 10,000 families had been successfully moved, voluntarily, to accommodations with secure tenure and basic amenities. Several factors underpin its success. The Mumbai Metropolitan Regional Development Authority in charge of the railway project had been willing to give up some of the powers normally held by government agencies in such resettlement projects, giving responsibility to the NGOs for determining eligibility, obtaining information on the community and allocating housing, for example – all functions that offer opportunities for corruption and rent-seeking. However, because the local community had long-standing relationships with the national NGOs, there was a trust and lines of communication that was a resource for the success.

Households agreed the criteria for allocating accommodations and in the new settlements, families formed lending cooperatives to assist families who had lost income as a result of the move. It is evident that the mutual trust and flexibility on the part of both community and government agencies were very much part of enabling poor people to act collectively for their own benefit and that of wider urban society.

Sources: toilets compiled from Mitlin and Satterthwaite (2004); railway dwellers' resettlement (World Bank, 2003a).

Figure 5.11 *Means for ensuring better access to environmental services by low-income groups*

....

● Reducing the cost of better quality housing, infrastructure, services – keeping down unit costs, changing the 'official' standards required
● Using credit as a means to allow low-income households to afford/spread costs/cope with fluctuating incomes
● Recovering costs from users and using these to finance other improvements
● Strengthening community organisations to increase their capacity to improve conditions themselves, to negotiate with others, secure additional resources and to contest measures that may impoverish them.

....

barrier to ensuring that they are able to contribute to financing those improvements, as shown in Figure 5.11.

Conclusion

Whilst the Green Agenda has tended to dominate western environmental thinking and the actions of international institutions of development such as the World Bank and the United Nations, there is now a better understanding that it is the immediate adverse effects on survival for the urban poor of such basic processes as cooking, washing and working which ensure that the environmental challenges at the household level are of no less global proportions than global warming itself. Sustainable urban management in developing countries as illustrated through this chapter evidently requires interdependent actions across all levels of the hierarchy. If the actions of community groups are to be replicated widely to deliver environmental improvements on this scale, decentralised and democratic city and national governance is essential for enabling local groups to organise and for valuing their 'voice'. External assistance is required at all levels: in building capacity and competence amongst local authority planners and in fostering consensus and leadership within communities. All actions depend on new partnerships built on new approaches to understanding as well as new kinds of interventions.

In continuity with the lessons learned about promoting sustainable rural livelihoods, urban development in the future must focus on the welfare needs of the poorest sectors of the towns and cities of the developing world. The urban environments of the poor are extremely hazardous to human health and the people themselves represent a substantial resource for the improvement of these environments. Enabling poor communities to take control of their own development is the starting point for achieving levels of urban development and environmental change which are unlikely to be met by international and/or government finances. Very often this also involves safeguarding the needs of specific groups within poor communities against more powerful economic interest groups.

It is also evident that the Brown Agenda of the majority of urban residents of developing countries encompasses challenging issues of the immediate future which are explicitly interdependent. They are simultaneously about generating an income to live day by day and the reality of resource degradation and danger. Unemployment is closely related to poverty and in turn to hazardous and deteriorating living and working conditions. The challenge of sustainable development includes a shift away from narrow sectoral programmes in urban development towards approaches which can address and utilise these interdependent concerns.

Furthermore, lessons are also being learnt within the developed as much as the developing world that a well-functioning urban system also depends on social stability, equity, integration and justice (UNCHS, 1996). Sustainable urban development requires new policies which reduce poverty and other forms of deprivation, but which are also socially inclusive. These are further factors lying behind the essential need for improved local governance to ensure that city authorities address specific local needs and are accountable to all citizens within their jurisdiction.

This chapter has considered the major constraints on and necessary conditions for sustainable urban development at a variety of levels, from community organisation to international political and economic activities. However, prospects for sustainable urban development are also tied closely to those of securing sustainable rural livelihoods. Rural-to-urban migration remains an important force in urban growth. Policy and practice in such areas as economic support for agricultural produce and urban food pricing will therefore have an important effect on the movement of people from rural areas to the towns and cities. The challenges and opportunities of sustainable development lie in providing security for individuals in meeting their basic needs in urban and rural areas; only then will they be able to take a long-term view of development and the environment.

Discussion questions

* List the key features of historic patterns and processes of urbanisation in the industrialised world and compare these with those of the developing countries.
* Compile the evidence behind the suggestion that the challenges of the Brown Agenda are now close to home for residents in cities of the developing world.
* What are the environmental impacts of cities on surrounding rural regions? Think widely to include impacts on livelihood systems and relations between and within households in rural areas using your understanding of the previous chapter.
* From the case studies illustrated (and any wider research), categorise the ways in which NGOs have been important in local urban environmental improvements.

Further reading

Hardoy, J., Mitlin, D. and Satterthwaite, D. (2001) *Environmental Problems in an Urbanising World*, Earthscan, London.

McGranahan, G. and Satterthwaite, D. (2002) 'The environmental dimensions of sustainable development for cities', *Geography*, 87,3, pp. 213–26.

Potter, R.B. and Lloyd-Evans, S. (1998) *The City in the Developing World*, Addison Wesley Longman, Harlow.

Rakodi, C. and Lloyd-Jones, T. (eds) (2002) *Urban Livelihoods: A People-Centred Approach to Reducing Poverty*, Earthscan, London.

UNCHS (2001) *Cities in a Globalising World: Global Report on Human Settlements, 2001*, United Nations Centre for Human Settlements (HABITAT), Earthscan, London.

6 Sustainable development in the developing world: an assessment

Summary

- The challenges and opportunities of sustainable development have been revealed as increasingly complex and varied as further and new 'interests' in sustainability are declared and as enhanced understanding of the operation of global systems has been delivered through these different channels.
- There has recently been a rapid development of tools for assessing sustainable development targets and outcomes, but there continue to be challenges for capturing processes of change and the more qualitative dimensions of sustainability.
- The notion of 'common futures' is used to assess recent evidence of progress towards sustainable development at a number of scales in terms of the extent to which more inclusive patterns and processes or areas of widening dispute and difference are revealed.
- Assessing the financial needs to implement sustainable development is problematic. There is much evidence that more sustainable patterns can be created without large finances and also that there are many barriers that are not closely linked to income. Ongoing challenges of debt relief and enhancing the global benefits of further trade expansion in particular are argued to be more important than questions of levels of targeted finance for conservation or aid per se.
- Whilst there have been substantial successes towards more sustainable development interventions based on community participation, these outcomes require changes also by institutions beyond the local level. Processes of empowerment involve difficult political challenges and community participation cannot be considered a panacea for sustainable development.

Introduction

It has been seen through the preceding chapters of this book that the notion of sustainable development encompasses a wide range of concerns. It includes the capacity of the planet to absorb the changes brought about by human activities and of the substantially compromised development opportunities for many people in the world, particularly in the developing countries. From the outset, in the investigation of the varied definitions and use of the term in Chapter 1, it was clear that there are different 'interests' in sustainable development and contested views of what should occur (the priorities for action and the nature of envisioned change) in future. As a result, the practice of sustainable development has to be understood as an inherently political and conflictual endeavour with those with more power best able to influence outcomes in their favour (Peet and Watts, 2004; O'Riordan, 2000).

The preceding chapters of this book have confirmed that the idea of sustainable development has been a strong influence in shaping many changes in conservation and development worldwide: in terms of the way individuals act, business interests operate and communities organise themselves, for example, but also in directing the nature of state activities, in prompting the formation of new international institutions, and in fostering new ways in which all such organisations relate to each other in the search for patterns and processes of change which are sustainable. One of the aims of the book was to highlight this 'institutional learning' and, through an assessment of the outcomes for people and environments on the ground in recent years, to identify the continued challenges for further moves towards sustainability. However, as more and more institutions of development are declaring an interest in 'sustainable development' as a policy goal (as O'Riordan (2002: 30) suggests, 'sustainable development is an unavoidable concept these days'), and further issues (such as global security) are increasingly articulated in terms of sustainable development, the requirement identified in Chapter 1 for continued critical questioning of the political nature of sustainable development becomes more important. The experiences of more sustainable processes and outcomes (as in Chapters 4 and 5) confirm that sustainability rests on *inclusivity* and *reconciling* different needs and interests at the local level. Furthermore, it has been seen that new opportunities for sustainable development have emerged when previously dominant interests are challenged: as NGOs, for example, engage in international fora on environment and development, as rural development professionals work in more participatory ways that value local knowledges and priorities, and as women are empowered to pursue more strategic gender interests as well as their practical concerns within natural resource management. Without continued critical reflection therefore, opportunities for more sustainable development are likely to be missed or compromised.

This chapter reflects on the progress being made towards more sustainable development. Firstly, it identifies the advances made in developing systems and indicators for assessing such progress. Subsequently, the chapter considers the prospects of future change in terms of a number of important tensions (amid the significant changes in practice) that have emerged through the substantive chapters of the book.

Assessing progress towards sustainable development

In 1987, the WCED urged the development of new ways to measure and assess progress towards sustainable development. However, just as arriving at common and accepted definitions of sustainable development was seen in Chapter 1 as a substantial and ongoing challenge, this is viewed also in terms of the development of indicators for measuring sustainable development. For example, since 1992, the United Nations has been working to develop a set of indicators based on the chapters of Agenda 21, for use by individual countries, but these are acknowledged to be still in the development stages. For some authors, trying to 'tie down and measure' sustainability is a 'futile exercise in measuring the immeasurable' (Bell and Morse, 1999: xii), the impossibility of the endeavour stemming from their understanding of sustainability not as a single thing, but a complex term open to a variety of interpretations depending upon the 'various perceptions of the stakeholders in the problem context' (p. 100). Clearly, through this text, the variety of natural conditions, differences in human values and the range of interests from place to place have been apparent. Furthermore, the holistic nature of sustainable development (the many interdependent dimensions) and the importance of temporal scale (intergenerational issues) present substantial challenges for the development of indicators which fundamentally seek to break down a complex system into its component parts. For others, however, whilst recognising the problems involved in the measurement of any parameter of sustainable development, this has to

> somehow be reconciled with the reality that everyone has a role to play in achieving sustainability – whether it is in policy development or consumption decisions. To make the right decisions we all need credible, accessible and timely information. Hence the advent of the indicator.
>
> (Chambers *et al.*, 2000: 15)

Similarly, the World Bank considers that whilst what is meant by sustainability will continue to evolve, 'in general, people value what they measure. One of the biggest challenges is how to measure all our assets and our progress towards sustainable development' (2003a: 15).

The challenge of moving towards indicators of sustainable development has been taken up by a range of actors in civic, academic and development communities. In Chapter 3, it was seen how companies are now reporting to stakeholders (including consumers) not just in terms of financial excellence but also social and environmental performance (so-called 'triple bottom line accounting'). Similarly, the Millennium Development Goals (Chapter 1) can be considered as key indicators of sustainable development, the common set of interdependent goals for international development defined by international institutions and adopted by 150 heads of state or government in 2000. All the MDGs are specific, quantifiable and directly measurable (Potter *et al.*, 2004). Many governments, departments and local authorities are also keen to be seen as accountable and transparent to their constituents and also are using indicators to monitor their commitments and achievements. For example, in 1999, the UK government published its strategy for sustainable development entitled 'Quality of Life counts' within which it is stated that:

> Sustainable development is about ensuring a better quality of life for everyone, now and for generations to come. It means a more inclusive society in which the benefits of increased economic prosperity are widely shared, with less pollution and less wasteful use of natural resources. *To know whether we are meeting that goal, we need to be able to measure what is happening and monitor progress.*
>
> (DETR, 1999: 3 emphasis added)

Towards this end, the strategy identified 15 'headline indicators' that would give the broad overview of trends and progress towards the objectives identified for sustainable development. A further core set of approximately 150 indicators were also identified that focused on more specific issues and areas for action. The headline indicators are seen in Figure 6.1. Figure 6.2 confirms the multiple functions that indicators are considered to perform within the UK strategy.

Evidently, the arena of assessing the progress of actions towards sustainable development is complex and there are many suggested frameworks for development of different types of indicator (see Bell and Morse, 1999, 2003; www.iisd.org). Some of the main approaches currently in use and developed by different institutions at various

Figure 6.1 *The headline indicators in the UK sustainable development strategy*

....

Themes, issues and objectives *Headline indicators*

....

Maintaining high and stable levels of economic growth and employment

1	Our economy must continue to grow	Total output of the economy (GDP and GDP per head)
2	Investment (in modern plant and machinery as well as research and development) is vital to our future prosperity	Total and social investment as a percentage of GDP
3	Maintain high and stable levels of employment so everyone can share greater job opportunities	Proportion of people of working age who are in work

Social progress which recognises the needs of everyone

4	Tackle poverty and social exclusion	Indicators of success in tackling poverty and social exclusion (children in low-income households, adults without qualifications and in workless households, elderly in fuel poverty)
5	Equip people with the skills to fulfil their potential	Qualifications at age 19
6	Improve health of the population overall	Expected years of healthy life
7	Reduce the proportion of unfit housing stock	Homes judged unfit to live in
8	Reduce both crime and people's fear of crime	Level of crime

Effective protection of the environment

9	Continue to reduce our emissions of greenhouse gases now, and plan for greater reductions in longer term	Emissions of greenhouse gases
10	Reduce air pollution and ensure air quality continues to improve through the longer term	Days when air pollution is moderate or higher
11	Improve choice in transport; improve access to education, jobs, leisure and services; and reduce the need to travel	Road traffic
12	Improve river quality	Rivers of good or fair quality
13	Reverse the long-term decline in populations of farmland and woodland birds	Populations of wild birds
14	Re-use previously developed land in order to protect the countryside and encourage urban regeneration	New homes built on previously developed land

Prudent use of natural resources

15	Move away from disposal of waste towards waste minimisation, reuse, recycling and recovery	Waste arisings and management

....

Source: DETR (1999).

Figure 6.2 *The intentions of the national core set of indicators*

· ·

- To describe whether we are achieving sustainable development overall
- To highlight key national-scale policy initiatives relevant to sustainable development and to monitor whether we are meeting key targets and commitments in those areas
- To educate the public about what sustainable development means
- To raise public and business awareness of particular actions which they need to take in order to achieve more sustainable development
- To report progress to international audiences
- To make transparent the trade-offs and synergies between sustainable development objectives

· ·

Source: DETR (1999: 16).

Figure 6.3 *Indicators for measuring sustainability*

· ·

Some of the main approaches to developing indicators of environmental sustainability are the following:

- **Extended national accounts**
  Green Accounts System of Environmental and Economic Accounts. United Nations. A framework for environmental accounting
  Adjusted Net Savings. World Bank. Change in total wealth, accounting for resource depletion and environmental damage
  Genuine Progress Indicator. Redefining Progress, and Index of Sustainable Economic Welfare. United Kingdom and other countries. An adjusted GDP figure reflecting welfare losses from environmental and social factors

- **Biophysical accounts**
  Ecological Footprint, Redefining Progress. World Wildlife Fund and others. A measure of the productive land and sea area required to produce food and fibre, and in renewable form, the energy consumed by different lifestyles within and among countries

- **Equally weighted indexes***
  Living Planet Index. World Wildlife Fund. An assessment of the populations of animal species in forests, freshwater and marine environments
  Environment Sustainability Index. World Economic Forum. An aggregate index spanning 22 major factors that contribute to environmental sustainability

- **Unequally weighted indexes***
  Environmental Pressure Indexes. Netherlands, EU. A set of aggregate indexes for specific environmental pressures such as acidification or emissions of greenhouse gases
  Well-being of Nations. Prescott-Allen. A set of indexes that captures elements of human well-being and ecosystem well-being and combines them to construct barometers of sustainability

- **Eco-efficiency**
  Resource Flows. World Resources Institute. Total material flows underpinning economic processes

- **Indicator sets**
  UN Commission for Sustainable Development and many countries.

· ·

* Equally weighted indexes are those whose components are equally weighted and then aggregated while unequally weighted indexes give some components greater weight than others
Source: World Bank (2003a).

scales are shown in Figure 6.3. In 1999, practitioners and researchers in the field of indicators and evaluation from five continents were brought together by the International Institute for Sustainable Development based in Canada. The outcome is known as the Bellagio Principles (they were endorsed in Italy) and they provide guidelines for the assessment process as a whole, from establishing the vision of sustainable development through to ensuring that the continued capacity for assessing progress exists (see Figure 6.4).

Figure 6.4 *The Bellagio Principles for Assessment*

....

1 Guiding vision and goals

Assessment of progress toward sustainable development should:

● be guided by a clear vision of sustainable development and goals that define that vision

2 Holistic perspective

Assessment of progress toward sustainable development should:

● include review of the whole system as well as its parts

● consider the well-being of social, ecological, and economic sub-systems, their state as well as the direction and rate of change of that state, of their component parts, and the interaction between parts

● consider both positive and negative consequences of human activity, in a way that reflects the costs and benefits for human and ecological systems, in monetary and non-monetary terms

3 Essential elements

Assessment of progress toward sustainable development should:

● consider equality and disparity within the current population and between present and future generations, dealing with such concerns as resource use, over-consumption and poverty, human rights, and access to services, as appropriate

● consider the ecological conditions on which life depends

● consider economic development and other, non-market activities that contribute to human/social well-being

4 Adequate scope

Assessment of progress toward sustainable development should:

● adopt a time horizon long enough to capture both human and ecosystem time scales thus responding to needs of future generations as well as those current to short-term decision-making

● define space of study large enough to include not only local but also long-distance impacts on people and ecosystems

● build on historic and current conditions to anticipate future conditions – where we want to go, where we could go

Figure 6.4—*continued*

5 Practical focus

Assessment of progress toward sustainable development should be based on:

- an explicit set of categories or an organising framework that links vision and goals to indicators and assessment criteria
- a limited number of key issues for analysis
- a limited number of indicators or indicator combinations to provide a clearer signal of progress
- standardising measurement wherever possible to permit comparison
- comparing indicator values to targets, reference values, ranges, thresholds, or direction of trends, as appropriate

6 Openness

Assessment of progress toward sustainable development should:

- make the methods and data that are used accessible to all
- make explicit all judgements, assumptions, and uncertainties in data and interpretations

7 Effective communication

Assessment of progress toward sustainable development should:

- be designed to address the needs of the audience and set of users
- draw from indicators and other tools that are stimulating and serve to engage decision-makers
- aim, from the outset, for simplicity in structure and use of clear and plain language

8 Broad participation

Assessment of progress toward sustainable development should:

- obtain broad representation of key grassroots, professional, technical and social groups, including youth, women, and indigenous people – to ensure recognition of diverse and changing values
- ensure the participation of decision-makers to secure a firm link to adopted policies and resulting action

9 Ongoing assessment

Assessment of progress toward sustainable development should:

- develop a capacity for repeated measurement to determine trends
- be iterative, adaptive, and responsive to change and uncertainty because systems are complex and change frequently
- adjust goals, frameworks, and indicators as new insights are gained
- promote development of collective learning and feedback to decision-making

10 Institutional capacity

Continuity of assessing progress toward sustainable development should be assured by:

- clearly assigning responsibility and providing ongoing support in the decision-making process
- providing institutional capacity for data collection, maintenance, and documentation
- supporting development of local assessment capacity

One of best known practical methods for exploring the human impacts on environment has been the 'ecological footprint' through which an audit or quantification of human use of nature is made in relation to the assessed biophysical constraints of the globe as an indicator of sustainability. The starting point in ecological footprinting is that all organisms make some impact on earth. That impact then relates to the 'quantity' of nature that is used to sustain consumption patterns and the key question is of whether that load exceeds what nature can support. Footprint analysis estimates the area of land that would be necessary to sustainably support those consumption patterns. It is clearly related to the notion of carrying capacity, but rather than asking 'how many people can the earth support?', ecological footprint analysis asks 'how much land do people require to support themselves?' (Chambers *et al.*, 2000: 59). Most commonly footprint analysis has been calculated and expressed for countries, regions and cities, but it can also be applied to products where the 'Environmental Rucksack' is the total amount of energy and raw materials required to extract, transport and manufacture a good. All such analyses rest on the fundamental premise that it is possible to estimate with reasonable accuracy the resources consumed and waste generated and in turn whether these can be converted to an equivalent biologically productive area necessary to support those functions (Wackernagel, 1998). The precise methods and calculations used will depend on the level of detail required, the data available and the purpose of the assessment. Footprinting is not without its critics, but is generally accepted as 'a great step forward' (Levett, 1998: 67) particularly for capturing ecological and spatial/ distributional aspects of sustainability (it is less good on economic aspects) and in assisting the visualisation of human impacts on the earth. Its 'simplicity' is proving to be valuable in assisting public understanding and in presenting a starting point for debate towards better planning.

In short, the work on developing indicators of sustainability raises the issue of sustainable development as a goal or a process of change. Great care is needed when understanding and interpreting any particular set of indicators or achievements as measured. As has been highlighted throughout the text, sustainability is a complex and contested notion with various interpretations and differentiated interests in the nature of future change. However, it has also been seen in a range of arenas (particularly within Chapter 3) that access to information, greater transparency and accountability, for example, have been powerful forces for change. It has also been seen how a lack of democracy, together with social conflict and environmental injustice, all threaten resources and jeopardise intergenerational well-being. The continued development of indicators, particularly into the social spheres of sustainability, will be an important part of further actions towards sustainability. Additional work is also needed (as identified in Chapter 4) in enhancing participatory methods for monitoring and evaluating all kinds of policy and projects, i.e. assessing change through processes that include people being affected by impacts or affecting those outcomes. Only in this way will it be understood whether projects are making a difference that matters to the people who are living with those changes.

A common future?

Throughout the text there has been substantial evidence provided for the global nature of sustainable development. In short, unprecedented rates and degrees of environmental, economic and political change currently impact on and connect people and regions across the globe, as seen in Chapter 1. The detail of these processes of change and interaction (the 'challenges of sustainable development' of Chapter 2) confirmed that suffering from environmental degradation is almost universal in the sense that contemporary pollution has an international impact and local pollution problems are repeated the world over (Yearley, 1995). Furthermore, deprivation in its many guises is also a problem which affects individuals, communities and countries worldwide. In addition, concerns for the *justices* involved in sustainable development, for how environmental degradation (and conversely, environmental improvements and interventions in environmental management) are distributed across society (as well as spatially) are recognised as issues for industrialised countries as much as for those involved in international development. Whilst the priority within the text was to focus predominantly on the particular environment and development challenges and progress in the developing world, the interdependence of different regions of the world was demonstrated repeatedly: where change in any one element of the world's atmospheric system, for example, has implications for the functioning of the system as a whole (and all organisms living within it); where an increasingly globalised economic system was identified as operating through geographical differences (of both the physical and human environments); and where individual human rights of freedom are now understood to connect to global security and to the global challenge of sustainable development.

The number of international fora held in recent decades around issues of environment and development (most notably UNCED at Rio de Janeiro in 1992 and the WSSD in Johannesburg in 2002) as well as the expansion of Multilateral Environmental Agreements was presented in Chapter 3 as evidence that the common nature of the global challenge of sustainable development has been recognised at the highest political level. An understanding of *common* futures was also seen to underpin the activities of transnational social movements. Whereas in the past, international non-governmental organisations, for example, operated to connect groups of people in one place (who had the finances) to those elsewhere in need (i.e. linkages based on 'sympathy' for others), increasingly people and places of the globe are being linked in empathy and solidarity. Transnational social movements currently connect people globally through what are understood as related and shared struggles and resistances in the spheres of environment, economy and culture.

However, the chapters of the book have also presented evidence of *difference* and *disputed* understandings of the future challenges in sustainable development. For example, it is widely argued (by academics and representatives of developing world governments) that the sustainable development agenda at the international level is *not* commonly shared, but rather, dominated by a more narrow 'northern' interest. In short, the argument is that the concern is for issues of 'Global Environmental Change, GEC' (such as the implications of climate warming and biodiversity conservation on future generations) rather than for international distributive issues of poverty that impact on current generations. Furthermore, as suggested by Leach and Mearns (1996), global images of shared environmental crises get a lot more airing than local views of those supposedly experiencing the problems.

During the UNCED proceedings of 1992, for example, the protracted negotiations between governments over the climate convention are considered by Redclift (1996) to reflect the *mutually incompatible* demands of the industrialised and developing regions. At Rio the northern countries focused on the conservation of the 'sinks' (i.e. the tropical rainforests, largely), whilst those countries of the South wanted the causes of climate change to be tackled. In Chapter 3, it was also seen that tension continues such as over the 'fairness' of the targets within the Kyoto protocol. These are set differently for the industrialised countries and the developing world in recognition of their varied capacities to respond to climate warming, but disputes over the targets have been part of the delay in fulfilling the commitment made by the international community to translate the climate convention into legally binding practice. Furthermore, the increasingly retrenched position of the Bush administration from a number of 'common' international environmental commitments illustrates also how environmental agendas can be very different even within regions.

In Chapter 3 it was seen that the World Summit on Sustainable Development in 2002 was important in reaffirming poverty (and inserting globalisation for the first time) within the international agenda. The legacy, however, of the dominant GEC agenda is substantially entrenched. For example, Reid (1995) reflects that whilst the report of the WCED (notably titled *Our Common Future*) was about *people* and future development and environment challenges for the global community, by the time of the Rio conference, there had been a 'drift' from this initial concern with the effects of development on people, to an agenda fundamentally about 'how dominant economic interests could be maintained within ecological constraints' (p. 229). Kirkby *et al.* (1995) have also pointed to the lack of concern at UNCED about poverty and distributional issues: 'In fact, as a comparison between the report [WCED] and the conference [UNCED] shows, the lack of relationship between them is bewildering, when one is explicitly a follow up to the other' (Kirkby *et al.*, 1995: 11). For Middleton and O'Keefe (2003) the origins of this emphasis on the environment and the effects of its destruction on human lives (rather than for the causes of poverty) go back even further; '*since* the Stockholm conference [of 1972] most effort has been devoted to fixing a damaged environment, rather than attacking the causes of the damage, *many of which are also the causes of poverty*' (p. 5 – emphasis added). Reid (1995: 230) concludes that,

> the major events since Rio have done little to alter the impression that we are content to allow sustainable development to become ecological sustainability. To economic interests, ecological sustainability ('saving the planet') appears to be a more compelling challenge than sustainable development ('meeting people's needs today and in the future').

Some of the challenges of overcoming these entrenched agendas have been seen in the text, as issues of GEC are more amenable to technical and political solutions than poverty and international inequality, as seen in Chapter 2. It is also easier to express, monitor and assess sustainable development in objective terms (Bell and Morse, 1993) giving further support to the power of the work of economists and ecologists rather than social and political scientists

(Reid, 1995). But there is evidence of change. As also seen in Chapter 2, the Intergovernmental Panel on Climate Change that has historically been involved in the most extensive modelling of climate change scenarios and prospective spatial impacts, is now working with the understanding that different 'pathways of development' (i.e. what happens in practice in economic, political and social terms) are frequently more important than climate change itself in influencing the scale and distribution of global and regional impacts (Parry, 2004).

Critical consideration of the notion of 'common futures' in the global challenges of sustainability were also identified in the arena of trade (particularly within Chapters 3 and 4). Whilst proponents of free trade (and neo-liberal development ideas generally) emphasise the global benefits that will flow from enhanced trade and economic activity, the campaigns of NGOs such as Oxfam are centred around how the international trade rules currently *don't* constitute a 'level playing field'. Their argument is that multilateral trade arrangements do not constitute a *common* starting point nor do they present equal opportunities for development in the near future. Furthermore, the Oxfam campaign looks to expose the unfairness and inequality now occurring, whereby certain countries of the world (the less developed nations) are expected (and conditioned to do so under structural reform programmes) to act in certain ways (i.e. open their economies and markets to trade and foreign investment), whilst others (more powerful countries like the US, the UK and Japan) continue to operate protectionist policies.

Perhaps most explicitly, the text has consistently revealed quite *different* environmental concerns that challenge less developed regions of the world in comparison to industrialised countries. As Redclift (1992: 26) identified:

> In urbanised, industrial societies, relatively few people's livelihoods are threatened by conservation measures. The 'quality of life' consider-ations which play such a large part in dictating the political priorities of developed countries surface precisely because of the success of industrial capitalism in delivering relatively high standards of living for the majority (but by no means all) of the population. In the South, on the other hand, struggles over the environment are usually about basic needs, cultural identity and strategies of survival.

Difference in environmental concerns has also been illustrated through an understanding of the priorities of poorer and more wealthy households within rural and urban contexts of the developing world. At all scales, the more economically powerful groups are generally more able to displace their environmental problems onto others in different places and/or into the future (McGranahan and Satterthwaite, 2002). There were also many examples given in the text of contested priorities in sustainable development within communities, often underpinned by differences in power according to wealth, but also by gender, for example. In Chapters 4 and 5, the substantial challenges for sustainable development in practice that emerge through the requirement to understand heterogeneous communities at the local level and to engage in participatory processes of research and planning were seen.

Growth and poverty

Sustainable development is being pursued in the twenty-first century in a significantly different political and economic context from that of the late 1980s, when the World Commission on Environment and Development reported. As seen in Chapters 1 and 2, since the 1980s, the world economy has moved from recession to a period of reinvigorated growth, has encompassed the collapse of communism in Eastern Europe and the former Soviet Union and seen the continued growth and maturity of the 'newly industrialising countries' of the Pacific Rim. Sustainable development is now being pursued in the context of the acknowledged globalising world economy, that has brought 'new ecological problems and different ecological politics' (Peet and Watts, 2004: 4).

In 1987, reviving economic growth was central to the recommendations made by the WCED. However, the quality of such growth had to change (becoming less energy-intensive, for example) and it needed to be more equitable to deliver basic needs to the poorest sectors of society across the globe. Under such circumstances, the WCED was optimistic that simultaneous environmental improvements could be achieved. In contrast to earlier understandings of the global challenge of the environment such as within the World Conservation Strategy (IUCN, 1980) and the 'uncomfortable' challenge that the recommendations presented to capitalist growth (Adams, 2001), mainstream environmentalism shifted with the Brundtland Report (and confirmed at the UNCED conference in 1992) to a 'comfortable reformism'. The focus became on issues of global environmental change (as seen in the section above) which were considered to be 'amenable to mitigation'. The recommendations and solutions proposed therefore rested on minor changes to the existing economic system, on better planning and use of technology and on the more careful use of capital, all of which lay 'firmly within the bounds of conventional political and economic thinking' (Adams, 2001: 103). As such, the argument is that the conception of both development and the environment into the 1990s remained heavily technocentrist, industrialist and modernist as it was in the 1950s and 1960s.

It was seen in Chapter 1 how neo-liberal ideas about what constituted 'development' and how it would be achieved became dominant in the 1990s: in the industrialised world through the politics of Reagan and Thatcher, for example, and in the developing world through the influence of the World Bank and the IMF and the programmes of macro-economic reform (SAPs) that increasingly became the condition for the receipt of continued finances for development. It was also seen in Chapter 3 how such thinking pervaded and was reinforced by other multilateral institutions such as the World Trade Organisation and the policies of bilateral aid organisations. In short, the prescription was that economic growth to the benefit of all would be secured through opening up national economies to the workings of the free market. However, by the end of the decade, experience on the ground, including a number of crises within major economies such as those in South-East Asia and Latin America (Indonesia in 1998 and Argentina in 1995 and 2002 for example), suggested that the economic gains made through such models could be very quickly reversed. Through the text, a range of challenges to this model for development has been seen, from theorists within the post-development school to the mass demonstrations mounted against the WTO on behalf of civil society organisations.

In Chapter 3, a number of changes in development practice were seen to have been made in the light of these outcomes. For example, structural adjustment programmes have been replaced by Poverty Reduction Strategy Papers as the principal strategic documents around which the World Bank and IMF as well as other donors coordinate their assistance to low-income countries. Part of the intention is that the latter would overcome some of the weaknesses of the former through the way in which they were developed by individual national governments and through much more explicit and open participatory processes that include representatives of the World Bank and IMF but also other donors and civil society. PRSPs are required to set out coherent plans for reform focused on poverty reduction and to identify the financing needs. Up to this point, whilst

NGOs had been involved in various kinds of collaboration with the World Bank with respect to their project lending, policy-based lending for structural reform remained beyond the reach of civil society groups. PRSPs constituted an acknowledgement on behalf of the World Bank that 'one size does not fit all' in terms of prescriptions for structural reform; rather, policies need to be tailored to the specific conditions and needs of particular countries as defined by multiple stakeholders. As Watkins commented some years ago,

> Nobody today questions the case for economic reforms aimed at reducing destabilising budget deficits, establishing realistic currency alignments, and restoring balance-of-payments viability. The challenge is to reach these objectives in a manner which protects the vulnerable, is socially inclusive rather than exclusive, and which establishes a foundation for sustainable economic growth.
>
> (1995: 10)

Recently, a new Operational Directive (that defines the mandatory policies and procedures of the World Bank) has been adopted, within which 'adjustment lending' has been renamed 'development policy lending'. The World Bank has been engaged in a two-year process of consultations with academics, governments, civil society groups and private sector representatives around the world towards finding a 'different way of doing things' and 'shedding a different light' on the impacts on previous adjustment lending (SAPRIN, 2004). Structural adjustment lending in the past had been characterised by very prescriptive conditions on recipient governments (see Figure 1.8), the measures imposed had met with extensive public opposition and public citizens had been excluded from the decision-making processes involved. The new focus is intended to move away from any prescriptive list of policies to a much broader range of issues (including strengthening health and education sectors), to ensure broader participation in government policy-making (through civil society engagement in PRSPs) and to better address the environmental and social effects of economic change (World Bank, 2004). SAPRIN is a global network of civil society organisations that was established in the mid-1990s (in recognition of the weaknesses and detrimental outcomes of structural reform in the past) to expand and legitimise the role of civil society in economic policy-making and to strengthen an organised challenge to structural reforms by citizens (SAPRIN, 2004). In 1996, it was invited by the then President of the World Bank, James Wolfensohn, to have a major role in the World Bank process of consultations towards changing their policies and procedures. It is too soon to assess the impact of the new directive, but moving away from a 'one size fits all' model of development and ensuring greater environmental and social accountability on behalf of the World Bank was seen in Chapter 3 to be hugely important in influencing the prospects of more sustainable outcomes in development.

Despite the limitations considered in the above section concerning the continued dominance of northern concerns in mainstream sustainable development, there is evidence that poverty and distributional issues are now a more important part of the development agenda. In particular, understanding has grown regarding the problems created by globalisation. In continuity with the World Bank's recent recognitions that development policy lending needs to be tailored to the unique character of each country's approach to poverty reduction and the nature of their own institutions, there has been a reworking of the understanding that 'a rising tide' of economic globalisation will *necessarily* 'lift all'. One illustration is in the subtitles of the two White Papers on International Development presented by the UK government. Both were titled, *Eliminating World Poverty*, but whilst the first was subtitled *A Challenge for the Twenty-First Century* (DFID, 1997), the second was *Making Globalization Work for the Poor* (DFID, 2000).

> Managed wisely, the new wealth being created by globalisation creates the opportunity to lift millions of the world's poorest people out of their poverty. Managed badly and it could lead to their further marginalisation and impoverishment. *Neither outcome is predetermined.*
> (DFID, 2000: 15 emphasis added)

Similarly, there is an emerging recognition that whilst trade has been an 'indispensable engine' for economic growth across the world throughout human history (UNDP, 2003b: xi), the lessons of the push for trade liberalisation over the last century have revealed that 'the expansion of trade guarantees neither immediate economic growth nor long-term economic or human development' (p. 1). The United Nations Conference on Trade and Development also asserts that 'international trade is vital for poverty reduction in all developing countries. But the link between trade expansion and poverty reduction is neither simple nor automatic' (UNCTAD, 2004: 10, *emphases added*). Just as with the World Bank above, the United Nations Development Programme has recently engaged in a project involving academics, civil society and a series of consultations with governments towards 'reversing the current disaffection with globalisation' (UNDP, 2003b: xi). The conclusion is that the multilateral trade regime needs to be better aligned with broader objectives of human development, with helping poor people everywhere to gain the opportunities to build a better life for themselves and their communities. The 'vision' that has emerged from these consultations and the principles on which a human development-oriented trade regime should be operationalised are shown in Figure 6.5. In continuity with the emerging principles at the World Bank, it is considered by the UNDP that the multilateral trade regime needs to reflect the *differences* between developing countries and industrialised countries more effectively; to give policy space for the coexistence of diverse development strategies and to permit asymmetric rules that favour the weakest members where required. Developing countries, for example, need to have greater flexibility in developing their agricultural policies to achieve food security and to protect the most vulnerable, including women. In the arena of the environment, flexibility needs to be ensured so that developing countries are enabled to design appropriate solutions according to their own development and environment priorities and without fear of trade sanctions.

Evidently, oversimplistic theories of state or market delivering development are now being substantially reworked in the twenty-first century, in theory and in practice, encompassing a much more nuanced understanding of the capacities and limitations of both, and indeed, the opportunities that lie in the 'third arena' of civil society. The evidence through this text of major institutions in development now working in different ways with multiple interests is cause for optimism. However, as Adams (2001: 381) suggests, 'there is no easy reformist solution to the dilemma and tragedy of poverty'. Ongoing efforts are required to decentralise power and initiative in development planning globally and nationally. Fundamentally, as argued succinctly by Reid (1995: 228), 'a development model that extends economic domination, imposes external solutions, measures progress in materialist rather than human terms, degrades the planet and impoverishes people, is itself impoverished'.

Figure 6.5 *The visions for trade in the future*

....

- Trade is a means to an end, not an end in itself
- Trade rules should allow for diversity in national institutions and standards
- Countries should have the right to protect their institutions and development priorities
- No country has the right to impose its institutional preferences on others

....

Source: UNDP (2003b).

Financing sustainable development

In Chapter 3 it was seen that finances from the World Bank targeted to the areas of environment and natural resource management specifically have risen in recent years. Furthermore, monies to the Global Environment Facility (GEF) since 1991 have constituted additional funding for some of the poorest countries to take on conservation efforts (that are acknowledged to carry added costs) in areas explicitly related to the challenges of the global commons. However, other important institutions remain underfunded. UNEP (the institution created following the 1972 UN Conference on the Human Environment to function as the international coordinating and watchdog body), for example, currently has a budget of around US$60 million annually. In contrast, the US Environmental Protection Agency has an annual budget of US$7.8 billion (Potter *et al.*, 2004: 274).

In Chapter 2, it was seen that the Brundtland Commission had estimated that the cost for developing countries of bringing environmental legislation up to US standards was in excess of US$5 billion. Subsequently, the UNCED secretariat in 1992 estimated that an extra US$125 billion every year in aid would be required to implement its action plan (Agenda 21) worldwide. However, as considered in Chapter 1, many of the problems of environment and development identified at the Rio conference got worse through the 1990s and the finances identified as necessary to implement Agenda 21 generally did not materialise. Furthermore, official development assistance fell to record low levels by the turn of the century, as discussed in Chapter 3. Recently, there has been enhanced debate surrounding how these levels of official development assistance must rise if the Millennium Development Goals (listed in Figure 1.12) are to be met. Whilst any of these assessments need to be considered with a degree of caution simply in terms of the difficulties of calculating such financial needs and the political nature of these statistics (many being made to support particular sectoral and regional interests, as identified by O'Riordan, 2000), the continued mismatch between what is pledged at these international meetings and what is actually forthcoming, is a concern that requires monitoring.

As O'Riordan stated in 2000, sustainable development is often not about large aid transfers. There were many examples in Chapters 4 and 5 of low-cost initiatives, training events, meetings with local government and the like that have shown that support for capacity building is often more effective in moving towards more sustainable processes and patterns of development than provision of concessional assistance per se. Through these chapters, it was also seen that more sustainable processes are being built through addressing those diverse aspects of poverty that are *not* necessarily closely linked to income, but, rather, are focused on the barriers to inclusion and development that come through lack of access to information or a lack of voice and democracy. The importance of these factors was seen in some of the changes that have been made on behalf of major international institutions and by business as well as in cases of local empowerment illustrated in Boxes M, P and Q. This is not to deny that significant barriers to sustainable development do indeed come through lack of resources per se – in influencing access to basic sanitation and other environmental improvements on behalf of low-income groups or in limiting the capacities of district, city, regional and national authorities with responsibilities for environment and development. Many regional and national conservation institutions now depend on foreign aid (Leach and Mearns,1996) and the continued role of 'outsiders' (dependent often on donor finances) was also seen in Chapters 4 and 5. The current attention given to raising levels of official development assistance (such as forwarded by the UK government in 2005 using its position of chair of the G8 countries), combined with the role of alliances such as 'Make Poverty History' (a UK network of charities, trade unions, campaign groups and celebrities mobilising around opportunities in 2005 to fight poverty and trade injustices) are sources for optimism.

However, it was also identified in Chapter 3 that levels of finance flowing inwards to developing countries through aid remain swamped by outflows in terms of interest on debts owed (see Table 3.2). From 1999, the 'Enhanced HIPC' announced by the World Bank, the IMF and a number of G8 countries has enabled more developing countries to qualify for relief on their debts owed to the international financial institutions. There have been statements recently by these countries that bilateral debts could also be cancelled in the near future. Historically, there have been few votes for northern governments in international development issues, so that there has been little pressure to challenge the status quo or to enhance development aid specifically (Reid, 1995). Indeed, O'Riordan (2000) goes further to question the degree to which industrialised countries have a genuine interest in change, 'since the current pattern of economic gain and political power is institutionally ensnared in non-sustainable development. Arguably, it is the non-sustainability that retains this institutional order' (p. 30). However, the 2004 example of the tsunami that struck many countries in Asia and the subsequent public response (involving unprecedented levels of monies pledged to charity organisations in industrialised countries including the UK and Australia, for example) may be an indication that public awareness of global realities and social justice is rising and could translate into political changes in those countries. As public donations for the disaster exceeded those of official disbursements in the UK, for example, the government was forced to declare that it would match those amounts in immediate relief assistance. Bilateral and multilateral debt repayments of those stricken countries have also been suspended for a period, suggesting that new spaces for rethinking the legacy of former lending to developing countries are being created.

Just as aid flows into developing countries are now exceeded by outflows in terms of debt repayments, so too have official aid disbursements been superseded as the principal source of investment finances in developing countries. As seen in Chapter 1, private capital flows worldwide, mainly in the form of direct foreign investment, have exceeded ODA many times through and beyond the 1990s and have been the driving force behind the increasingly integrated international economy that characterises the contemporary economic era. However, such investment in the developing world has been seen to be concentrated in a small number of countries in South-East Asia and Latin America in particular (and has also been proven to be highly speculative and transitory). Furthermore, trade itself is increasingly taking place not between countries, but within companies, the power of which was seen to exceed the total income of the countries in which they make their investments. If more countries are to share more equitably in global prosperity and trade is to work to create economic opportunities in the developing world and support secure and sustainable livelihoods, further reforms to the international trading system are evidently required, as argued in the section above. There are also ongoing challenges for sustainable development of ensuring that TNCs become more accountable to the peoples and environments in which they operate, as seen in Chapter 3.

Working with 'community'

Issues of low levels of economic development, the problems of debt and the challenge of finding policies to foster new economic opportunities in ways which enhance human development and the natural resource base, are substantial. Furthermore, whilst many of the shifts towards more sustainable development patterns and processes have been seen to have been effected without large transfers of financial resources, many rest on very significant shifts in political power. In particular, it has been seen that the empowerment of local communities is a necessary condition of sustainable development and poverty alleviation; too often in the past, development processes have served to undermine local control over the resources on which they depend and have led to increased insecurity of livelihood and environmental degradation. But transferring and/or creating power and control within community groups in developing countries depends on many interrelated actions across the hierarchy of levels, as considered throughout the text. Whilst such actions may not be expensive, they do require difficult political decisions and often profound (and unsettling) changes. This applies as much to consumers in the more industrialised countries, professionals in development research and amongst government leaders in international and national negotiations, as it does to city planners, NGO staff, and to men and women in the communities of the developing world themselves. But continued changes are required. As Reid (1995: 229) asserts, 'ultimately we are all degraded by the destitution we allow to persist'.

There has been substantial evidence presented through this text of various institutions in development 'finding' community to the benefit of local peoples and environments. Of particular note, perhaps, have been the southern based NGOs such as SEWA in Chapter 4 and SPARC in Chapter 5 that are now recognised nationally and internationally to be host to substantial expertise and capacity in terms of working at the local level across a variety of sectors in sustainable development that constitutes (and has instilled in many local examples) momentum for further change. However, there have also been examples given whereby the prospect for sustainable change depends on wider political and economic factors that shape outcomes, including the authority in future of 'traditional institutions' over common property resource management and the longevity of donor finances (both seen in Chapter 4 to influence the practice of Community Based Natural Resource Management, for example). Figure 6.6 displays the characteristics of interventions from the viewpoint of what are understood as the features of successful community-driven initiatives in contrast with those of outside funding agencies. As Adams (2000) has stated, whilst there have been many initiatives that seek to co-opt local interests, built on a belief that they are operating in the interests of some wider constituency, fundamentally, 'development planning is centralized and imposed' (p. 381). The suggestion is that despite the mounting evidence on the ground to support the theories for more flexible, diverse (and radical) courses for change towards sustainable development, there remain significant barriers. It remains the case, for example, that many donors have procedures that require outputs to be defined at the outset, which may present problems for valuing local priorities or indeed for enabling local communities to take advantage of new opportunities created (Satterthwaite, 2003). Many donors continue to be 'unwilling or unable to support processes whose objectives are to transform the interactions between the state and the poor' (p. 17).

In this respect, the current enthusiasm with which the Millennium Development Goals have been taken up by international institutions and donors and are increasingly becoming the new conditionality vehicles for aid to developing countries requires some cautious interpretation. Whilst many of the MDGs are central to sustainable development in that they demand better outcomes in areas that affect poorer groups, as seen in Chapter 1, they are externally defined (and driven) and are concerned with measurable outcomes (rather than those known important facets of sustainable development processes such as the accountability of local governance that are harder to measure). As donors are increasingly keen to be seen to be working towards the achievement of these goals, there is a danger for the developing countries of 'strategy fever'. More and more, developing countries are required to respond to a 'battery' of international obligations, legal requirements, planning frameworks and initiatives such as PRSPs, NEAPs, LA21 as well as the MDGs (Dalal-Clayton, 2003). Not only do these requirements put a strain on institutions that already have limited capacity, but they carry the possibility of duplication of effort and a reduction in policy coherence. Furthermore, there is considerable doubt concerning the knowledge of local area contexts or real engagement with local communities that these international agencies and the experts that they draw on have (Satterthwaite, 2003).

It has been seen through this text that whilst there is wider understanding within a variety of agencies of the shortcomings of externally-imposed and expert-oriented research and development practice and that community participation has become a pervasive alternative discourse, it does not offer an unproblematic panacea for sustainable development. As Cooke and Kothari (2001) have strongly

Figure 6.6 *Comparing the characteristics of community-based and donor initiatives*

....

Characteristics of many successful community-driven initiatives	*Project characteristics which make implementation easy for outside funding agency*

....

Modest external funding available to support many and diverse initiatives in different locations	Large capital sum provided to one project; managing many 'low-cost' projects is too costly in staff time
Multisectoral, addressing multiple needs of low-income groups	Single sector, because managing a multisectoral project implies coordinating different sections in the donor agency and different government agencies or departments within the project, which is time-consuming
Implementation over many years – less of a project and more of a longer-term process to improve conditions and services, and to improve relations between low-income communities and external agencies (including local government)	Rapid implementation (internal evaluations of staff performance in funding agencies are often based on the volume of funding supervised and the speed of implementation)
Substantial involvement of local people (and usually their own community organisations) in defining priorities, developing project design, and implementation	Project largely designed by agency staff (usually in offices in Europe or North America) or by consultants from the funding agency's own nation
Project implemented collaboratively with community-based organisations, often local NGOs, local government and, often, various government agencies or ministries	Project implemented by one construction company or government agency
High ratio of staff costs to total project cost (in part because the initiative sought to keep down costs and to mobilise resources locally)[a]	Low ratio of staff costs to total project cost (because this is seen within the agency or its funders as a measure of 'efficiency')
Capacity to change in response to changing local circumstances or external factors (or because of a recognition that new approaches are needed to increase effectiveness)	Very limited capacity to change from what was specified in the project documentation
Difficult to evaluate using conventional cost–benefit analysis because of multiple benefits	Easy to evaluate by focusing on the achievement of quantitative outcomes that

and many qualitative improvements, including many that may not have been anticipated in the original proposal	were identified and specified in the original project document
Little or no direct import of goods or services from abroad	High degree of import of goods or services from funding agency's own nation

Note:[a] This was not always the case, and careful preparation may mean a low proportion of staff costs to total costs, especially if the initiative grows.
Source: Satterthwaite (2003).

articulated, the complexities of power and power relations can still be misunderstood and misused in interventions within this agenda; an enthusiasm for participatory methods in research can drive out others with advantages not delivered by those tools and there may well be decision-making processes that are not participatory that are equally valid in practice. Unjust or 'tyrannical' uses of power (the title of their book) can characterise participatory development processes and practices as much as within the agendas they have sought to contest.

Conclusion

The achievements made towards sustainable development as detailed in this book have been secured without revolutionary political and economic change in the world system. But they have involved a reassessment on behalf of individuals, nations, NGOs and international institutions of the constraints and opportunities of development and the environment, of the criteria for success in the use and protection of the resources of the world and of notions of human progress and well-being in the twenty-first century. The shortfalls which have been identified are confirmation that continued progress depends on factors that include government intervention 'into a dynamic economic system whose overriding motor drive is the desire to maximise profits' (Smith, 1991: 272–3) and also individual understandings and personal reassessments of needs, of commitment to the wider community and of obligations to future generations. Indeed, these challenges are interrelated in that ensuring that governments do indeed take the required and appropriate actions for sustainable development (including within multilateral fora as well as within national boundaries) demands continued pressure from individuals, NGOs and representatives of business, commerce and industry. As Reid (1995: 235) has stated:

Sustainable development confronts, not just society, but each of us at the heart of his or her purpose. It invites us to give practical support to the values of social equity, human worth and ecological health; it questions our readiness to involve ourselves in the struggle for change; it challenges our willingness to contribute in greater measure to the activities of NGOs and dedicated individuals who campaign on our behalf; and it asks us to accept that the small beginnings from which so many successful campaigns have started reside within ourselves.

It has been seen that assessing progress towards the achievement of more sustainable development processes is a challenge in itself. Whilst increasing the material wealth of those in poverty is one 'quantitative' dimension of sustainable development, well-being is now recognised to encompass also 'qualitative', non-economic values such as democracy and dignity. The latter dimensions are criteria for successful sustainable development which have regularly been overlooked within past processes of development and are part of the explanation for the patterns of poverty and environmental deterioration described in this book. Progress towards the more qualitative aspects of sustainable development is hard to ascertain: they are long term and multi-faceted, but nevertheless essential for ensuring the ecological, social and cultural potential for supporting economic activity in the future.

Critically, the quantitative and qualitative dimensions of sustainable development are inseparable and mutually reinforcing. The examples in this book of successful sustainable development projects confirm the positive synergism to be gained from prioritising local knowledge and needs in programmes which enable communities to improve their own welfare and that of the environment. The outcome is seen to be greater than the sum of the parts: benefits are gained from addressing the environment and development together which have not been achieved through separate programmes as people gain security against becoming poorer and, in so doing, achieve the power to participate in further change, for example. It is these characteristics of success which give optimism for future sustainable development. However, there can be no single or neatly defined prescription for change. There are no 'blueprints' for sustainable development: sustainable development actions depend on embracing complexity and working to reconcile different interests in environment and development. It is not possible to predict what the likely needs of future generations will be, the nature of technological progress that will be made or the precise outcomes of global warming. Flexible solutions are required as the nature of the 'problem' evolves and as policies, programmes and projects proceed. However, these are not justifications for inaction today. The obligation of the current generation is both to use and to protect the resources of the world in ways that meet human development opportunities more equitably today, but which do not preclude options for such actions tomorrow.

References

Actionaid (2003) *GM Crops – Going Against the Grain*, available online, www.actionaid.org.

Adams, A. (1993) 'Food insecurity in Mali: exploring the role of the moral economy', *IDS Bulletin*, 24,4, pp. 41–51.

Adams, W.M. (1990) *Green Development*, Routledge, London.

—— (2001) *Green Development: Environment and Sustainability in the Third World*, second edition, Routledge, London.

Adams, W.M. and Hulme, D. (2001) 'Conservation and community: changing narratives, policies and practices in African conservation', in Hulme, D. and Murphree, M. (eds) *African Wildlife and Livelihoods: The Promise and Performance of Community Conservation*, James Currey, Oxford, pp. 9–23.

Adeel, Z. (2004) 'Focus on water issues: perspectives at the end of the International Year of Freshwater', *Global Environmental Change*, 14, pp. 1–4.

Agrawal, A. and Gibson, C.C. (1999) 'Enchantment and disenchantment: the role of community in natural resource conservation', *World Development*, 27,4, pp. 629–49.

Ainger, K. (2002) 'Earth Summit for sale', *New Internationalist*, no. 347, pp. 20–2.

Allen, J. and Hamnett, C. (eds) (1995) *A Shrinking World? Global Unevenness and Inequality*, The Shape of the World: Explorations in Human Geography series, no. 2, Oxford University Press, Oxford.

Allen, T. and Thomas, A. (eds) (2000) *Poverty and Development into the Twenty-First Century*, Oxford University Press, Oxford.

Arnwell, N.W., Livermore, M.J.L., Kovats, S., Levey, P.E., Nicholls, R., Parry, M.J. and Gaffin, S.R. (2004) 'Climate and socio-economic scenarios for global-scale climate change impact assessments: characterising the SRES storylines', *Global Environmental Change*, 14, pp. 3–20.

Atkins, P.J. and Bowler, I.R. (2001) *Food and Society: Economy, Culture, Geography*, Arnold, London.

Auty, R. (1993) *Sustaining Development in Mineral Economies: The Resource-Curse Thesis*, Routledge, London.

Bankoff, G., Frerks, G. and Hilhorst, D. (eds) (2004) *Mapping Vulnerability: Disasters, Development and People*, Earthscan, London.

Bannon, I. and Collier, P. (eds) (2003) *Natural Resources and Violent Conflict: Options and Actions*, World Bank, Washington.

Banuri, T. and Spanger-Seigfried, E. (2001) *Strengthening Demand: A Framework for Financing Sustainable Development*, IIED and International Networking Group, London.

Banuri, T., Boston, S. and Bigg, T. (eds) (2002) *Financing for Sustainable Development*, IIED, London.

Barbier, E.B. (1987) 'The concept of sustainable economic development', *Environmental Conservation*, 14,2, pp. 101–10.

Barrett, H. and Browne, A. (1995) 'Gender, environment and development in sub-Saharan Africa', in Binns, J.A. (ed.) *People and the Environment in Africa*, Wiley, London, pp. 31–8.

Barrow, C.J. (1995) *Developing the Environment: Problems and Management*, Longman, London.

Bartelmus, P. (1994) *Environment, Growth and Development: The Concepts and Strategies of Sustainable Development*, Routledge, London.

Bartone, C., Bernstein, J., Leitmann, J. and Eigen, J. (1994) *Towards Environmental Strategies for Cities*, Routledge, London.

Basel Action Network (2002) *Exporting Harm: The High-Tech Trashing of Asia*, Basel Action Network, Seattle.

Bass, S. and Dalal-Clayton, B. (2004) 'National sustainable development strategies', in Bigg, T. (ed.) *Survival for a Small Planet: The Sustainable Development Agenda*, Earthscan/IIED, London, pp. 101–20.

Beall, J. (1997) 'Thoughts on poverty from a South Asian rubbish dump', *IDS Bulletin*, 28,3 pp. 73–90.

Bebbington, A. (2004) 'Movements and modernisations, markets and municipalities: indigenous federations in rural Ecuador', in Peet, R. and Watts, M. (eds) *Liberation Ecologies: Environment, Development, Social Movements*, second edition, Routledge, London, pp. 394–421.

Beder, S (2002) *Global Spin: The Corporate Assault on Environmentalism*, revised edition, Green Books, Totnes, Devon.

Bell, S. and Morse, S. (1999) *Sustainability Indicators: Measuring the Immeasurable?*, Earthscan, London.

—— (2003) *Measuring Sustainability: Learning from Doing*, Earthscan, London.

Bernstein, H., Crow, B. and Johnson, H. (eds) (1992) *Rural Livelihoods: Crises and Responses*, Oxford University Press, Oxford.

Bigg, T. (2004) 'The World Summit on Sustainable Development: was it worthwhile?', in Bigg, T. (ed.) *Survival for a Small Planet: The Sustainable Development Agenda*, Earthscan/IIED, London, pp. 3–22.

—— (ed.) (2004) *Survival for a Small Planet: The Sustainable Development Agenda*, Earthscan/IIED, London.

Biswas, A.K. (1993) 'Management of international waters', *International Journal of Water Resources Development*, 9,2, pp. 167–89.

Biswas, M.R. and Biswas, A.K. (1985) 'The global environment: past, present and future', *Resources Policy*, 11,1, pp. 25–42.

Blaikie, P. and Brookfield, H. (1987) *Land Degradation and Development*, Methuen, London

Bloom, D.E., Canning, D. and Jamison, D.T. (2004) 'Health, wealth and welfare', *Finance and Development*, March, pp. 10–15.

Bown, W. (1994) 'Deaths linked to London smog', *New Scientist*, 25 June, p. 4.

Braidotti, R., Charkiewicz, E., Hausler, S. and Wieringa, S. (1994) *Women, the Environment and Sustainable Development: Towards a Theoretical Synthesis*, Zed Books, London.

Bramble, B. (1997) 'Financial resources for the transition to sustainable development', in Dodds, F. (ed.) *The Way Forward: Beyond Agenda 21*, Earthscan, London, pp. 190–205.

Brown, L.R. (ed.) (1996) *Vital Signs, 1996/1997: The Trends That Are Shaping Our Future*, Earthscan, London.

Bryant, R.L. and Bailey, S. (1997) *Third World Political Ecology*, Routledge, London.

Buckles, D. (ed.) (1999) *Cultivating Peace: Conflict and Collaboration in Natural Resource Management*, International Development Research Centre, Canada.

Buckles, D. and Rusnak, G. (1999) 'Conflict and collaboration in natural resource management', in Buckles, D. (ed.) *Cultivating Peace: Conflict and Collaboration in Natural Resource Management*, International Development Research Centre, Canada, pp. 1–10.

Cairncross, F. (1995) *Green Inc.: A Guide to Business and the Environment*, Earthscan, London.

Campbell, B., Mandondo, A., Nemarundwe, N. and Sithole, B. (2001) 'Challenges to proponents of common property resource systems: despairing voices from the social forests of Zimbabwe', *World Development*, 29,4, pp. 589–600.

Carlsen, L. (2004) 'The people of corn', *New Internationalist*, no. 374, pp. 12–13.

Castree, N. (2003) 'Uneven development, globalisation and environmental change', in Morris, D., Freeland, J., Hinchliffe, S. and Smith, S. (eds) *Changing Environments*, Oxford University Press, Oxford, pp. 275–312.

Chambers, N., Simmons, C. and Wackernagel, M. (2000) *Sharing Nature's Interest: Ecological Footprints as an Indicator of Sustainable Development*, Earthscan, London.

Chambers, R. (1983) *Rural Development: Putting the Last First*, Longman, London.

—— (1988) 'Sustainable rural livelihoods: a key strategy for people, environment and development', in Conroy, C. and Litvinoff, M. (eds) *The Greening of Aid: Sustainable Livelihoods in Practice*, Earthscan, London, pp. 1–17.

—— (1993) *Challenging the Professions: Frontiers for Rural Development*, Intermediate Technology Publications, London.

—— (1994) 'Foreword', in Scoones, I. and Thompson, J. (eds) *Beyond Farmer First: Rural People's Knowledge, Agricultural Research and Extension Practice*, Intermediate Technology Publications, London, pp. xiii–xvi.

—— (1997) *Whose Reality Counts?* Intermediate Technology Publications, London.

Chambers, R., Pacey, A. and Thrupp, L.A. (1989) *Farmer First: Farmer Innovation and Agricultural Research*, Intermediate Technology Publications, London.

Chissick, R. (1990) 'The gender trap', *Guardian*, 4 December.

Christian Aid (2004) *Fuelling Poverty*, London.

Chuta, E. and Leidholm, C. (1990) 'Rural small scale industry: empirical evidence and policy issues', in Eicher, C.K. and Statz, J.M. (eds) *Agricultural Development in the Third World*, second edition, Johns Hopkins University Press, Baltimore, pp. 327–41.

Clarke, R. and King, J. (2004) *The Atlas of Water: Mapping the World's Most Critical Resource*, Earthscan, London.

Clayton, K. (1995) 'The threat of global warming', in O'Riordan, T. (ed.) *Environmental Science for Environmental Management*, Longman, London, pp. 110–31.

Cleaver, H. (1999) *Computer-linked Social Movements and the Global Threat to Capitalism*, www.eco.utexas.edu/facstaff/cleaver, accessed 7.04.03.

Cohen, B. (2004) 'Urban growth in developing countries: a review of current trends and a caution regarding existing forecasts', *World Development*, 32,1, pp. 23–51.

Colchester, M. (1990) 'The International Tropical Timber Organisation: kill or cure for the rainforests?', *Ecologist*, 20,5, pp. 166–73.

—— (1994) 'The new sultans: Asian loggers move in on Guyana's forests', *Ecologist*, 24,2, pp. 45–52.

Commonwealth Secretariat (1989) *The Langkawi Declaration on the Environment*, Marlborough House, London.

Connor, S. (2003) 'UN donates £19 million to clean up Russia's polluted Arctic shores', *Independent*, 23 October.

Conroy, C. and Litvinoff, C. (1988) *The Greening of Aid: Sustainable Livelihoods in Practice*, Earthscan, London.

Conway, G.R. (1987) 'The properties of agroecosystems', *Agricultural Systems*, 24, pp. 95–117.

—— (1997) *The Doubly Green Revolution: Food for All in the 21st Century*, Penguin, London.

Corbridge, S. (1987) 'Development and underdevelopment', *Geography Review*, September, pp. 20–2.

—— (1999) 'Development, post-development and the global political economy', in Cloke, P., Crang, P. and Goodwin, M. (eds) *Introducing Human Geographies*, Arnold, London, pp. 67–75.

Cooke, B. and Kothari, U. (eds) (2001) *Participation: The New Tyranny?* Zed Books, London.

Craig, G. and Mayo, M. (eds) (1995) *Community Empowerment: A Reader in Participation and Development*, Zed Books, London.

Crow, B. (2000) 'Understanding famine and hunger', in Allen, T. and Thomas, A. (eds) *Poverty and Development in the Twenty-First Century*, Oxford University Press, Oxford, pp. 51–74.

Dalal-Clayton, B. (2003) 'The MDGs and sustainable development: the need for a strategic approach', in Satterthwaite, D. (ed.) *The Millennium Development Goals and Local Processes: Hitting the Target or Missing the Point?* IIED, London, pp. 73–92.

Dankelman, I. and Davidson, J. (1988) *Women and Environment in the Third World*, Earthscan, London.

Davies, S. (1993) 'Are coping strategies a cop out?', *IDS Bulletin*, 24,4, pp. 60–72.

DEFRA (2004) *Recycling and Waste*, www.defra.gov.uk/environment/waste/, accessed 2.04.04.

Department of Environment and Natural Resources (1995) *Philippine Environmental Quality Report*, 1990–95, Manila.

Department for International Development (1997) *Eliminating World Poverty: A Challenge for the 21st Century*, Department for International Development, Government Stationery Office, London.

—— (2000) *Eliminating World Poverty: Making Globalization Work for the Poor*, Department for International Development, Government Stationery Office, London.

—— (2001) *Addressing the Water Crisis: Strategies for Achieving the International Development Targets*, Department for International Development, London.

Desai, V. and Potter, R.B. (eds) (2002) *The Companion to Development Studies*, Arnold, London.

DETR (1999) *Quality of Life Counts. Indicators for a Strategy for Sustainable Development in the UK: A Baseline Survey*, Department of the Environment, Transport and the Regions, London.

Developments Magazine (2000) Issue 12, Department for International Development, London.

Devereux, S. (1993) 'Goats before ploughs: dilemmas of household response sequencing during food shortages', *IDS Bulletin*, 24,4, pp. 52–9.

—— (1999) *Theories of Famine*, Harvester Wheatsheaf, New York.

Dicken, P. (2003) *Global Shift: Reshaping the Global Economic Map in the Twenty-First Century*, fourth edition, Sage Publications, London.

Dickenson, J., Gould, B., Clarke, C., Mather, C., Prothero, M., Siddle, D., Smith, C. and Thomas-Hope, E. (1996) *A Geography of the Third World*, second edition, Routledge, London.

Dixon, C. (1990) *Rural Development in the Third World*, Routledge, London.

Dodds, F. (ed.) (1997) *The Way Forward: Beyond Agenda 21*, Earthscan, London.

—— (2002) *Earth Summit 2002: A New Deal*, Earthscan, London.

Doyle, T. and McEachern, D. (2001) *Environment and Politics*, second edition, Routledge, London.

Drakakis-Smith, D. (2000) *Third World Cities*, second edition, Routledge, London.

Dunn, K. (1994) 'Killing the ripest crop', *CERES*, 26,5.

Edge, G. and Tovey, K. (1995) 'Energy: hard choices ahead', in O'Riordan, T. (ed.) *Environmental Science for Environmental Management*, Longman, London, pp. 317–34.

Edwards, M. and Gaventa, J. (eds) (2001) *Global Citizen Action*, Earthscan, London.

Ehrlich, P.R. (1968) *The Population Bomb*, Ballantine, New York.

Elliott, J.A. (1996) 'Resettlement and the management of environmental degradation in the African farming areas of Zimbabwe', in Eden, M.J. and Parry, J.T. (eds) *Land Degradation in the Tropics: Environmental and Policy Issues*, Pinter, London, pp. 115–25.

—— (2002) 'Towards sustainable rural resource management in sub-Saharan Africa', *Geography*, 87,3, pp. 197–204.

Escobar, A. (1995) *Encountering Development: The Making and Unmaking of the Third World*, Princeton University Press, Princeton.

Finger, M. (1994) 'Environmental NGOs in the UNCED process', in Princen, T. and Finger, M. (eds) *Environmental NGOs in World Politics*, Routledge, London, pp. 186–213.

Flaherty, J., Veit-Wilson, J. and Dornan, P. (2004) *Poverty: The Facts*, fifth edition, CPAG, London.

Ford, L.H. (1999) 'Social movements and the globalisation of environmental governance', *IDS Bulletin*, 30,3, pp. 68–74.

Frank, A.G. (1967) *Capitalism and Underdevelopment in Latin America*, Monthly Review, London.

Friedmann, J. (1995) 'Where we stand: a decade of world city research', in Knox, P.L. and Taylor, P.J. (eds) *Cities in a World System*, Cambridge University Press, Cambridge, pp. 21–37.

Friends of the Earth (1999) *The IMF: Selling the Environment Short*, Friends of the Earth, Washington, also available online at www.foe.org/international

—— (2002) *Marketing the Earth: The World Bank and Sustainable Development*, www.foe.org, accessed 18.06.04.

Geheb, K. and Binns, J.A. (1997) 'Fishing farmers or farming fishermen? The quest for household income and nutritional security on the Kenyan shores of Lake Victoria', *African Affairs*, 96, pp. 73–93.

George, S. (1992) *The Debt Boomerang*, Pluto Press, London.

Gittings, J. (2002) 'China bans toxic American computer junk', *Guardian*, 1 June.

Global People's Forum (2002) *The Global People's Forum Civil Society Declaration*, www.worldsummit2002.org/download/ GlobalPeopleDeclaration.rtf, accessed 27.04.04.

Goldsmith, E., Allen, R., Allaby, M., Davoll, J. and Lawrence, S. (eds) (1972) *Blueprint for Survival*, Penguin, Harmondsworth.

Gourlay, B. (2003) 'This digital age will benefit poor countries only if we truly care', Open Eye, *Independent*, 3 June.

Greenpeace (2003) *Playing Hide and Seek: How the Shipping Industry, Protected by Flags of Convenience, Dumps Toxic Waste on Shipbreaking Beaches*, www.Greenpeaceweb.org/shipbreak/, accessed 9.03.04.

Guardian (1992) 'The new waste colonialists', 14 February.

Guardian and ActionAid (2003) *Trade: An Insight into the Way the World Does Business*, Guardian Newspapers, 8 September.

Guijt, I. and Shah, M.K. (1998) *The Myth of the Community: Gender Issues in Participatory Development*, Intermediate Technology Publications, London.

Gupta, A. (1998) *Ecology and Development in the Third World*, second edition, Routledge, London.

Guttman, P. (2003) 'What did WSSD accomplish? An NGO perspective', *Environment*, 45,2, pp. 21–8.

Gywnne, R.N. (1999) 'Globalisation, commodity chains and fruit exporting regions in Chile', *Tijdschrift voor Economische en Sociale Geografie*, 90,2, pp. 211–25.

—— (2002) 'Export processing and free trade zones', in Desai, V. and Potter, R.B. (eds) *The Companion to Development Studies*, Arnold, London, pp. 201–6.

Halle, M. and Borregaard, N. (2004) 'The trade and environment agenda post-Johannesburg', in Bigg, T. (ed.) *Survival for a Small Planet: The Sustainable Development Agenda*, Earthscan Publications/IIED, London, pp. 32–45.

Halweil, B. (2002) 'Farming in the public interest', in World Resources Institute, *State of the World, 2002*, pp. 51–74.

Hardoy, J.E. and Satterthwaite, D. (1989) *Squatter Citizen: Life in the Urban Third World*, Earthscan, London.

Hardoy, J.E., Mitlin, D. and Satterthwaite, D. (1992) *Environmental Problems in Third World Cities*, Earthscan, London.

—— (2001) *Environmental Problems in an Urbanising World*, Earthscan, London.

Harriss, B. and Crow, B. (1992) 'Twentieth century free trade reform: food and market deregulation in sub-Saharan Africa and South Asia', in Wuyts, M., Mackintosh, M. and Hewitt, T. (eds) *Development Policy and Public Action*, Oxford University Press, Oxford, pp. 199–230.

Hart, R.A. (1997) *Children's Participation: The Theory and Practice of Involving Young Citizens in Community Development and Environmental Care*, Earthscan, London.

Hasan, A. (1988) 'Orangi Pilot Projects', in Conroy, C. and Litvinoff, C.

(eds) *The Greening of Aid: Sustainable Livelihoods in Practice*, Earthscan, London.

Hayter, T. (1989) *Exploited Earth: British Aid and the Environment*, Earthscan, London.

Heijmans, A. (2004) 'From vulnerability to empowerment', in Bankoff, G., Frerks, G. and Hilhorst, D. (eds) *Mapping Vulnerability: Disasters, Developments and People*, Earthscan, London.

Hettne, B. (2002) 'Current trends and future options in development studies', in Desai, V. and Potter, R.B. (eds) *The Companion to Development Studies*, Arnold, London, pp. 7–11.

Hewitt, K. (1997) *Regions of Risk: A Geographical Introduction to Disasters*, Longman, London.

Hewitt, T. (2000) 'Half a century of development', in Allen, T. and Thomas, A. (eds) *Poverty and Development into the Twenty-First century*, Oxford University Press, Oxford, pp. 289–308.

Hildyard, N. (1994) 'The big brother bank', *Geographical Magazine*, June, pp. 26–8.

Hill, A.G. (1991) 'African demographic regimes: past and present', paper presented at the Conference of the Royal African Society, Cambridge, April.

Hirsch, T. (2000) 'Scaling the electro-scrap mountain', *Guardian*, 30 April.

Hodder, R. (2000) *Development Geography*, Routledge, London.

Holmberg, J. and Sandbrook, R. (1992) 'Sustainable development: what is to be done?', in Holmberg, J. (ed.) *Policies for a Small Planet*, Earthscan, London, pp. 19–38.

Huckle, J. and Martin, A. (2001) *Environments in a Changing World*, Prentice-Hall, Harlow.

Huggler, J. (2004) 'The price of dignity for Fatima?', *Independent*, 9 December.

Hulme, D. and Infield, M. (2001) 'Community conservation, reciprocity and park–people relationships: Lake Mburo National Park, Uganda', in Hulme, D. and Murphree, M. (eds) *African Wildlife and Livelihoods: The Promise and Performance of Community Conservation*, James Currey, Oxford, pp. 106–30.

Human Geography series, no. 2, Oxford University Press, Oxford, pp. 143–82.

Hunt, C. (1996) 'Child waste pickers in India: the occupation and its health risks', *Environment and Urbanisation*, 8,2, pp. 111–74.

ICLEI (1997) *Local Agenda 21 Survey: A Study of Responses by Local Authorities and Their National and International Associations to Agenda 21*, International Council for Local Environmental Initiatives.

International Federation of Red Cross and Red Crescent Societies (2002) *World Disasters Report*, Kumarian Press, USA (Connecticut).

IPCC (2001) *Climate Change, 2001: Synthesis Report*, Watson, Robert T. and the Core Writing Team (eds), Cambridge University Press, Cambridge.

IUCN (1980) *World Conservation Strategy*, International Union of Conservation of Nature and Natural Resources, UNEP, WWF, Geneva.

Jackson, C. (1995) 'Environmental reproduction and gender in the Third World', in Morse, S. and Stocking, M. (eds) *People and Environment*, UCL Press, London, pp. 109–30.

Johnston, R.J., Taylor, P.J. and Watts, M.J. (eds) (2002) *Geographies of Global Change: Remapping the World*, second edition, Blackwell, Oxford.

Johnston-Hernandez, B. (1993) 'Dirty growth', *New Internationalist*, no. 246, pp. 10–11.

Kelly, M. and Granwich, S. (1995) 'Global warming and development', in Morse, S. and Stocking, M. (eds) *People and the Environment*, UCL Press, London, pp. 69–107.

Kiely, R. (1998) 'Introduction: globalisation, (post-) modernity and the Third World', in Kiely, R. and Marfleet, P. (eds) *Globalisation and the Third World*, Routledge, London, pp. 1–22.

Kiely, R. and Marfleet, P. (eds) (1998) *Globalisation and the Third World*, Routledge, London.

Kirkby, J., O'Keefe, P. and Timberlake, L. (eds) (1995) *The Earthscan Reader in Sustainable Development*, Earthscan, London.

Knox, P. L. (2002) 'World cities and the organisation of global space', in Johnston, R.J., Taylor, P.J. and Watts, M.J. (eds) *Geographies of Global Change: Remapping the World*, second edition, Blackwell, Oxford, pp. 328–39.

Knox, P.L. and Marston, S.A. (2001) [1998] *Places and Regions in Global Context*, second edition, Prentice-Hall, New Jersey.

Koch, M. and Grubb, M. (1997) 'Agenda 21', in Owen, L. and Unwin, T. (eds) *Environmental Management: Readings and Case Studies*, Blackwell, London, pp. 455–9.

Korten, D.C. (1990) *Getting to the Twenty-First Century: Voluntary Action and the Global Agenda*, Kumarian Press, New York.

—— (2001) 'The responsibility of business to the whole', in Starkey, R. and Walford, R. (eds) *The Earthscan Reader in Business and Sustainable Development*, Earthscan, London, pp. 230–41.

Leach, M. and Mearns, R. (1991) *Poverty and Environment in Developing Countries: An Overview Study*, final report to ESRC and ODA, IDS, Sussex.

—— (eds) (1996) *The Lie of the Land: Challenging Received Wisdom on the African Environment*, James Currey, Oxford.

Lee, K., Holland, A. and McNeill, D. (eds) (2000) *Global Sustainable Development in the Twenty-First Century*, Edinburgh University Press, Edinburgh.

Lees, C. (1995) 'Midwives say they murder female babies', *Times*, 20 August.

Leonard, H.J. (1989) *Environment and the Poor: Development Strategies for a Common Agenda*, Transaction Books, Oxford.

LeQuesne, C. and Clarke, C.A. (1997) 'Trade and sustainable development', in Dodds, F. (ed.) *The Way Forward: Beyond Agenda 21*, Earthscan, London, pp. 167–78.

Levett, R. (1998) 'Footprinting: a great step forward, but tread carefully – a response to Mathis Wackernagel', *Local Environment*, 3,2, pp. 67–74.

Lindner, C. (1997) 'Agenda 21', in Dodds, F. (ed.) *The Way Forward: Beyond Agenda 21*, Earthscan, London, pp. 3–15.

Lipton, M. (1977) *Why Poor People Stay Poor: Urban Bias in World Development*, Temple Smith, London.

Lynch, K. (2005) *Rural–Urban Interactions in the Developing World*, Routledge, London.

Malena, C. (2000) 'Beneficiaries, mercenaries, missionaries and revolutionaries: unpacking NGO involvement in World Bank financed projects', *IDS Bulletin*, 31,3, pp. 19–34.

Marray, M. (1991) 'Natural forgiveness', *Geographical Magazine*, 63,12, pp. 18–22.

Mather, A.S. and Chapman, K. (1995) *Environmental Resources*, Longman, London.

Mawhinney, M. (2002) *Sustainable Development: Understanding the Green Debates*, Blackwell, Science, Oxford.

McCormick, J. (1995) *The Global Environment Movement*, second edition, Wiley, London.

McGranahan, G. and Murray, F. (eds) (2003) *Air Pollution and Health in Rapidly Developing Countries*, Earthscan, London.

McGranahan, G., and Satterthwaite, D. (2002) 'The environmental dimensions of sustainable development for cities', *Geography*, 87,3, pp. 213–26.

McGranahan, G., Ecocuidad, L., Satterthwaite, D. and Velasquez, L. (2004) 'Striving for good governance in urban areas: the role of Local Agenda 21s in Africa, Asia and Latin America', in Bigg, T. (ed.) *Survival for a Small Planet: The Sustainable Development Agenda*, Earthscan/IIED, London, pp. 121–34.

McGranahan, G., Jacobi, P., Songsore, J., Surjadi, C. and Kjellen, M. (2001) *The Citizens at Risk: From Urban Sanitation to Sustainable Cities*, Earthscan, London.

McNeill, D. (2000) 'The concept of sustainable development', in Lee, K., Holland, A. and McNeill, D. (eds) *Global Sustainable Development in the Twenty-First Century*, Edinburgh University Press, Edinburgh, pp. 10–29.

Meadows, D.H., Meadows, D.L., Randers, J. and Behrens III, W.W. (1972) *The Limits to Growth*, Universe Books, New York.

Medina, M. (2000) 'Scavenger cooperatives in Asia and Latin America', *Resources, Conservation and Recycling*, 31, pp. 51–69.

Middleton, N. and O'Keefe, P. (2003) *Rio Plus Ten: Politics, Poverty and the Environment*, Pluto Press, London.

Middleton, N., O'Keefe, P. and Moyo, S. (1993) *Tears of the Crocodile: From Rio to Reality in the Developing World*, Pluto Press, London.

Mitchell, G. and Dorling, D. (2003) 'An environmental justice analysis of British air quality', *Environment and Planning A*, 35, pp. 909–29.

Mitlin, D. and Satterthwaite, D. (2004) *Empowering Squatter Citizens: Local Government, Civil Society and Urban Poverty Reduction*, Earthscan, London.

Mohan, G. (2002) 'Participatory development in practice', in Desai, V. and Potter, R.B. (eds) *The Companion to Development Studies*, Arnold, London, pp. 51–4.

Mohan, G., Brown, E., Milward, B. and Zack-Williams, A.B. (2000) *Structural Adjustment: Theory, Practice and Impacts*, Routledge, London.

Momsen, J.H. (2004) *Gender and Development*, second edition, Routledge, London.

Mortimore, M. (1989) *Adapting to Drought: Farmers, Famines and Desertification in West Africa*, Cambridge University Press, Cambridge.

Moser, C. (1995) 'Women's mobilisation in human settlements', in Kirkby, J., O'Keefe, P. and Timberlake, L. (eds) *The Earthscan Reader in Sustainable Development*, Earthscan, London, pp. 298–302.

Mosley, P. (1995) *Aid and Power: The World Bank and Policy Based Lending*, Routledge, London.

Mullen, J. (2002) 'Rural poverty', in Desai, V. and Potter, R.B. (eds) *The Companion to Development Studies*, Arnold, London, pp. 147–51.

Murray, C. (2002) 'Rural livelihoods', in Desai, V. and Potter, R.B. (eds) *The Companion to Development Studies*, Arnold, London, pp. 151–5.

Myers, N. and Myers, D. (1982) 'Increasing awareness of the supranational nature of emerging environmental issues', *Ambio*, 11,4, pp. 195–201.

Najam, A. (2004) 'Towards better multilateral environmental agreements: filling the knowledge gap', in Bigg, T. (ed.) *Survival for a Small Planet: The Sustainable Development Agenda*, Earthscan/IIED, London, pp. 74–84.

Narayan, D. with Patel, R., Schafft, K., Rademacher, A. and Koch-Schulte, S. (2000) *Voices of the Poor: Can Anyone Hear Us?* Oxford University Press, Oxford.

Neefjes, K. (2000) *Environments and Livelihoods: Strategies for Sustainability*, Oxfam, Oxford.

New Internationalist (2001) *Do or Die: The People Versus Development in the Narmada Valley*, no. 336.

—— (2002) *Inside Business: How Corporations Make the Rules*, no. 347.

—— (2004) no. 365.

—— (2004) 'Resource wars: the facts', *Wars for Africa's Wealth*, no. 367, pp. 18–19.

Observer (2003) 'Fire and floods worldwide', 17 August.

O'Riordan, T. (1981) *Environmentalism*, second edition, Pion, London.

—— (1995) *Environmental Science for Environmental Management*, Longman, London.

—— (2000) 'The sustainability debate', in O'Riordan, T. (ed.) *Environmental Science for Environmental Management*, second edition, Pearson Education, Harlow, pp. 29–62.

Oxfam (2002) *Rigged Rules and Double Standards: Trade, Globalisation and the Fight against Poverty*, www.maketradefair.com, accessed 21.07.05.

Parry, M. (2004) 'Viewpoint: global impacts of climate change under the SRES scenarios', *Global Environmental Change*, 14, p. 1.

Patnaik, U. (1995) 'Economic and political consequences of the green revolution in India', in Kirkby, J., O'Keefe, P. and Timberlake, L. (eds) *The Earthscan Reader in Sustainable Development*, Earthscan, London, pp. 146–50.

Pearce, F. (1997) 'The biggest dam in the world', in Owen, L. and Unwin, T. (eds) *Environmental Management: Readings and Case Studies*, Blackwell, London, pp. 349–54.

—— (1998) 'Arsenic in the water', *Guardian*, 19 February.

—— (2001) 'Arsenic victims get legal aid to sue scientists', *Independent*, 27 July.

Pearson, R. (2001) 'Rethinking gender matters in development', in Allen, T. and Thomas, A. (eds) *Poverty and Development into the 21st Century*, Oxford University Press, Oxford, pp. 383–402.

Peet, R. and Watts, M. (2004) *Liberation Ecologies: Environment, Development, Social Movements*, second edition, Routledge, London.

Pelling, M. (ed.) (2003) *Natural Disasters and Development in a Globalising World*, Routledge, London.

Pepper, D. (1984) *The Roots of Modern Environmentalism*, Croom Helm, London.

—— (1996) *Modern Environmentalism: An Introduction*, Routledge, London.

Popham, P. (1997) 'Parents are paid to have the daughters India lost', *Independent*, 30 March.

Potter, R.B. and Lloyd-Evans, S. (1998) *The City in the Developing World*, Longman, Harlow.

Potter, R.B., Binns, J.A., Elliott, J.A. and Smith, D. (2004) *Geographies of Development*, second edition, Addison Wesley Longman, Harlow.

Power, M. (2003) *Rethinking Development Geographies*, Routledge, London.

Pretty, J. (1995) *Regenerating Agriculture: Policies and Practices for Sustainability and Self-Reliance*, Earthscan, London.

—— (2002) 'Regenerating agriculture', in Desai, V. and Potter, R.B. (eds) *The Companion to Development Studies*, Arnold, London, pp. 170–5.

Pretty, J. and Ward, H. (2001) 'Social capital and the environment', *World Development*, 29,2, pp. 209–27.

Rakodi, C. (2002a) 'Economic development, urbanisation and poverty', in Rakodi, C. and Lloyd-Jones, T. (eds) *Urban Livelihoods: A People-Centred Approach to Reducing Poverty*, Earthscan, London, pp. 23–34.

—— (2002b) 'Prosperity or poverty? Wealth, inequality and deprivation in urban areas', in Desai, V. and Potter, R.B. (eds) *The Companion to Development Studies*, Arnold, London, pp. 253–7.

Rakodi, C. and Lloyd-Jones, T. (eds) (2002) *Urban Livelihoods: A People-Centred Approach to Reducing Poverty*, Earthscan, London.

Rao, P.K. (2000) *Sustainable Development*, Blackwell, Oxford.

Reardon, T. (2001) 'Rural nonfarm employment and incomes in Latin

America: overview and policy implications', *World Development*, 29,3, pp. 395–409.

Redclift, M. (1987) *Sustainable Development: Exploring the Contradictions*, Routledge, London.

—— (1992) 'Sustainable development and popular participation: a framework for analysis', in Ghai, D. and Vivian, J.M. (eds) *Grassroots Environmental Action: People's Participation in Sustainable Development*, Routledge, London, pp. 23–49.

—— (1996) *Wasted: Counting the Costs of Global Consumption*, Earthscan, London.

—— (1997) 'Sustainable development: needs, values, rights', in Owen, L. and Unwin, T. (eds) *Environmental Management: Readings and Case Studies*, Blackwell, London, pp. 438–50.

Reed, D. (ed.) (1996) *Structural Adjustment, the Environment and Sustainable Development*, Earthscan, London.

Reid, D. (1995) *Sustainable Development: An Introductory Guide*, Earthscan, London.

Reij, C., Scoones, I., and Toulmin, C. (eds) (1996) *Sustaining the Soil: Indigenous Soil and Water Conservation in Africa*, Earthscan, London.

Renner, M. (2002) 'Breaking the link between resources and repression', in Worldwatch Institute, *State of the World*, Earthscan, London, pp. 149–73.

Resor, J.P. (undated) *Debt for Nature Swaps: A Decade of Experience and New Directions for the Future*, www.fao.org/docrep/, accessed 19.01.05.

Rich, B. (1994) *Mortgaging the Earth: The World Bank, Environmental Impoverishment and the Crisis of Development*, Earthscan, London.

Rigg, J. (1997) *SouthEast Asia*, Routledge, London.

Robinson, G.M. (2004) *Geographies of Agriculture: Globalisation, Restructuring and Sustainability*, Pearson Education, Harlow.

Rose, D. (2003) 'Record heat wave closes Mont Blanc to tourists', *Observer*, 17 August.

Rostow, W. (1960) *The Stages of Economic Growth: A Non-Communist Manifesto*, Cambridge University Press, Cambridge.

Routledge, P. (2002) 'Resisting and reshaping destructive development: social movements and globalising networks', in Johnston, R.J., Taylor, P.J. and Watts, M.J. (eds) *Geographies of Global Change: Remapping the World*, Blackwell, Oxford., second edition, pp. 310–27.

Rowell, A. (1996) *Green Backlash: Global Subversion of the Environmental Movement*, Routledge, London.

Sanchez, R. (1994) 'International trade in hazardous wastes: a global problem with uneven consequences for the Third World', *Journal of Environment and Development*, 3,1, pp. 137–52.

SAPRIN (Structural Adjustment Participatory Review International Network) (2004) *Structural Adjustment: The SAPRIN report: The Policy Roots of Economic Crisis, Poverty and Inequality*, Zed Books, London.

Satterthwaite, D. (2002a) 'Urbanisation and environment in the third world', in Desai, V. and Potter, R.B. (eds) *The Companion to Development Studies*, Arnold, London, pp. 262–7.

—— (2002b) 'Urbanisation in developing countries', in Desai, V. and Potter, R.B. (eds) *The Companion to Development Studies*, Arnold, London, pp. 243–7.

—— (ed.) (2003) *The Millennium Development Goals and Local Processes: Hitting the Target or Missing the Point?*, IIED, London.

Satterthwaite, D. and Tacoli, C. (2002) 'Seeking an understanding of poverty that recognises rural–urban differences and rural–urban linkages', in Rakodi, C. and Lloyd-Jones, T. (eds) *Urban Livelihoods: A People-Centred Approach to Reducing Poverty*, Earthscan, London, pp. 52–70.

Satterthwaite, D., Hart, R., Levy, C., Mitlin, D., Ross, D., Smit, J. and Stephens, C. (1996) *The Environment for Children: Understanding and Acting on the Environmental Hazards that Threaten Children and Their Parents*, Earthscan, London.

Schurmann, F.J. (2002) 'The impasse in development studies', in Desai, V. and Potter, R.B. (eds) *The Companion to Development Studies*, Arnold, London, pp. 12–15.

Schwarz, W. (1991) 'They're not waving but drowning', *Guardian*, 25 January.

Scoones, I. and Thompson, J. (eds) (1994) *Beyond Farmer First: Rural People's Knowledge, Agricultural Research and Extension Practice*, Intermediate Publications, London.

Seitz, J.L. (2002) *Global Environmental Issues: An Introduction*, second edition, Blackwell, Oxford.

Sen, A.K. (1981) *Poverty and Famine: An Essay on Entitlement and Deprivation*, Clarendon, Oxford.

Seyfang, G. (2003) 'Environmental mega-conferences: from Stockholm to Johannesburg and beyond', *Global Environmental Change*, 13, pp. 223–8.

Shaw, M., Dorling, D., and Mitchell, R. (2002) *Health, Place and Society*, Pearson Education, Harlow.

Shepherd, A. (1998) *Sustainable Rural Development*, Macmillan, Basingstoke.

Shiva, V. (1989) *Staying Alive*, Zed Books, London.

—— (2000) *Stolen Harvest: The Hijacking of the Global Food Supply*, Zed Books, London.

Simon, D. (2002) 'Neo-liberalism, structural adjustment and poverty reduction strategies', in Desai, V. and Potter, R.B. (eds) *The Companion to Development Studies*, Arnold, London, pp. 86–92.

Smith, A.H., Lingas, E.O. and Rahman, M. (2000) 'Contamination of drinking water by arsenic in Bangladesh: a public health emergency', *Bulletin of the World Health Organisation*, 78,9, pp. 1093–1103.

Smith, P.M. (1991) 'Sustainable development and equity', in Smith, P.M. and Warr, K. (eds) *Global Environmental Issues*, Hodder and Stoughton, London, pp. 243–85.

Speth, J.G. (2003) 'Perspectives on the Johannesburg Summit', *Environment*, 45,1, pp. 25–9.

Starke, L. (1990) *Signs of Hope: Working Towards Our Common Future*, Oxford University Press, Oxford.

—— (ed.) (1997) *Vital Signs: 1996–97: The Trends That Are Shaping Our Future*, Earthscan, London.

Starkey, R. and Walford, R. (eds) (2001) *The Earthscan Reader in Business and Sustainable Development*, introduction by the editors, 'Defining sustainable development', Earthscan, London.

Stock, R. (1995) *Africa South of the Sahara: A Geographical Interpretation*, Guildford Press, London.

Stohr, W.B. and Taylor, D.R.F. (1981) *Development from Above or Below? The Dialectics of Regional Planning Developing Countries*, Wiley, Chichester.

Taylor, A. (2003) 'Trading with the environment', in Bingham, N., Blowers, A. and Belshaw, C. (eds) *Contested Environments*, Wiley, Chichester, pp. 171–212.

Third World Network (1989) 'Toxic waste dumping in the Third World', *Race and Class*, 30,3, pp. 47–57.

Thomas, A. (2000) 'Meanings and views of development', in Allen, T. and Thomas, A. (eds) *Poverty and Development into the Twenty-First Century*, Oxford University Press, Oxford.

Thomas, A. and Allen, T. (2001) 'Agencies of development', in Allen, T. and Thomas, A. (eds) *Poverty and Development into the Twenty-First Century*, Oxford University Press, Oxford, pp. 189–218.

Thompson, B. (2003) 'IT: problem or solution?', *Developments Magazine*, DFID, London, pp. 32–4.

Todaro, M.P. (1997) *Economic Development in the Third World*, seventh edition, Longman, London.

Todaro, M.P. and Smith, S.C. (2003) *Economic Development*, eighth edition, Pearson Education, Harlow.

Traisawasdichai, M. (1995) 'Chasing the little white ball', *New Internationalist*, no. 263, pp. 16–17.

Turner, R.K. (1988) *Sustainable Environmental Management*, Belhaven, London.

UNCHS (United Nations Centre for Human Settlements) (HABITAT) (1996) *An Urbanising World: Global Report on Human Settlements*, Oxford University Press, Oxford.

—— (2001) *Cities in a Globalising World: Global Report on Human Settlements, 2001*, United Nations Centre for Human Settlements (HABITAT), Earthscan, London.

UNCTAD (2003) *World Investment Report, 2003*, United Nations, New York and Geneva.

—— (2004) *The Least Developed Countries Report: Linking International Trade with Poverty Reduction*, United Nations, New York and Geneva.

UNDP (1993) *Human Development Report*, Oxford University Press, Oxford.

—— (1996) *Human Development Report*, Oxford University Press, Oxford.

—— (1998) *Human Development Report*, Oxford University Press, Oxford.

—— (1999) *Human Development Report*, Oxford University Press, Oxford.

—— (2001) *Human Development Report*, Oxford University Press, Oxford.

—— (2002) *Human Development Report*, Oxford University Press, Oxford.

—— (2003a) *Human Development Report*, Oxford University Press, Oxford.

—— (2003b) *Making Global Trade Work for People*, Earthscan, London.

UNICEF (2004) *The State of the World's Children, 2004. Official Summary*, UNICEF, New York.

United Nations (2000) *United Nations Millennium Declaration*, United Nations, New York.

—— (2003) *World Urbanisation Prospects: The 2003 Revision*, United Nations, New York.

—— (2004) *World Urbanisation Prospects: The 2003 Revision*, Dept of Economic and Social Affairs, New York, available online: www.un.org/esa/population/publications/wup2003report

Upton, S. (2004) 'The international framework for action: is the CSD the best we can do?', in Bigg, T. (ed.) *Survival for a Small Planet*, Earthscan/IIED, London, pp. 85–100.

Van Rooy, A. (2002) 'Strengthening civil society in developing countries', in Desai, V. and Potter, R.B. (eds) *The Companion to Development Studies*, Arnold, London, pp. 489–94.

Vidal, J. (1998) 'Woman power halts work on disputed Indian dam', *Guardian*, 13 January.

Vorley, B. and Berdegue, J. (2001) *The Chains of Agriculture*, IIED, London.

Wackernagel, M. (1998) 'The ecological footprint of Santiago de Chile', *Local Environment*, 3,1, pp. 7–25.

Walker, G., Fairburn, J., Smith, G. and Mitchell, G. (2004) *Environmental Quality and Social Deprivation*, R&D Technical Report E2–067/1/TR, www.environment-agency.gov.uk/commondata, accessed 30.1.04.

War on Want (2004) *Profiting from Poverty: Privatisation Consultants, DFID and Public Services*, War on Want, London.

Watkins, K. (1995) *The Oxfam Poverty Report*, Oxfam, Oxford.

Watts, M.J. (1983) *Silent Violence: Food, Famine and Peasantry in Northern Nigeria*, University of California Press, Berkeley.

—— (1994) 'Living under contract: the social impacts of contract farming in West Africa', *Ecologist*, 24,4, pp. 130–4.

—— (2004) 'Violent environments: petroleum conflict and the political ecology of rule in the Niger delta, Nigeria', in Peet, R. and Watts, M. (eds) *Liberation Ecologies: Environment, Development, Social Movements*, Routledge, London, second edition, pp. 273–98.

Watts, M.J. and Peet, R. (2004) 'Liberating political ecology', in *Liberation Ecologies: Environment, Development, Social Movements*, second edition, Routledge, London, pp. 3–47.

Werksman, J. (1995) 'Greening Bretton Woods', in Kirkby, J., O'Keefe, P. and Timberlake, L. (eds) *The Earthscan Reader in Sustainable Development*, Earthscan, London, pp. 274–87.

—— (ed.) (1996) *Greening International Institutions*, Earthscan, London.

White, B. (1997) 'Agroindustry and contract farmers in upland West Java', *Journal of Peasant Studies*, 24,3, pp. 100–36.

WHO (2000) *Global Water Supply and Sanitation Assessment 2000 Report*, WHO, Geneva.

—— (2003) *The World Health Report, 2003*, WHO, Geneva.

—— (undated) *Children's Environmental Health*, www.who.int/ceh/en/, accessed 30.04.2004.

Willett, S. (2001) 'Introduction: globalisation and insecurity', *IDS Bulletin*, 32,2, pp. 1–12.

Willis, K. (2005) *Theories of Development*, Routledge, London.

World Bank (1990) *World Development Report*, Oxford University Press, Oxford.

—— (1992) *World Development Report*, Oxford University Press, Oxford.

—— (1994) *World Bank and the Environment, Fiscal 1993*, World Bank, Washington.

—— (1997) *World Development Report*, Oxford University Press, Oxford.

—— (2000) *World Development Report*, Oxford University Press, Oxford.

—— (2001) *Making Sustainable Commitments: An Environment Strategy for the World Bank*, World Bank, Washington.

—— (2003a) *World Development Report: Sustainable Development in a Dynamic World*, World Bank, Washington.

—— (2003b) *Annual Report, 2003*, World Bank, Washington.

—— (2003c) *Environmental Matters at the World Bank, Annual Review*, World Bank, Washington.

—— (2004) *From Adjustment Lending to Development Policy Lending: Update of World Bank Policy*, Operations Policy and Country Services, Washington, August 2004, accessed via http/inweb18.worldbank.org (21.7.05).

—— (2005) *From Adjustment Lending to Development Policy Support Lending*, www.worldbank.org, accessed 04.02.05.

World Commission on Environment and Development (1987) *Our Common Future*, Oxford University Press, Oxford.

WRI (World Resources Institute) (1992) *World Resources, 1992–93*, Oxford University Press, Oxford.

—— (1994) *World Resources, 1994–95*, Oxford University Press, Oxford.

—— (1996) *World Resources, 1996–97: The Urban Environment*, Oxford University Press, Oxford.

—— (2003) *World Resources, 2002–04*, Oxford University Press, Oxford.

Yearley, S. (1995) 'Dirty connections: transnational pollution', in Allen, J. and Hamnett, C. (eds) *A Shrinking World? Global Unevenness and Inequality*, The Shape of the World: Explorations in Human Geography series, no. 2, Oxford University Press, Oxford.

Young, E.M. (1996) *World Hunger*, Routledge, London.

Zaman, A. (2001) 'Poison in the well', *New Internationalist*, no. 332, pp. 16–17.

Index